IGNORE THE
FEAR

FIONA QUINN

First published in Great Britain 2019
Reprint 2020

LEMON PUBLISHING

Edited by Liz Marvin and Aileen McKay

ISBN: 978-1-9163191-0-3

Photographs by LM_edia

For my mum

FIONA QUINN

Contents

Foreword by Sean Conway

Land's End to John O'Groats is an iconic route that has fuelled the imagination of many intrepid explorers and adventurers for centuries. Pioneers cycled and walked it back in the 1800s and, from then on, as soon as a new form of transport was invented it wasn't long before someone used it to have their own adventure discovering what the best island in the world has to offer. Someone has hit a golf ball all the way, another person has pushed a bed (and slept in it), and there was even someone who did the entire journey living only off nuts. It's Great British eccentricity at its best and I love it, so much so that I have completed the route six times in five different ways. Swimming, cycling (twice), running, sailing, and driving.

As much of an iconic experience as it is, and everyone who does it exclaims passionately how much it changed their lives, it's still very rare for people to do it more than once, and in different ways – especially human powered. So rare in fact that I could only find a handful of people who've both cycled and walked or run it. Considering that over 4000 people have climbed Everest and a dozen have reached the moon, this makes Fiona's achievement of both cycling and walking it all the more impressive. She didn't stop there though. After that she then decided to attempt the extremely daunting task of stand up paddleboarding the route. This very much piqued my interest.

There is something magical about travelling on water, especially the ocean. You're at the mercy of the elements, fighting nature in her ferociousness and beauty all at once. Even if you're not that far off shore, the truth is that for miles in all directions there is nothing. It's there where you meet the real you, and it forces you to become the person you never knew you could be. It's so simple and yet so powerful.

Fiona's stand up paddleboard adventure certainly tested her to the limits. Having had a bad experience in water when she was a child, and then to put herself in a situation that pushes on that fear, week after week, is no mean feat. Along the way she lost sight of shore to paddle some 40 miles across the Irish Sea, becoming the first woman to do so. Through all of the challenges she faced, it was her belief in herself and those around her that enabled her to keep moving forwards.

And in completing the journey she put herself into an even smaller category of people in the world. A category that, as far as I am aware, only has two people in it... and I am the other one. She has completed Britain's most famous route in three separate forms of human-powered transport.

Well done, Fiona. Keep pushing those boundaries and thinking big. You're an inspiration to many and it's an honour to have been around to witness you achieve your goals and dreams. Never stop.

Sean Conway

SUP Britain Route

Map provided by ZeroSixZero

Prologue

We set up our tent on a grassy field overlooking the sea, just to the south of St Ives, Cornwall. This would be home for the next four days as I started my world record attempt. In the car was my paddleboard, dry bags, and all the other kit I'd need. From clothing and food supplies to trackers and radios. We'd spent the last couple of weeks gathering all we could in preparation. As we checked through everything after setting the tent up, the sun went down and the drizzle started up. *I think it's all there. I hope it is. I've never done anything like this before.*

It was now 8.30pm on Friday 20th of April 2018. Liam Morrell, my photographer, and I shuffled over to the campsite restaurant to get warm and have dinner. Looking around us, we felt slightly out of place. Dressed as you'd expect for an adventure, we looked a tad dishevelled. Plus, we'd arrived with all our bits of tech that needed charging and we felt slightly cheeky asking to plug in a million things in what turned out to be a much nicer restaurant than we'd expected. Luckily they didn't mind and, as we waited for dinner to arrive, the reality that this was now actually happening began to sink in.

Am I crazy? I thought.

And I wasn't the only one thinking it. As my start date had drawn closer, friends still didn't believe I was going to actually do this. 'Aren't you worried it won't all come together in time?' they'd ask. 'At what point will you give up and call it off?'

But I never had any intention of calling it off. Even a lack of funding, support boat, and skipper the night before I was due to start couldn't stop me. The potential regret at not trying was too big to quit. I had to go for it. I had to make a start and hope that it would all come together – that everything I would need to support me as I paddled from Land's End to John O'Groats would appear in time.

This was it. The weather forecast was good for the first time in weeks. It was *the* day: the start of another adventure. Everything had been leading up to this. It was finally here and the nerves were building up big time. While Liam scoffed down a huge steak, I could barely stomach my mushroom and spinach tagliatelle, which he was more than happy to finish for me. We sat quietly with our own thoughts. I was far more nervous than I usually am before starting a big challenge. I knew that it was not only because this was the biggest, most complicated challenge I'd ever taken on, but because I'm scared of the sea. And for the next three, four months *(longer? I wondered)* every day that conditions allowed, I would be out on the Atlantic Ocean, then the Irish Sea, then the North Sea, on a stand up paddleboard.

Eight hundred miles, eighty-one days, six crew members, four pods of dolphins, one support boat, and an uncountable number of paddle strokes later, I sat there waiting... bobbing on my board as my crew took Shogun into the shallow harbour at John O'Groats. It was an overcast day, although not overly cold or too windy, so it didn't take much to linger in the North Sea waiting for my grand finale. The kelp gently swayed in the water beneath my board as I easily manoeuvred my paddle back and forth to keep myself roughly in one spot. The brightly coloured houses that sat on the coastline next to the tiny harbour beckoned me ashore – the only colour punctuating the grey landscape.

It's a remote destination really only visited for its significance as the most north-easterly settlement on mainland Britain, or to catch the ferry over to Orkney. There's little else here.

The official sign that stands tall – the wild sea and Orkney Islands beyond to the north – marks the start or end point of lots of journeys and I know it well. And, having started my JOGLE walk and ended my LEJOG cycles here, I know there's also a nice café with a locally brewed Thistle cider waiting with my name on it.

Liam and Aileen got the boat tied up against the seawall and, cameras in hand, they started to wave me over. A small crowd had gathered. Literally about five members of the public had been intrigued enough to stand and wait for my arrival, having just learnt why there's a paddleboarder out in the North Sea.

I got back onto my feet after having sat waiting on my board for about thirty minutes, which, in itself, created a kind of anti-climax to the whole endeavour. Then I paddled in. Not wanting to rush, I took my time, savouring the moment, enjoying the cheers and clapping of my mini welcoming crowd. With the harbour ramp in sight it felt almost surreal. *Did I actually paddle here? Is it all about to be over? Is Liam getting this drone shot from the right angle?*

I was nervous about the final step off my board. The ramp was covered in slimy, green seaweed and I didn't want to fall over and look like an amateur in front of the crowd. That would be a rather inelegant end to the months of effort... As I gingerly lifted my board under my arm and began walking up the ramp, Aileen ran down with Liam's camera to capture the moment. It turned out to be probably one of my favourite shots from the end: a ridiculous grin, tanned hands and feet, and the knowledge that I'm still scared of the sea.

I was still an amateur, and yet there I was. Look how far I'd come. And all it took was to put one paddle stroke after another, after another, after another.

Usually you hear this bit of the story at the end; the description of that finish line feeling is the draw to keep you reading on. But I'm telling it to you now for a reason. This adventure is not about that iconic sign. It's not about 800 miles, world records, or trying to claim a title. If anything, it's about the start.

Getting to the starting line of anything in life, not least an adventure, is by far the hardest. All those points at which you could decide that it's too hard, that it's not going to work, that you might look stupid if you try (and, my gosh, what would happen if you failed?). But this is a story about what happens when you lean in to that possibility of failure; when you don't stop pushing to make something happen, because the alternative of regretting what could have been is far worse.

So, let's start at the beginning and as we mean to go on. Starting is not about being ready – that's by far the least important aspect to getting started. For me, the key to starting is your 'why.' It's the question I get asked the most – 'why do you do it?' – and truthfully if the answer is ever 'because I thought I should' or 'because that's what you're supposed to do,' then sometimes that's a good reason *not* to do something. Don't do it for likes or for kudos. Do it for shits and giggles, do it for adventure stories, or because you have this niggling feeling that unfathomably compels you to do it. Do it against the odds. Do it *because* you're an amateur. Do it to show yourself what you're capable of and to test your wits against your own expectations. But, most of all, do it because the idea of it simply makes you smile.

You'll need your why even before you set off. In those moments before the start when you could quit, when everyone gives you the opt-out option:

'But people like you don't do things like this.'

'When will you call it a day and come for a pint?'

'You don't *have* to do this, you know...'

And you'll need your why once you've started. At the start of every day, those mini starts need your why too. It's your motivation to get your tired limbs out of your sleeping bag at 3am, when you're utterly exhausted and the last thing you want to do is face a cold, dark morning and slog it out against unfavourable weather conditions, doing something that no-one else can really appreciate or understand.

And if your why is strong enough, it doesn't matter if you only cover one mile today. One mile is better than none. One mile is moving forwards.

So what's my why then? Why did I decide that I should end up at John O'Groats on a paddleboard?

1

For a love of cake

The daunting gap

I remember being about five years old. Still small enough to push through the tightly knit branches as they spiralled up the tree, my arms and legs getting scratched each time I wiggled through, tree sap sticking to the palms of my hands as I clung on to each new branch that lifted me higher...

I could see the next tree about three metres away to my right. Its outstretched tentacles waved at me in the gentle breeze, calling me over, and, feeling like a bear in its natural habitat, I wondered if I could climb between the two. Could I cross this daunting gap between known and unknown, and end up over there, from this tree to the next, via its flimsy branches?

Then, all of a sudden, I was jolted from my thoughts.

"Fiona, what the hell are you doing? Get down from there!"

I was adventurous as a kid. I remember exploring the woods with my older brother, kicking up huge piles of autumn leaves and generally running wild around Steeple Bumpstead, the small village in north Essex where we grew up. Then we moved to a big town and I became a teenager.

I was no longer wild. But I didn't fit in with this urban jungle either.

Losing my sense of adventure and my innate daring to go beyond what I knew had a real impact on more than just how dirty my clothes were at the end of the day. In truth, I left a part of myself out there – in the wild. I was a shy, awkward teenager. I lost my confidence, had low self-esteem, and never dared to wonder if there was somewhere I could be other than right where I was.

So, I followed the all too familiar path laid out before all good middle class girls – get good grades, go to university, secure a graduate job, climb the career ladder. This was what my life began to look like. I figured out how to write a good essay or report and, from school until the end of university, I managed to deliver what the tutors wanted from me. Essentially, I became successful in line-toeing.

At first I revelled in it. Being near the top of the class and seeing that lovely A written on my assignments confirmed that I was indeed good enough, I was what people wanted, I was a success. I noticed that the people around me thought differently of me since I'd started gaining this sort of official approval; where they'd ignored me before, they now valued my input and ideas, and I found a lot of comfort in that. But, truthfully, nothing exciting ever comes from being comfortable.

Then came the summer of 2009. I'd just graduated with an MA in European Real Estate from Kingston University at exactly the same time as the property and financial worlds were imploding around us in a global financial crisis. Jobs were few and far between. Things were beginning to get uncomfortable...

Nonetheless, I got my first corporate job through an application I'd made for a summer internship. I didn't get the internship I'd applied for (not so much as an acknowledgement of my application) but come one Friday afternoon at the end of the summer, the HR department rang me to say they needed a new graduate to do work experience on a major contract – starting the following Monday. And that's how, at the drop of a hat, I found myself working in a big glass building next to St Paul's in central London.

This was one of the largest surveying firms in the world. Most real estate graduates would have bitten off their right arm to get work experience or a job there. So at twenty-two I was on minimum wage, doing a four-hour round commute from my parents' house near Cambridge into the City every single day.

I was exhausted. The work was dull and repetitive: I was effectively cold-calling commercial property agents day-in, day-out asking if they'd managed to find tenants for our clients' empty properties. Given the economic conditions, the answer was invariably 'no'. Adding this cycle of rejection to the soul-sapping travelling and the pitifully low pay, it's safe to say I didn't love my first experience of corporate life. But maybe there was something I was missing, I thought – a system that I hadn't cottoned on to yet that would enable me to be good at this, to figure out how to toe the line, and actually start enjoying it. This was what I was supposed to do, after all. I was supposed to be good at this!

I asked the associate director I was working with for a chat to see how the land lay, to see what my options were. But it didn't go to plan. Our discussion mostly consisted of her patronising me for not automatically knowing how things worked, finishing up with her expressing a dislike of me leaving on time each day to catch my train home to Cambridge, pointing out that everyone else in the office was often there from 8am to 8pm, if not later.

'Fiona,' she said, concluding her feedback, 'you're here to work until you *break*!'

Well, maybe it was the stress she was under, but honestly I think she just viewed this as the only way of working. She was corporate through and through, literally prepared to break herself for her job and she clearly expected everyone else to do the same. She would come in when she was really sick – promptly infecting the rest of the team – as if she were a martyr for the client. Nothing mattered more than the work and time was constantly against us: every day was a rush, full of pressure and anxiety, and not a second spare for me to ask about anything I was struggling with.

As I handed in my notice to our boss just six weeks after I started, I didn't mention her comments, although they were the fuel I had needed to leave. I didn't fit into this male dominated, power dressing, heavy drinking lifestyle – and being told I was there to work until I *broke* made this as clear as day. Somehow, in that moment, something clicked in my mind. Despite feeling like this job was what I was supposed to do, I realised that I was completely unable to be myself in this context. It was also then that I realised I don't actually have to do what I'm 'supposed' to do. This is my life – mine! And I have the power to choose what I do with it.

I found my way back to my five-year-old self up in that tree, wondering whether those branches could hold her weight. I'd regained that confidence to imagine that I could be somewhere different, to explore somewhere new, and to cross that daunting gap between known and unknown.

After leaving that job I understood that it's all a choice. I don't have to get a corporate job. I don't even have to work in real estate. I don't have to stick to my degree. It doesn't matter how much money I earn or where I live; it only matters that I make choices that enable me to be who I want to be and do things that make me happy – so long as my bills are paid, of course.

That's not to say that the choices on the table are always easy or favourable. Life is hard. It doesn't always go our way and sometimes we have to make incredibly difficult and painful choices. But, whatever the situation, we do always have a choice. And in that moment my choice was where to go next.

While we graduated that year into the worst job market for two decades, I still truly felt that we were the lucky ones. We were entering the workplace when great change was afoot and we had the opportunity to go out into the world with a new approach and seek out different opportunities to our parents. It felt like there was a groundswell of people who were ditching chasing huge salaries, or devoting their twenties to working their ass off in order to eventually become a director in a big firm. Instead, they were seeking healthier, more productive, and more innovative approaches to work. And the traditional goals – money, job titles, accumulating stuff – they just didn't define success in the same way anymore, at least not for me.

With this approach in mind, I decided to dive straight into setting up my first business, in the hope it would enable me to be more self-directed. I'd developed a real interest in sustainability during my degree and was keen to run an ethical business. I was also fascinated by nature and how natural ingredients can be so much better for us than the synthetic products we tend to load onto our skin every single day. So, I decided to set up an online business selling Soil Association certified organic skincare products from British brands. And that's how Saffron Organic came to be.

I was eager to see what I could make happen, despite not having a clue what I was doing. I began to pull things together: the website, products, marketing. I loved the challenge of it all, but it soon became apparent that I needed to earn a living while it got off the ground. As much as I didn't want to chase a corporate nightmare, I also didn't fancy spending the whole of my twenties living with Mum and Dad, and I knew that this business was going to take a while to start bringing in a salary. Determined to make things work, I got myself a research job at my old university and moved back to London, spending all my spare time trying to sell organic products online.

The problem was, as I'd never run a business before and I didn't know anyone with experience to share, I hadn't considered that there might be ways of structuring Saffron Organic other than the obvious online shop. Like many people at the time, I'd only ever been taught about the traditional approach: find a big idea to make you a millionaire; magically source a huge cash injection to get started; invest a lot of time developing it (in secret, of course, so no-one steals your idea); and then launch it into the world and hope it doesn't sink. Ta-dah!

Except this isn't a winning strategy. In fact, it's pretty much a sure-fire way to lose lots of money in most cases. It's also a strategy that has, in a lot of industries, been turned on its head over the past ten years. Start-up now, particularly in tech, is all about quick and cheap prototypes, constantly iterating and building a product through collaboration. What a difference a decade makes.

It took me four years to admit to myself that I wasn't having fun or making any money. It could have been a big successful business – just not for me. Even though it didn't work out, I don't see my first attempt at a start-up as a failure: I learnt so much about what I'm capable of, and about what was missing from my approach. Most notably, I learnt that the model and approach I'd used for Saffron Organic didn't work with how I work, and it would take more attempts before I began to learn exactly what 'my way' looks like.

Everyone needs a tribe

When I finally made the decision to close Saffron Organic in 2014, it was a relief to not have it hanging over me any more. At the same time, I was made redundant from my job at the university, which – honestly – also felt like a big positive. It was a great opportunity to take on board what I'd learnt over the past four years and put it into practice by finding a totally new direction.

As I began to reach out to those around me to chat about the future, I couldn't find anyone who saw the world in the same way I did: most of them were focused on a 'proper job' or were rolling out a detailed five-year business plan. I wanted neither of those things. I just wanted an opportunity to explore what I was good at, what made me happy, and which (of many) business ideas I could potentially make work.

In my quest to seek out like-minded people, I found myself sitting in a field with a hundred strangers at a brand new microfestival. Run by Escape the City, Escape to the Woods was focused on enabling career change and start-ups, and it was full of people looking for an alternative approach to life and work. On the last day, after the early morning mist had cleared from the surrounding fields and we'd polished off a hearty breakfast, we all crowded into a large tent to listen to a 30-something, ginger-haired guy chat to us about a life lived more adventurously.

'Forget the big adventures,' he proclaimed. 'They're great if you have the time, but most of us don't have a few spare years. Instead, look for the adventurous opportunities in everyday life. Seek out the small, the tiny, or even the micro-adventures that add a dash of fresh air, open green space, and the feeling of fear to your day.'

It turned out that this man, Al Humphreys, knew a thing or two about adventure. He might have started out with big, grand adventures – most notably cycling around the world and walking 1000 miles across the Empty Quarter, a vast sand desert in the south of the Arabian Peninsula – but he was now championing the micro approach.

Bored of your nine-to-five? Why not mix it up with a five-to-nine micro-adventure sleeping wild for the night? Leave your desk at 5pm and hop on a train to a scenic spot to watch the sun set. Snuggle down into your sleeping bag after a few beers and wake up with a beautiful sunrise as your alarm. Admittedly, it's not the best night's sleep you'll ever have but, boy, will it make you appreciate your bed when you get home!

The thing about micro-adventures, as Al so eloquently put it, is that there is so much out there just waiting to be explored. We're incredibly lucky to be living in the UK, with all this stunning scenery on our doorsteps, and yet we so often get stuck in our daily routines. But the only thing you will never be able to create more of in your life, is time.

Seriously, remember that. Write it down.

Time is limited, so use it wisely. Whether that's sixty-four hours over the weekend, fifteen hours overnight between working days, or even one hour in your lunch break, it's all there to be made the most of. In fact, I wrote most of this book by getting up an hour earlier before work every day – one hour each morning, setting myself a 1,000 word target – and then I'd get on with the rest of my day. It's amazing just how much that single extra hour adds up to. And, of course, there are so many other exciting things that you could do with that extra time in your day: go swim in a river, go for a bike ride with your child, paint, dance, learn to code, start a business, do yoga outside, learn a language, or bake a cake... Stop for a moment right now and think about it: how would *you* spend an extra hour?

Returning to that festival in the woods – despite it requiring the use of a tent for the weekend – I'll happily admit that, at this point, back in 2014, I would never have called myself a camper. Once, when I was a teenager, I'd visited the Isle of Wight to help my friend, Anna Smith and her parents on their annual fortnight away, where they took kids who wouldn't otherwise get a holiday. Now, that's a lovely thing to do, taking disadvantaged kids on a camping holiday; but, unfortunately, sleeping in a tent for two weeks in the same location resulted in an infestation of black beetles and earwigs. I spent one night sitting bolt upright, unable to sleep for fear of ingesting one of said bugs, and I saw a black beetle scurry along the top of Anna's sleeping bag towards her open mouth as she slept – well, that was, I thought, enough to put me off it for life. And for those ten years since, up until this point in a field with one hundred strangers and Al Humphreys, it had been.

But there's something magical about being surrounded by people who see the world the same way you do. They make you realise it's OK. It's OK to be scared and to not have a clue, but to try anyway – whether it's on an adventure or in any other area of your life. So there I was, at the end of a long weekend desperate for more hugs from strangers and more fuel for my business ideas... plus I'd now been given this new idea about the possibility of adventure! Little did I know what an enormous impact that such a little concept, like spending just one night under the stars, was due to have on my life.

Al had sold it so well – that micro-adventures are incredibly accessible, non-committal, and most importantly, *fun* things to do. They don't have to lead anywhere, be part of a greater plan, or be a 'success' in any way. They're just for you. For one night, you get to do something you otherwise wouldn't do and to see things differently in the process.

So, the following spring, I found myself standing underneath the clock at Waterloo station in London with a big rucksack on my back stuffed with a sleeping bag, and a bottle of wine, waiting for two girlfriends to join me. When we reached the other end of the train line, the sun dipped low in the sky over a small village in Kent. We wandered around the village seeking out a shop to buy snacks for the next morning before the most critical part of any adventure – heading to the pub.

Following a very nice burger and chips, stuffed full to fuel a slightly cold night under the stars, we headed off in search of a hill. Having never done this before, one of my friends, Zita Helena was so excited that when she got chatting to someone on our meanderings through the village, she promptly exclaimed what we were doing and asked for recommendations of locations for sleeping out. While we managed to gather numerous puzzled looks, perhaps rather unsurprisingly, local knowledge of wild camping spots was lacking.

So, we hiked through some fields towards the nearest hill we could see and settled down to devour the wine. At the planning stages we had invited another friend of ours, Matt Trinetti. But, as one-by-one we found ourselves needing to go for a wee, we were very glad that we weren't in the company of any men. It was hardly a discrete location in which to whip your trousers down! At this point, kit wasn't really on my radar. So it was only once we were snuggled up next to a hedge that we found ourselves starting to think through how all the necessities actually work when doing this wild camping thing.

We'd had the foresight to buy bivvy bags at least – if you haven't encountered one before, a bivvy bag is basically a large waterproof sack that goes over your sleeping bag to keep it dry, in theory. But, not knowing if we'd ever want to do this again, we'd opted for the cheapest possible ones we could find. And while a £4.99 emergency bivvy bag might feel luxurious in a life or death situation, these luminous orange models made us look like we were trussed up in body bags and the lack of breathability meant that our sleeping bags were wet from the inside anyway with condensation.

But, as the sun finally dipped below the horizon, our accommodation truly came into its own. The views over the rolling hills that stretched out before us were stunning, only enhanced by my first experience of watching slow-moving trains glow in the darkness. There's something hypnotising about watching them as they roll through the patchwork of hills every now and again. It's a sight that I love to this day, wondering where they're all going, knowing that I get this special spot to myself for the night after the last one has passed through... just so long as they're not so close you have to listen to them chugging away, of course.

It's an odd concept, wild camping. Even with an upgraded bivvy that breathes, why choose to sleep out under the stars? Most normal people wouldn't even entertain the idea of sleeping outside when they have a perfectly good bed at home or could just book a cosy room in a B&B.

I'd met Zita and Lisa, my buddies for that first wild camping trip, a few months earlier on an entrepreneurship course run by Escape the City (the same people who'd organised the microfestival in the woods). We were all at a point in our lives when we lusted after the *new* – something different to offer us a new perspective, a new experience, and a new story. We wanted more from our lives than just a nine-to-five job and the usual day-to-day experience. So that's how we found ourselves sleeping in the long grass of a random field, waking up to a star-lit sky every hour or so (I've learnt since that wild camping is rarely a good night's sleep!).

From that first night I went on to wild camp with other friends in a whole variety of locations in and around London, and down in the southwest of England. Through exploring the worlds of adventure and startups, it seemed that a willingness to push yourself in the outdoors and to develop a business often overlapped in many ways, and I was lucky enough to find groups of people who saw the world from a similar perspective. They were curious, full of ideas, hope, and enthusiasm. They too had no idea where they wanted to end up, just that they wanted to try and see if – over there through the bushes, beyond the tree line, and over the other side of the valley – there might be something exciting, whether that turned out to be a new lifestyle, a new business or career, or a new experience. We were all keen to help each other get there and happily open to wherever we might end up.

The truth is that no one of us is an isolated island. We need support, we need connections, we need feedback and ideas. We need to laugh, to share stories, and to navigate the ups and downs together. Finding people who were like me, challenging society's norms and expectations, was one of the most important factors in creating my own way and taking those first tentative steps on a path towards living more adventurously.

Adventure is all about cake

Around the same time as my redundancy, at the age of 26, I started dating a guy who was seriously into cycling. A year later we were a six-bike household (four his, two mine). I found that I loved cycling. Weekends were often spent hopping on our bikes outside our one-bed flat in Surbiton and gliding down the lush, green Surrey hills that I'd come to appreciate, stopping at cafés along the way, or pottering into central London along the River Thames.

Since school, I'd not done much sport at all. There was my brief flirtation with cheerleading at university (that's totally a sport, right?) – I attended a social event where we all watched *Bring It On*, plus one training session, after which I decided it wasn't for me. My friend, Sarah Dominey who was on the same course as me at university, played a fair bit of sport, often joining a hockey or lacrosse team when she moved somewhere new. And I could see the attraction. It's a great way to get to know people locally, but organised sport just doesn't really appeal all that much to me: I don't like the commitment of having to be somewhere every week at a set time and working towards someone else's goals.

But in cycling I'd definitely found my sport-based calling. I can do it on my own schedule, I can go where I want to, and I can do the type of cycling that I find fun. And despite the fact that it's something you can do solo, it's actually really sociable – cyclists are so friendly. The speed is perfect for covering nice distances and yet still slow enough to enjoy the scenery. You can carry everything you need on your bike and, of course, there are the mandatory cake stops – did I mention those? When the going gets tough you get the benefit of a downhill to counteract the up, and you can coast on flat sections. All in all, it doesn't really feel like exercise. It's just fun! I really do love it.

I got my first bike as an adult on the Cycle to Work scheme before I was made redundant and opted for a Specialized Vita Comp hybrid bike – light enough to be nimble on the roads, but sturdy enough to handle towpaths and gentle off-road sections. A solid, middle-of-the-road bike, which also turned out to be the most stolen bike in London due to its saleability on the second-hand market... This was my main bike which took me everywhere, from small local rides to 60+ milers; but, for fear of it being nicked, I rarely left it locked up outside, which limited its day-to-day use a little.

My second bike was an old and very rusty Dutch style bicycle with a soft padded saddle, a big, not-so-shiny bell, and broken gears. It also had a lovely wicker basket on the front and I tied an old basket from a charity shop onto the rack at the back too. A neighbour had given it to me as she never used it and it was perfect for nipping into my local town centre, or back and forth to the allotment I had at the time. Those baskets accommodated both soil-covered potatoes and bags of shopping alike, and the rust on its surface ensured that I didn't have to worry about it getting stolen. It was also the perfect bike for riding in regular clothes: no padded shorts needed and it was even ladylike if I was wearing a skirt!

My bike wasn't the only rusty thing about my start to cycling as an adult though. The first big route that Nick and I did together involved a 'little ride,' as he described it, over the unrelenting Surrey hills. Constant ups and downs, with no flat sections to rest and regain my composure. I'd not cycled since I was about 14 and I don't think Nick had appreciated just how unfit I was. Not only did I not have any kind of general fitness, but there were muscles I used on that ride that I didn't even know I had. It ended with him thinking I was laughing at how ridiculously hilly it was, when I was actually crying behind my sunglasses. Not a great start.

Luckily though, that didn't put me off and we toned down our rides from then on until I started to find my cycling legs. The hills were the hardest to start with. Even the smallest incline would make my legs scream at me to stop – it was like they just simply refused to work uphill. But, like most things, the more you do it the easier it becomes, and soon enough my body started to adapt and it became easier and more enjoyable.

A few months in I decided I needed something to test myself, so I signed us up for the British Heart Foundation London to Brighton bike ride: 60 miles from Clapham Common in south London through the rolling countryside of Sussex, culminating in the legendary Ditchling Beacon, before sweeping down to Brighton's seafront. A giant of a hill with twists and turns that more often than not defeats its opponents, Ditchling Beacon is not for the faint-hearted or those who haven't found their cycling legs yet. I had no delusions that I'd make it up that section without getting off to push, but the rest sounded like a great day out. It's a huge community event, the route is lined with local Scout clubs putting on barbecues, and the thousands of cyclists taking part makes for a supportive and fun atmosphere.

In terms of training, well, I have to admit there wasn't any... I figured we had all day to get there, and surely it couldn't be that hard. Right? However, after just ten miles, I started to think that this No Training strategy was potentially a mistake as I was so slow and already pretty shattered. Nick, however, was prepared. He'd decided to ride his heaviest bike, knowing he wasn't going to get anywhere quickly with me in tow. Ten hours later, at around 7.30pm, we eventually got to Brighton, just in time to get the last event-organised bus back to London.

While Nick's take on it might have been different, I actually didn't see the lack of training as a mistake. Yes, it was a lot harder than it would have been had I trained. But for me what mattered was that I started, that I did something, that I took action and challenged myself. I had no intention of being good, simply of starting. It's an approach that I have to say I love for its simplicity and lack of pressure. Just throwing myself into something new! It's OK to be a bit rubbish at first – everyone is. I learnt a lot more about myself and about what I was capable of by simply having a go and, in the months that followed, I kept cycling. And that was when I really began to love it. As the weeks passed, I felt myself growing stronger *and* I'd just cycled London to Brighton on no training – now I could do anything!

Seven years after quitting that graduate job, I was onto my second business, turning a community vegetable box scheme into a social enterprise. But, as I edged closer to the big three-oh, things were beginning to shake up in my life beyond that new-found love of cycling and wild camping. I was having to make some hard choices that I knew were right for me, but which left me in a rather difficult place.

For a start, I had to face the fact that my two-and-a-half year relationship with Nick was coming to an end just at the point when most people my age start to get married. My parents had divorced the year before which had resulted in a family split. I was no longer speaking to my dad. On top of that, my mum, who was finally free from an unhappy marriage, had just been diagnosed with stage 3 breast cancer and I was now going to be caring for her.

I tried my best to support my mum through her treatment. It was tough. I had to move out of the flat I'd shared with Nick and I didn't have a proper income as I was solely working on the new business, which couldn't pay a proper salary yet. I was dividing my time between ferrying my mum to hospital in Cambridgeshire and trying to keep the business afloat in London.

Mum was in hospital for a second time, about to have the main operation to remove the cancerous breast, and at the same time they would reconstruct a new one using tissue from her stomach – there are pros to everything, right? She got a free tummy tuck on the NHS, we joked between us. I tentatively asked the nurse if it was possible for a district nurse to visit mum after the surgery at home, because I would have to go to London two days later for the business.

The nurse turned to me with an eyebrow raised and said in a loaded tone, "Some things in life are more important than work. You should be looking after your mum, not going to work!" Her words punched me in the gut and ripped out my heart in one fell swoop. I couldn't hold back the tears. I had already felt like this was a risky operation, and if anything went wrong, this could be the last time I'd ever see her. Yet this nurse had found a way to make me feel even worse.

So that was a 'no' then. Luckily the operation went well and Mum's wonderful neighbours were able to look out for her while I had to be in London. She ended up with a flat stomach and a new boob and got the all clear after a year of surgery, chemo, and radiotherapy.

Supporting my mum through her cancer treatment only made me want to get outside even more. I wanted to live my life to the full because I'd been rather brutally reminded that it can be over so very quickly. I craved a personal challenge, alone time, and thinking space. I craved a different story to the one I'd been living out over the past two years.

My business – again – wasn't making me happy, so a couple of months after Mum's op I closed it, this time remembering to 'fail quickly'. I then began searching for ways to explore my newfound interest in adventure. It had started with the micro-adventures, but now I was keen to combine this with my love of cycling (and cake stops) in order to take my adventures to the next level.

So, I began brainstorming ideas for what I could do next. I liked the idea of a triathlon, adding some other sports into the mix, but, unsurprisingly, the organised nature and time restrictions of an actual triathlon didn't appeal. I decided to make up my own. I wanted something with a starting line that was easy for me to get to and had the option of local support from friends in case it all went pear-shaped.

Still wanting to stay close to home in case Mum needed me, I looked at a map and the River Cam called my name. From what I'd learnt by listening to the handful of people I knew in the adventure world, doing a source to sea adventure seemed to be a thing. So, I opted for a triathlon the length of the river: first cycling the full length, then walking it, then finishing off by stand up paddleboarding (SUP) the navigable section in the middle – I didn't fancy getting swept out to sea at the coastal end of the river, and the first 20 miles are too shallow to paddle in.

Starting in spring 2016, I took my time and spent a long weekend here and another there, completing each of the three disciplines, one at a time. I cycled it first with my friend, Chantell Frost over two days. Then I went back to walk it on my own a couple of weeks later and finished off with the SUP route, on which I was joined by nine friends and a dog.

It was funny. Standing there at the start of the walk was the most ridiculous I have ever felt. When you have a friend by your side on a wild adventure, somehow it doesn't seem so weird;

but on my own I felt like a complete plonker. What the hell was I doing? *I've got four days ahead of me walking next to this river. If people ask me what I'm doing they're going to think I'm crazy.*

I have to say though, Jelly Babies do make everything a little better. As I got going, and those sugary treats began jumping into my mouth, everything started to look rosier and no-one even stopped to ask what I was doing. On the one hand it was liberating that no-one cared, but on the other it was a bit disappointing. And so it became a fun highlight of my day trying to strike up a conversation with the people I passed and casually mention what I was doing, just to see the baffled looks on their faces.

I relish that feeling of doing something a bit different, a bit weird, a bit pointless – but, at the same time, great fun. It reminds me that different is possible. I can cross that daunting gap between known and unknown, so long as there's cake or Jelly Babies waiting on the other side.

It was July by the time I'd finished all the legs of my triathlon along the River Cam and I'd fallen in love with adventuring – particularly the stage when I was alone on the walk, as that's when I'd dreamt up new ideas of fun ways to get from A to B, both literally and from a career perspective. I'd thought about how I'd like my life to be different, what kind of work I'd like to focus on next, who I'd like to work with, and in what kind of role I thought I could be most valuable. I'd come home from each section of the triathlon brimming with ideas about what my next big goal should be.

2

Facing my fears

How big could I go?

It was a blustery day at the start of April 2017. The wind was threatening to blow me backwards, but the sun shone brightly and I was a few days into my biggest adventure yet. Walking along the edge of the A838 on the north-west coast of Scotland, I'd come to a section overlooking a beautiful, sheltered, sandy bay with turquoise waters gently lapping at the shore. Throwing my 15kg backpack down on the grass, I sat down beside it and gazed out to sea.

Beyond those four days along the River Cam, I'd never done a long distance walk before. But then I had found myself wanting to explore more of the UK, and to really test myself in a new way, and this walk would certainly do that. Plus, after my attempt at cycling the classic British adventure, Land's End to John O'Groats (LEJOG), the previous year hadn't quite worked out, I was keen to go back, heading south this time: from John O'Groats down to Cornwall.

Back in autumn 2016, after the fun I'd had on my River Cam triathlon in the spring, I'd loaded up my hybrid bike with a sleeping bag and tent (and a few other bits), then set off solo and self-supported from Land's End. It was easy enough to plan – with none of the currency or language issues that I might have had to think about if I'd gone abroad – and I was looking forward to exploring more of the country I call home.

The most south-westerly corner of Cornwall, Land's End, for those who haven't been, is a bit of an odd tourist amusement park. The sign at the edge of a 100-metre cliff looks out to sea. Squint, and you'll see the Isles of Scilly! This sign is cordoned off during opening hours, meaning you have to pay if you want to actually touch it (official photos are extra!). The South West Coast Path stretches out promisingly in either direction, running along the cliff edge, offering rugged wilderness and beautiful views on a sunny day. A mess of accommodation, games machines, restaurants, and gift shops spoil the view inland.

Getting out of this weird location as soon as I could, I cycled north, navigating by paper map and occasionally my phone. I was following National Cycle Routes (NCRs) and had arranged to stop off at friends' places along the way. I loved the excitement of discovering different parts of the country. First struggling with the Cornish hills, and from there camping in pub gardens (one pub owner even gave me the key to his pub!) and, of course, all the many cake stops kept me going as I battled my way through Birmingham and over the Yorkshire moors, until I finally found myself north of the border. I'd officially cycled to another country! On day eighteen of the adventure, I was following NCR 7 through the Cairngorms... 800 miles down and 200 to go. The heavens opened and rain pelted me relentlessly all day. I was soaked through and freezing cold in the early October chill. After getting lost, I had to push my bike over what felt like a mountain to get back on track and by the time I was on the cycle route again I couldn't stop shaking.

Surrounded by eerie, grey mountains on all sides, leaking clouds still hung low in the sky. The cycle path that snaked next to the A9 was so gravelly that I couldn't maintain any kind of speed to get warm, and the cold continued to bite at my fingers, making it painful just holding onto the handlebars. Shaking uncontrollably, I realised that I had no option but to seek a way out. It was past the end of the tourist season up in the Scottish Highlands, so what few B&Bs are dotted around in this sparsely populated wilderness were closed.

Eventually, I came across a house in the middle of nowhere, down a small lane off the A9, and knocked hopefully on the door with my best 'please help me' face at the ready. While looking slightly put out at being interrupted, the couple who lived there let me come in and thaw out while they got their grandchildren some lunch. I huddled by the fire, getting as close as I could without burning myself, but after an hour I was still frozen to the bone and would start shivering again as soon as I moved away from the heat.

They agreed that it would be foolish for me to keep going, so they dropped me at the local train station some 20 miles away – for a fee – and I got a train to Inverness. I found myself a hostel and then continued onwards with a mix of cycling and trains to get to John O'Groats. My first big adventure and I hadn't made it... not how I'd wanted to. I'd set out to cycle every mile and I'd failed.

But, despite that, I'd bloody loved it! I'd loved being out in the wilderness and reliant only on myself. I'd loved the freedom of my self-propelled transport. I'd loved exploring the varied regions of our incredible country. On a bike, you see so much more, you feel every hill, and you can stare endlessly out into every horizon you meet in a way that you just can't on a train or in a car. I was hooked.

And while I might have failed to cycle the whole way, I had just cycled *800* miles, when before all I'd done was 80. It felt incredible.

Now, sitting next to my backpack and looking out at the North Sea, just a few days into my JOGLE walk, there was something else bobbing in my mind – something beyond the challenges that lay ahead on this walking adventure.

I was due to stay with a friend of mine, Sean Conway in about a month's time once I'd walked a casual 500 miles to the Lake District. I'd met him the year before and learnt of his own adventures, which had been a huge inspiration for me to go bigger still with mine. His best-known adventure is probably his 2013 swim the length of Britain, from Land's End to John O'Groats. He'd cycled LEJOG a few years previously and had since turned the cycle and swim into what he called the 'ultimate British triathlon' by running JOGLE dressed as Forrest Gump (as you do!).

No-one had ever swum LEJOG before Sean, and his record stood unchallenged for five years. Having sort of cycled LEJOG myself and now walking it, the idea of adding a water leg and creating my own British triathlon began percolating in my head. *Could I do that? Could I somehow travel LEJOG on the sea, out there in those freezing North Sea waters that were now crashing onto rocks in front of me?*

'Hell no!' was my answer. I was finding this walking malarkey hard enough. Just four days in, I'd already realised how much I hated walking with such a heavy pack. It was so unbelievably slow and incredibly painful. Everything hurt – from my feet to my ankles, from my legs to my back, from my shoulders to my hips.

That walk certainly delivered on my initial goal of testing myself in a new way. Not only was it frustratingly slow-going and generally very uncomfortable, but I also ended up getting seriously injured. I was rescued by strangers while in the Lake District after I'd developed acute tendonitis so badly in my left ankle that I couldn't move my foot even a millimetre without crying in pain.

This wonderful family took me first to the local minor injuries unit in Penrith, and an hour later they came back to check on me, feeling bad for just leaving me in the hospital alone, and invited me to stay with them for the night. As I was by myself, injured, and with nowhere to stay (Sean was still a two-hour drive south and wasn't due back from a trip until the following day), I was very grateful to say the least. It was such an incredibly generous offer, inviting some wild woman they'd picked up off the roadside into their home – their warmth and care was just amazing.

Once I'd been given crutches and some painkillers, I went back with this family to their lovely home, where they cooked me dinner and shared stories of hiking up some of the famous 214 Lake District peaks called Wainwrights, named after Alfred Wainwright who documented them in his historic guidebook. I had a long soak in their huge bath and snuggled up in a comfy bed, trying not to move my foot throughout the night. Lucky, as I felt a bit awkward imposing on strangers, the next morning, Lin Crosland, a friend-of-a-friend, came to pick me up. I stayed with her and her family on their farm overlooking Bassenthwaite Lake while I recovered.

Having had a week off recovering on crutches, and helping out where I could on the farm – feeding lambs and petting the dogs (a crucial job) – I got myself gently walking again. And two days later I made it to Sean's house in Windermere. After long chats about injuries, adventure careers, loving the Lake

District, and life in general, I pushed on towards Cornwall, which was by that point a mere 470 odd miles away.

Oh, the Lakes! I was now heading south out of the Lake District and had fallen in love somewhere along the way. The towering mountains are high enough to provide amazing views and a challenging climb to reach their peaks, while the glorious lakes themselves are endlessly inviting. It might have helped that it didn't rain once the whole time I was there but, I have to say, it's still my favourite place in the UK to date.

(If you've never been, I honestly don't know what you've been doing with your life. My top tip is to head to Pooley Bridge and walk the north section of the Ullswater Way. It's a real mixture of cow-dodging paths through grassy fields, wonderful woodland, and then the stunning vistas that open out over Ullswater Lake, with peaks rolling off into the distance beyond. And, if water's your thing, you can rent a kayak or boat to go exploring on the lake.)

As I reached Kendal, I was feeling stronger by the day, so I decided to up my daily mileage from 20 to 30 miles for six days straight in order to make up for the time I'd had off on crutches. Luckily, the tendonitis didn't come back during that week! However, it was a week of non-stop rain and at this point I realised the greatest flaw in my planning: footwear. As most of my route was on some form of path, what I actually needed was light, easy-to-dry footwear rather than heavy, supportive hiking boots. Unfortunately I had the latter, which, when combined with a relentlessly rainy week, meant putting on soaking boots every morning. And wet feet every day means one thing... trench foot. Yup, that condition they used to get in trenches during the First World War. It's not a disease – it's simply what happens to your skin when it's wet for a long time.

Trench foot is very painful (although not as acute as tendonitis). It essentially feels like there's sand in your boots grating on your raw feet as you walk, but it's actually just your skin disintegrating on itself. Plus, there's the blisters – extra deep so you can't pop them as there's too many layers of nerves to go through. All in all, not fun.

It was at this point that I came to realise what 'mind over matter' really means. My feet were literally coming apart, but I'd set myself 30-mile targets to reach every day. I was conscious that if I winced and hopped to try to make it hurt a little less, I'd just end up throwing something else out, like a hip or my back. So, after a day of very painful walking, I decided that I would take a different approach.

I stood myself up on the path, then, to get rid of any tension, I shook it all about (like I was doing the Hokey Cokey). I must've looked like a right idiot, but, once loosened up, I took a deep breath and simply began to walk as if nothing was wrong. I didn't think about walking or pain or anything to do with the reality of my current situation. Instead, I daydreamed of cake, beaches, and baths – *anything* other than what I was doing. And, after just five minutes of walking normally and thinking about ice cream, I noticed... nothing.

There wasn't one bit of pain, so long as I kept walking and avoided thinking about trench foot. The mind is way more powerful than the body.

The initial pains from walking with a heavy backpack had eased by this point, as my body had become used to it, and the more I got used to the pace, the easier it became mentally too. It's funny though: the more I endured during that walk, the more determined I was to get to the end. No matter what it took, I was hell bent on walking every single step the length of Britain. There was no way I'd get a train like I'd had to do with the cycle leg. The pain, the crutches, the disintegrating feet – none of it made me want to stop. In fact, it all made me want to do it even more. It wasn't because I *like* pain, I might add, but because the more I found myself able to overcome these hurdles, the more I wondered what else I was capable of.

And, by the time I walked up to the Land's End sign, 57 days and 993 miles after setting off from John O'Groats, I knew I was made of tough stuff. I knew that I could make it through anything, if only I tried hard enough.

After finishing the walk, I made the most of summer, enjoying lazy bike rides to the beach, working again and earning some money, seeing friends, having a shower every day, and living a pretty normal life. But, as autumn sneaked in, I figured I should go back and cycle LEJOG again from the beginning – just so that I could say I'd cycled the whole way. I went a slightly different route and this time I made it successfully to the end, cycling every mile.

With walking and cycling LEJOG now firmly under my belt, I started to wonder what I should do next, and if – perhaps – I'd dismissed a LEJOG triathlon too quickly. Could a sea-based LEJOG adventure actually be possible for me? Either way, there was one particular, personal hurdle to overcome first though...

A fear of the sea

I can't remember exactly how old I was. Six? I couldn't swim yet, but I enjoyed being in swimming pools, splashing around, and clinging to Mum when I was out of my depth. We were staying at a well-known national chain of holiday parks and on this particular day, my brother and I were enjoying going down the indoor water slide. Mum was positioned in the pool at the end to catch me when the slide spat me out, as the water was too deep for me to stand up.

After a few goes, I didn't want to stop, so I ran back up to queue for the slide with the other kids. When it came to my turn, I stepped up to the top of the slide. The instructor, a bored teenager, nodded for me to go and I excitedly threw myself into the rushing jet stream of water and down the plastic tube. My hands stretched out to my sides, steadying me as the power of the water threw me from side to side and the tube twisted and turned, my bum bumping over the ridges until I finally shot out the other end. This time, though, there were no arms outstretched waiting to catch me. No-one pulled me safely up to the surface.

Mum hadn't realised I'd gone back for another go. She was on the other side of the pool with my dad, and they initially had no idea I'd just plunged into the water.

Oddly, I don't remember any panic or thinking about drowning, but I did quickly realise that reaching my hands up to the surface and flailing them around didn't help me. Looking around under the water I saw the side of the pool about a metre away, so I frantically propelled myself in its direction until I could touch it, and eventually hauled myself out of the water.

I don't know how long I was under the water for, but, by the time I'd rescued myself, and was sitting on the edge, coughing and spluttering, my parents had raced over.

"Weren't there any lifeguards?" you might ask. And that's a very good question. One had spotted me from the other side of the pool and blew her whistle to alert her colleague, who was standing chatting to someone about three metres behind me. My mum had heard the whistle and, not seeing me anywhere, knew it must have been me and rushed to help. But the lifeguard standing within saving distance didn't hear the whistle or see me drowning.

After that incident, I learnt to swim with school swimming lessons like most kids and I was never that bothered about being in a pool – I guess because I knew I could save myself if I needed to. But from then on deep, open water made me nervous.

I don't know how I went from nearly drowning in a pool to being scared of deep, open water, but I think it's the element of control – or rather a lack thereof – that frightens me. I know I can save myself in a pool; I don't know if I could do that at sea.

Sean's length of Britain swim had seen him contend with masses of stinging jellyfish, reports of sharks in the waters, and wild storms that lead to the loss of the kayak from the back of his support boat (luckily all of the crew were fine). Given my fear of being in the sea there was still no way I was going to even contemplate matching Sean's four and a half month swim – I'd have to find another way.

Back in 2012, I visited my university friends, Sarah and James Dominey, who had moved out to Barcelona after graduation. While they were at work during the day, I entertained myself by exploring the city, going to the chocolate museum, and attending a cookery course (where I learnt how to make paella and crème Catalana, the local version of crème brûlée!). On my wanderings, I also stumbled upon this thing called stand up paddleboarding. I'd never heard of it before, but it looked fun and seemed to be done near the shore, meaning I wouldn't be going much out of my depth.

I met the instructor, Marc at the Base Nautica sports centre on one of the beaches just north of the city centre. It turned out I was the only one at the session – and I think this was the very first of Marc's new SUP business. Once I was kitted out in a wetsuit, we made our way down to the sea. We stood on the warm sand as he went through some theory elements, before he got me onto the board and paddling out to just the other side of the breaking waves. I listened to his explanations of the different paddle strokes and how to balance, and managed to get myself up from kneeling to standing. We paddled back and forth along the beach, constantly dealing with side-on swell, while I tried to find my feet with this completely new sport. It was exhausting but, unbelievably, around forty-five minutes in I'd still not fallen off the board, much to my instructor's dismay.

'You have to fall in so that you're not scared of it,' Marc said, laughing as he started trying to shove my board with his paddle.

'No! Don't you dare!' I fired back, not in the mood for his games. I had been just about OK up until this point, but the idea of falling off and into the sea was too much.

His game worked and I lost my balance, but, somehow, I managed to fall onto the board and ended up on all fours. I could see he was slightly put out that I still wasn't wet, but I didn't care. I'd had enough by that point and called an end to the session early. I was knackered.

Jump forward six years and I'd since SUPed on lakes and rivers back in the UK. It had been an altogether different experience to going in at the deep end in Barcelona – calm and relaxing, no rolling swell or pushy instructors to deal with, and I'd found it super easy to get on and off the board without the risk of getting wet. It didn't seem so bad after all... so when I found myself starting to seriously think about a water-based LEJOG route, I turned to Google to find out if anyone had ever attempted to SUP it.

The short answer was no. It turned out that a guy had paddleboarded across the Atlantic and I knew from friends in adventure circles that Charlie Head had paddleboarded sections of the English coastline (before bad weather had prevented him from heading up into northern Scotland) but, as far as I could tell, no-one had ever done LEJOG on a SUP.

Knowing about Sean's experiences from his swim, combined with my own fear of the sea and inexperience paddling off shore, meant that if I was going to do this kind of sea-based adventure, unlike my previous self-supported adventures, I'd need full support. There was no way I'd go out there alone. But when you start looking at supported adventure, the costs skyrocket immediately: a support boat, skipper and crew, a photographer to record it, canal permits, kit, and food and travel expenses. All this meant that if I was going to contemplate going down this route, I'd really need something that would grab headlines in order to be able to attract sponsors and cover the costs. *Well*, I thought, *three world firsts would surely be big enough!*

But why?

I'm not altogether sure *why* the idea of making my walk and cycle into a triathlon by paddleboarding LEJOG was so compelling to me. I was highly aware of my fear. The thought of actually being out at sea on a SUP made me feel sick. I had no clue how tides worked. I didn't know anything about boats or skippers. And I had no experience paddling on the sea beyond that one session in Barcelona.

On the face of it, I was the most scared, inexperienced, and unlikely person to take on such a ridiculous challenge, let alone to be the first person in the world to attempt it.

And my friends firmly agreed. When I told them, they'd humour me and say things like, 'Oh, that sounds like an interesting idea,' clearly thinking it was exactly that and only that – an idea. I don't think anyone actually believed for one second that I'd make it happen (except my mum, of course). I have these big, bizarre ideas every now and then, and only ever attempt some of them, so to friends this one was no different to the many that get left on the shelf. This was, after all, by far the most out there and therefore least likely to happen, so should surely be firmly tucked away at the back of that shelf, out of harm's reach.

Honestly, I think it was partly the sheer ridiculousness of it that appealed to me – the fact that no-one took me seriously, that they thought it was impossible, and that they certainly thought that *I* couldn't do it, even if they'd never say it so bluntly. The challenge of doing something so far out of my comfort zone, to push past all fear and expectation and do it anyway, drew me in.

What if I could face my fear? What if I could make the impossible possible? I've always been a bit headstrong. My mum would probably describe me as pretty determined, so once I get an idea in my head it's hard for me to shake it until I've given it a bloody good go.

There was something more about this though, something more than just an alluring idea. I couldn't and still can't quite put my finger on it. I just felt unfathomably compelled to do it. But I knew for sure that it was now or never, and that in one year, yet alone twenty, I couldn't deal with looking back and thinking, *what if I'd just tried – how different would my life be now?*

The plan

I sat staring at a map of Britain one cold November morning in 2017. *Do I actually want to do this,* I thought, *or am I just looking at this because it sounds like a cool idea?* With an emphatic *yes* already in my mind, I knew that it was as simple as that – decision made. Despite not having a clue how I'd make it happen, I was resolute that I had to see if it was possible. I decided that I was happy to work out the details over the next few months, and aim to leave by some point in April, when the weather should start to warm up and before the heat of the summer kicked in.

So, what to call it? The names of my previous adventures had been simple, for ease of talking about them and to make them easy to find if someone was searching for me online, so I continued my trend and that's how SUP Britain came into being. I threw together a simple page on my website with some basic headline points of what SUP Britain was and – suddenly – there it was, officially out in the world for everyone to see. I followed up with an announcement on social media, then settled in to prepare a plan with 5 months to go.

Even though I was thinking about paddling solo, no adventure – even an unsupported one – is ever truly a solo endeavour. The route planning, kit recommendations, moral support, finances, and general advice that get you to the starting line are all essential. Sure, it's one thing to learn some aspects on the job and being open to seeing what happens as you go, but, while I do love this approach, I'm not daft. I knew I would need to have a really good idea of how to handle some key aspects of the challenge if I wasn't going to die. Having people to call on for support is incredibly important in any aspect of my life, but particularly if I'm going one hundred percent out of my comfort zone and into potentially dangerous situations.

From the beginning, Sean was an incredible support. His knowledge from having done a similar route and his willingness to share insights from his extra eight years of experience in adventure were so welcome. Using his swim as my example, I quickly formulated a plan of how I'd tackle this expedition. Despite its enormous scale, it was actually quite simple in its approach. Just some fundamentals to get sorted, then all I would have to do was focus on the paddling... oh, and ignore the fears screaming at me from inside my chest, like some sort of alien trying to burst its way out.

Sean's route had seen him swim from Land's End in Cornwall, up the west coast of England then Scotland, and round the north at Cape Wrath to reach John O'Groats. The reasoning behind choosing the west coast was simply that it was shorter than going up the east, plus it dodged the busy Dover shipping lanes.

He had wanted to swim through the Caledonian Canal, which connects the west and east coasts of Scotland, providing a neat cut up through the middle of the country and avoiding the need to go around that brutal north west corner with the more dangerous waters. Despite repeatedly trying, he wasn't given permission to swim through the canal due to environmental reasons and so, unable to take this cut-through, Sean's route was one hundred percent sea-based.

Looking at Sean's west coast route, it seemed like a sensible option for me too. While there are some inland waterways that join up various parts of the country, there are none that stretch the whole length of Britain and, rather than split the route 50:50 sea to inland, I felt it would be easier to stick mainly to the sea for logistical simplicity, but with one critical difference.

The thought of paddling around Cape Wrath on that most north-westerly edge of mainland Scotland – a very fierce stretch of sea highly exposed to North Sea storms – did not fill me with excitement. Luckily, as a paddleboarder, I would be allowed to paddle through the Caledonian Canal and this would shorten my route by around 70 miles. And, having walked along most of the canal during my walk south from John O'Groats the previous spring, I already knew that it was a really beautiful part of the country.

So that was it. All the route planning I needed was the overall picture – just like on all my other adventures. Based on an estimate of my daily mileage, I plotted out a spreadsheet of where I thought I'd paddle to each day. Given that the support boat would get us to and from anchorages or harbours, I didn't worry too much about trying to plan to paddle to a suitable stopping place, calculating that I could let the boat take up that slack and ferry me back and forth.

However, in truth my estimated daily mileage of 12 miles was based on not very much at all. At this stage, I had never tried to paddle from point A to point B on the sea. So, I assumed that I could work with a paddling speed of two miles an hour for six hours a day (the length of one tide, as I now knew), and allow for a little more distance to be covered further north on my route as my ability improved.

When I emailed John Patrick this estimate he laughed. 'Are you planning on paddling *at all*? You'll probably drift faster than that!' he replied. John had gotten in touch with me via Facebook. I knew nothing about the sea or boats and I didn't have any contacts in the industry. I didn't think I knew a single sailor, or even had any friends of friends that I could call on. So, I had put the word out through social media.

'Any yachtmaster skippers fancy acting as support, following a terrified paddleboarder the length of Britain to set a world record?' was essentially what I had asked... not a bad offer if you ask me!

The little that I had found out about the sea from Google had suggested that a yachtmaster was the most experienced skipper you could find, and that was exactly what I needed. I wanted someone who could tell me what to do in terms of tide, harbours, boat stuff, and navigation – plus, I needed to be able to trust them to keep me and my photographer safe.

Facebook turned out to be a great source of connections for advice, but those actually willing to volunteer for such an attractive opportunity were thin on the ground though, most likely because I couldn't pay them. Totally self-funded at this point, I could only offer expenses – anyone willing to skipper, or be my photographer, would have to be able to and want to do it purely for the fun of it. An adventure of a lifetime, if you look at it in the right way...

Initially, I was dead set on getting one skipper for the whole trip. I refused to entertain the idea of having to manage skippers coming and going weekly, plus the added expenses of their travel to and from wherever we'd made it to that week, on top of everything else I would have to deal with during the expedition, just did not seem viable. I wanted crew that were committed and would back me wholeheartedly, without me having to constantly get new people excited about the trip while I was in the throes of tackling a couple of world records. Maybe this was asking too much, but it was the plan I wanted to make happen, so I was sticking with it.

I had one or two people get in touch to offer their skippering services. Funnily enough, they were all old, white men. Now, I have nothing against old, white men as individuals, but it truly just goes to show where the boating world is at... And I will say that the thing with some old, white men is that they have an over-inflated sense of knowing how things ought to be done. Yes, I had no idea about the sea, and I knew that, but I did have extensive experience in organising an adventure and in knowing my own abilities.

I set up a Skype meeting with one of these guys. When I asked what experience he had as a skipper, he proceeded to tell me about the time when he had captained a support boat for a race over in the Caribbean. *So far so good – what had he learnt from this experience?* I wondered.

'Well, the key to any of these kinds of endurance adventures, let me tell you, is nutrition,' he began. 'It's really important that you get your calorie intake right, with the right kind of food, of course. I can help you write out a nutrition plan...'

He was adamant that, as my skipper, he should be in charge of my nutrition. He continued, 'And you're going at the wrong time. April is no good. You have to start in June or July. Don't worry, I'm your guy. I'm going to be your skipper and you're going to start in June.'

I had to laugh.

Clearly this guy hadn't bothered to look at my website or social media. If he had, he'd have known right away that I'm powered by cake – and that it's a non-negotiable. And as for attempting to dictate when my adventure would begin and telling me who was going to be my skipper, it was very clear that this guy was not the one.

By January, though, time was ticking on and I still had no skipper. But I did have one call booked in with an Irish man who had found me via a Facebook post. He was a yachtmaster – tick – and was pretty much retired, so potentially had the full four-odd months that I thought SUP Britain was going to take free of other commitments – double tick.

As I excitedly explained my plan, John listened intently, and in his cheerful but calm Irish accent, he began to discuss ways to solve the problems I was yet to figure out. He offered me his carefully considered advice and it sounded like he thought my scheme was possible. Ridiculous, but possible.

After just five minutes on the phone with John, I knew I wanted him as my skipper. *This* was the guy. I instantly trusted him and I've come to learn that you should always trust your gut. John had the experience I was looking for and the right attitude to boot, which is almost more important when considering bringing someone onto an adventure support team. Plus, luckily, he didn't seem to think I was totally out of my mind and told me he was up for the challenge.

So, with my adventure pencilled in his diary, I set about utilising John's vast knowledge of the sea to try and make a more accurate plan of the distances I'd cover each day. I was very conscious that I'd rather overestimate how long it would take, than underestimate and feel disheartened at slow progress. But, after John's mickey-taking of my conservative 12-miles a day estimate, I figured that even with my complete lack of experience, I could definitely do better than 'drifting' pace. I notionally upped my mileage to 15 miles per day – if only to look less stupid, rather than based on any new, tangible information.

With the route planned (sort of), I turned my attention to the rest of my crew, equipment, and funding. Kit wise, I'd only ever paddled on an inflatable SUP before, so this seemed like the obvious option to go for – sticking with what I knew. I'd heard that hard boards, while quicker, have the potential to be less stable. Plus they would likely be painful to kneel on for a long period of time and, given my inexperience on the sea and fear of falling in, the likelihood that I'd kneel to begin with was quite high. I also knew that an inflatable board would make it easier for me to store it on the boat and transport it to and from the expedition, as they pack down to a suitcase-sized bag.

I was keen to get two boards: one shorter, wider board offering me a more stable option to start out with, and a faster, sleeker one for once I felt more comfortable. Additionally, having two boards would enable any friends, crew, or strangers I met along the way to paddle with me too, adding a social element to the adventure – and I was really drawn to that.

Clothing wise, I'd opted for an NRS summer wetsuit teamed with a brightly coloured PFD (personal flotation device) to keep me safe, plus the other essentials: sunglasses, a baseball hat, a waterproof case for my phone, a SPOT tracker with an SOS function in case things went really wrong, Aquapac drybags for the food and extra clothes I needed to carry on my board, and a SIGG insulated water bottle to keep my water chilled and fresh.

Then there was the small matter of a boat. To find the right vessel, I really needed the advice and guidance of someone who knew all about sailing – I didn't have a clue – so, turning to my network, I reached out to a couple friends of friends (of friends) for support.

Now, I wouldn't normally shell out £80 for a day ticket to an event, but the Royal Geographic Society's Explore weekend seemed like the perfect place to find some of this advice I needed. I wagered that if it led me to the right money, then this investment was nothing.

When I got there, I honed in on a funding talk. I found my way up to the members' library nestled on the top floor, surrounded by period architecture and the beautiful historic features of the society's 1875 building. The walls were lined – floor to ceiling – with old books, which contrasted with the polished finish of the glass-walled meeting rooms and modern furniture. It was suitably impressive. And the talk lived up to expectations too.

The guy giving the talk began by running through what sponsors are looking for, how to approach them, and what they need to make decisions. But he also stressed that you never know from the outside how things will align for an organisation: they might just be looking for something that had never crossed your mind, so you should be open about who you'll collaborate with. He explained that he and his partner had ended up getting sponsorship from a garage company for their cycling adventure across Europe because they wanted him to stop off en route at several branches to facilitate a team-bonding opportunity for employees. So, to get funding, I realised I would have to get creative.

A friend of mine, Spike Reid, had recently completed his own large-scale paddleboarding expedition, completing the first descent of the Ganges in India on a SUP. He'd been active in the adventure world for his whole career and was able to give me some advice on the sponsorship side of things: a logo and good photos, he explained, is key. Luckily, I knew a photographer I could call on.

David Altabev lived in London and worked in innovation management: he'd developed his love of photography on the side of his professional life and had been a photographer for social sport groups like Project Awesome, Midnight Runners, and the Uganda Marathon, as well as other adventurers too. Fortunately for me, David was more than happy to combine a trip he'd already been planning to Bristol with a quick photo shoot for SUP Britain.

I figured we should head to a suitably epic-looking coastal location to make me look gnarly and brave, even if I was feeling anything but at that point. We drove an hour over the border into Wales and along the coast to Southerndown. That day, the weather had decided to up the stakes and was blowing a gale, to say the least. As we pulled into the beach car park and sat

overlooking the sea, the heavens opened, and rain pelted the car –
the sea was as raw as the wind. I suppose this is what I'd been
looking for though. A greyish-brown raging backdrop to convey
the enormity (read: stupidity) of what I was trying to do.

We had arrived before high tide, giving us an hour or so
with the rocky beach exposed. I got changed into my wetsuit and
pumped up my board. David tried to direct me, but I was
honestly not having a great time: it was hard to hold my board
steady as the wind fought relentlessly to pull it out of my grip.
And it's not easy to look gnarly and brave when you're fighting
just to stay standing up.

At one point David looked at me with a straight face and
said, 'so, are you going out then?'

I looked at him, and then at the sea, and then back at
him. I laughed. 'In this? Are you crazy?'

'Surely this is what it's going to be like on the
adventure?' he asked, confused. 'If you can't go out in this, how
are you going to make it up the country?'

'These are terrible conditions. If I went out now, I'd
never even make it onto my board, plus you won't be able to see
me – the swell's too high. I'm just going to wait for good
weather on the trip,' I assured him confidently. He didn't look in
the least bit convinced.

'You know it's the *sea*, right? You're going to be
waiting a long time,' he retorted.

I could tell he'd just moved me from the box in his head marked 'maybe she's lost it' into the one that said 'she's definitely delusional.'

With David's shots under my belt, I cracked on with my sponsorship mission. It was a tricky one: my previous adventures had all been relatively cheap, going solo and self supported, which meant it was much easier to forget about sponsorship and just do whatever I wanted. But with this adventure I knew that the boat and crew would be far too expensive, costing in the region of twenty times what any of my other adventures had cost, so I needed cash sponsorship.

I already knew from speaking to a wide range of people that it's typically through existing contacts that you get given money if you're not already 'well known' in some capacity. So, I fired into this approach, emailing anyone and everyone I knew, or had ever come into contact with. The guard from South West Trains I had said 'morning' to last Tuesday, the postie from my childhood home, and the guy that did my MOT six years ago – you know, just to be thorough...

Having had no luck, I moved on to emailing complete strangers, each time trying to somehow pre-empt how my outlandish plan might be useful for them – for example, if their business related to the sea or the environment or women's empowerment. While this definitely produced more replies than emailing round the houses, nothing quite fitted.

Kit, on the other hand, was much easier to get my hands on. Brands were delighted to support me. Of the nine kit sponsors I had in the end, all were unendingly supportive – and at the end of the day, their real value wasn't so much in the free stuff (brilliantly helpful as that was!), but in their belief in me. They knew that I would try my best and that was all that mattered to them. They looked forward to my stories along the way, the message I would share of going beyond what you think you're capable of, and the content I was already starting to produce. From their comments and shares on social media to check-in emails, I really felt that these communications were from one human being to another. These might have been business decisions, but they were based in real human connection and that meant a lot.

So, my kit was sorted, but I still had to find another way to finance the expedition. In the meantime, next on the to-do list was an expedition photographer.

Setting up Skype, I got ready to chat to Liam in Dubai. He was out there working as a photographer for an outdoor company, filming and photographing kids for publicity materials for the centre. Doing the same activities week in, week out had been a good first photography job for him learning the ropes at the age of 22, but now he seemed keen to develop his photography further. I had some initial concerns about Liam's age when I got his application through, and these continued through our chat.

It wasn't quite a straight photography role that I had in mind – I'd called it 'photographer and media relations' in my posts about it online. I know exactly how much energy being on an adventure takes out of me and how little time there is left to do much else, so I was hunting for a photographer who would also take the initiative to gain as much media coverage as possible for SUP Britain, to the benefit of both of us and my sponsors, organising coverage on TV, radio, and online along the way. It was clear that Liam was keen to take on a role that could get his own work a lot of exposure, but I was hesitant about his ability to really push the adventure and get us coverage – his slightly shy and inexperienced demeanour did not convince me that he would take the lead and run.

Another photographer on my radar was Phil, a 30-something who had previously created a short wildlife film before selling it to a local tourism agency, so I knew that he had the confidence and creativity to both capture the content I needed and to push it out to the media. When we met, though, Phil seemed hesitant. He'd already half agreed to cycle across Europe with a friend and, very familiar with the lure of adventure, I could see that Phil's enthusiasm was for his own trip and not mine. Over the next week or so he changed his mind from initially saying that he could commit for the whole adventure, to dropping down to a couple of months, then, a few days later, just a couple of weeks.

It wasn't going to work. Above all else, I needed someone who would stick around – the last thing I wanted was to be left a crew member down midway through and have to divert my attention away from paddling to sort it out. So, while his answers to most of my questions had been brief, Liam did seem like a cool guy who – critically – I could get along with for several months on a small boat out at sea. And I reminded myself that he was only 22, so I couldn't, therefore, expect him to have the approach of someone in their thirties. Plus, as well as being committed, he seemed enthusiastic and up for learning, which I figured would be enough for him to grow into the role as the adventure went on. When I offered him the role, he happily accepted and I was excited to have him on board.

It was great to finally be making some progress with the planning and having my two main crew members on board felt like I'd cleared a huge hurdle. It was now February and I'd been pushing out my adventure plans across social media, snowballing more support.

One morning, an email came through from someone who turned out to be ranked third in the British SUP Association 2017 Women's SUP Surf series – clearly, the sea was her home. Cal Major had gotten in touch to let me know that she was going to SUP LEJOG, too, this year. Her route differed from mine, in that she would go inland from the Bristol Channel and through the canals, while I would go over the Irish Sea. She'd then pop back out somewhere around Liverpool and our routes would rejoin on Scotland's west coast as we both headed for John O'Groats via the Caledonian Canal.

What on earth? The last thing I wanted was to feel like I had to race anyone else – let alone someone so experienced – while I was desperately trying to face my fear. Until now, the idea of being the first person to SUP LEJOG was just a nice bonus for getting to the end... after all, thousands of people had walked and cycled LEJOG before I'd had a crack at it and I'd never tried to be the fastest. I'd just adventured at my own pace, in a way that felt right for me.

I started to wonder though, if having Cal paddling too was actually a great opportunity for both of us. I thought that our simultaneous bids would amplify our stories and therefore create even greater traction for our respective sponsors – here were two people both taking on an extreme world first, like Scott versus Amundsen racing for the South Pole... except that it was women and it was now and it would be happening right here on our doorstep. Historic! I emailed Cal back to see if she'd be up for chatting, but she didn't reply.

There was no way I'd let this put me off though. My adventure was very different to Cal's – different routes and for different reasons. I resolved to simply give it my best shot. I'd get there when I got there, whether first or second, all I could do was try.

Wipe out

I'd never trained for any of my previous adventures. The idea of getting fit by covering the same miles over and over again just didn't appeal. Instead, I see endurance adventures as being so long that my body has time to adapt – starting slowly at first and building up stamina as I go. And this approach felt right for this adventure. The last thing that I wanted to do was force myself to spend any longer than was necessary on the sea: I was conscious that I didn't want to scare myself out of doing it before I'd even got going. Plus, I figured that once I'd started, the momentum of being on an adventure, and the social pressure to finish, would help me to push through the fear I'd inevitably face.

Nonetheless, before taking to the sea, I thought it advisable to get at least a touch of experience, given the only ocean paddleboarding I'd done so far was that one session some six years ago in Barcelona. A friend of mine had been on a paddleboarding skills course with Tim Trew, who runs SUP Bristol with his partner Kate Ingham, and recommended contacting him for some advice on the kind of session that might help, given what I was setting out to do.

Tim is a wonderfully warm, friendly, and helpful guy. He's been paddleboarding for at least ten years and is an expert instructor – even teaching other instructors. Tim was excited to be able to offer some guidance on the expedition and, when we met in a cosy café in Bristol on a wet, winter's morning, he talked me through everything: from what kit to wear – *do I go for a wetsuit, dry suit or semi-dry?* – to other people I should contact for advice. He then suggested that he could take me out on the sea for a short, one-to-one session to give me some top tips. It was perfect.

Around a month before I was due to start, Tim and I headed out to Clevedon on the north coast of Somerset, just west of Bristol. We suited up (opting for wetsuits) and hopped onto the Marine Lake to start with. A lido right on the seafront, this little oasis of calm, flat water next to the rather scarily raging sea, was a great place for Tim to be able to assess my technique, which – surprisingly – he said was good. He gave me some guidance on how to get more power into my stroke, then we hit the sea.

It was a blustery day with a strong onshore wind and two feet of swell, creating a bleak landscape of browns and greys – murky waves crashed violently onto the beach. Needless to say, this ominous scene did nothing to quell my nerves. Tim went out on his own first to get a feel for the water. He made it look so effortless, riding the waves standing up, using his paddle to brace and stop himself from falling in, all with a huge smile on his face. This was clearly his happy place.

Then came my turn to join him. This was *not* my happy place. I was scared of being in the water and I was scared of looking like an idiot. I really didn't want to go out there, but I knew I had to. This was my opportunity to learn from someone who could teach me loads. So out we went.

The waves were breaking so close to the shore that I had to fight the sheer power of the water just to jump onto my board and get onto my knees. At the same time, the wind threatened to blow me off. Finally, I was on the board, but there was no way in hell I'd be standing up in this. Not only was I terrified of falling off and being pummelled by the waves, but I just didn't see the point of heading out if I was going to be back off the board the second I stood up. I fought to keep the board pointing directly into the wind, nose into the choppy swell as it crashed towards the shore. If my board turned even slightly side on, I'd get wiped out.

I tried to paddle out beyond the breakers but it was utterly exhausting. I looked around me. The reality of just how scared I was feeling began to sink in. I tried to control my fear, push it to one side, and get the job done. But, in that very moment, I knew that if I hadn't already made the adventure public, I would have been tempted to pull out – ear is such an overwhelming feeling and I knew I didn't want to spend months of my life feeling like this.

But, for now, I knew I had no choice but to keep paddling. *Almost there, just a little bit further.*

'Ahhhhhh!'

A wave caught me off guard and flipped the board, throwing me into the murky, churning sea. Treading water and trying to breathe, it took me a second to think what to do.

'Focus! Just get back on the board,' I told myself.

I still had a hold of my paddle, which was lucky – otherwise, I'd have been even more at the mercy of the waves. I reached out to pull the board back the right way up. In leaning across the top of the board to haul the far side over towards me, I somehow ended up underneath the board and submerged beneath the water. Grabbing the edge, I forced the board away from my head and gasped for air... I looked around. The waves were too high to see where Tim had gone.

'Don't panic, don't panic,' I kept telling myself as waves broke over me in quick succession, 'just get back on the board.'

Soon, Tim spotted me and waved for us to go into shore. I can't even remember if I did manage to get myself back on the board or if I just let the waves dump me on the beach but, either way, I'd just experienced my first fall off the SUP and it was not fun.

We stood back on dry land and chatted briefly, looking out to sea. The waves were still crashing ashore as aggressively as they had when we first arrived – the wind roared across the brown ocean stretching out before us. These were *not* conditions I would be going out in during SUP Britain. I'd simply wait for good weather. But, to Tim, this was normal: 'if you can't go out in this, you'll never make it up the country.'

I appreciated his point. It's definitely true that the sea in this part of the world is choppy far more often than not, but I decided that I was happy to wait – I was in no rush to race up the coast. Plus, I'd be getting onto my board each day from the support boat well offshore, so I wouldn't have to fight my way out over breaking waves every single time I wanted to set out. I'd simply need calm enough conditions beyond the breakers.

Honestly, I left my session feeling nervous about what was ahead, yet – weirdly – a little more prepared now that I'd actually fallen off my board. I knew that the only way I was going to feel more relaxed about my fear of the sea was to face it head-on. And I'd just done it!

I think Tim, on the other hand, left feeling like I didn't have a chance in hell.

Timing wise, I'd been thinking I'd set off in April and, as the end of March drew near, there seemed to be a potential good weather window to aim for in the second week of the month. But this was all very much dependent on me finding a boat, a skipper, and funding in time – plus, it was assuming that the weather window would hold out.

As I continued the hunt for a support boat, I found something that looked like it might work and booked a viewing. Liam had managed to leave his existing job a couple of weeks early to join SUP Britain, so was back from Dubai, ready to join me. I decided to pick him up from his mum's house and head down to Devon together for a bit of a recce and to view the boat.

Liam's mum, Rachel Pointing lives in Stevenage, just an hour's drive south from my mum's house, en route towards the West Country. I knocked on Rachel's door and Liam answered eagerly, all packed up and just grabbing his last few bits of kit. He was about a foot taller than me, lean, short brown hair swept slightly to the side and a stubbly beard, wearing jeans and a hoodie. I said a quick hello to Rachel and Liam's stepdad, Steve, who I think would have preferred that they'd had some time to get to know the weird woman who would be taking their son on a wild adventure before we set off. But, with a long drive ahead of us, we quickly loaded the car and hit the road – with two lovely good luck cards and some cake in tow.

The drive down was a great opportunity to get to know Liam. We swapped stories about our families and our careers to date: he told me about his plan to improve his guitar playing during the trip, then I shared stories from my previous adventures. It turned out that Liam had grown up on sport. Skateboarding, slacklining, fishing, surfing, kayaking, snowboarding, and messing about in boats... it seemed like there wasn't much that he hadn't tried his hand at. Liam had already packed a lot into his twenty-two years and I liked his approach – it seemed he was a keen learner, one who put in the hours to get good at a new sport and learn some tricks while he was at it. Liam had also worked as a sports instructor for kids, so he was used to being patient when people weren't very good at something, which would no doubt come in handy with me on this trip.

We also talked some more about what had motivated him to apply to join the expedition, giving me a clearer idea of what he wanted to get out of it all, as well as a sense of where he could contribute best. It turned out that it had been his girlfriend, Amy Buck who had pushed him to apply for the role, because, while he thought it looked cool, he didn't imagine that he was experienced enough. He was glad she had given him a nudge. After all, 'you don't ask, you don't get' is a great motto to live by.

Liam also explained that he'd been feeling really nervous during our Skype call – partly because he had felt too inexperienced for the role, but, amusingly, moreso because there had been an enormous snake in the room with him. It transpired that the only room on the site where he had been working that both had an internet connection and would be quiet enough for a call was where the resident snake had its tank, and he had been worried that it would escape mid-call and attack him.

'How do you feel about spiders?' I asked with loaded intent.

'I don't mind them – why?' he responded suspiciously.

'Well, I hate them, so I have a deal for you. If you get rid of the spiders on the boat, I'll get rid of the snakes!' We both chuckled.

'I'm not entirely sure that's a fair deal...'

'But, if ever there *is* a snake on board, you'll be glad we made this deal!'

'Ha, fair enough – deal!'

Getting to Falmouth, the first boat we viewed seemed like a great option for the expedition and the owner initially seemed keen to sell. He said his wife was increasingly ill and found herself unable to get aboard anymore. It was a 30-foot sailing yacht with three sleeping areas and a swim deck at the back of the boat, which – I explained to him – would be great for getting on and off my board more easily multiple times per day while bobbing out at sea. Offering his unsolicited opinion, he insisted that I wait until June to start, to the point where he refused to sell his boat to me, given I clearly had no intention of taking his advice.

Despite the boat viewing going nowhere, Liam and I headed to Durdle Door on Dorset's south coast to get a little paddling practice at a picturesque location. The sea was calm, there was barely any swell or wind, and the sun was shining, so I wasn't feeling too bad about going out. It did worry me, however, that Liam wasn't coming with me and would simply be watching and taking photos from the shore. If anything happened, I would be out there on my own. This made me nervous.

Liam's experience both in surfing and as a dingy and powerboat instructor meant that he had a pretty solid understanding of the sea – he certainly knew far more than me – so, this was where his teaching began. He explained that waves come in rough sets: a few smaller waves, followed by some bigger ones, then a lull before the cycle starts again. It all varies from beach to beach and depends on the conditions – but, even still, you can always watch and count them as they come in until you get a reasonable idea of when the bigger waves will give way to a calmer section. Then, you can launch your board during the lull and (hopefully) get out beyond the breakers before the next set rolls in.

This was also a lesson in topography: the surface make-up of a beach affects how waves break, meaning that in some places, waves will break gently far out from the shore then smoothly roll in, while others will create the conditions for a short, sharp breaking wave that dumps right onto the beach. This was a dumping beach.

We stood there ready to go, Liam watching the set come in, and then: 'go, go, go!' I ran with my board into the sea, jumped swiftly onto the board and started determinedly paddling my way out past the breakers. Then we both saw it. Liam had misjudged this particular wave set and a huge bank of water reared up, ready to drop itself right on top of me.

Since my experience in Clevedon with Tim, I'd been watching lots of surfing videos on YouTube, in the hope I might pick up some tips. I remembered learning that surfers often duck dive waves: that is, pushing the front of their boards down under the face of the approaching water to avoid getting caught up in the wave's breaking surface. This was the only option that sprang to mind in those seconds as the wave reared up. However, SUP boards (particularly inflatable ones) are much more buoyant than surfboards and there's no way even an experienced paddleboarder would be able to duck dive an inflatable SUP – the physics just don't work that way.

Nonetheless, I pushed down on the front of the board, not knowing what else to do. Amazingly, I didn't go under. The board somehow swung around 180 degrees and I was now surfing the wave back into shore. I was astonished! I'd just managed to avoid getting wiped out by a huge wave and I was thrilled to not be in the water...

Suddenly, my paddle caught at the side of the board and the wave pulled me sideways into the water, rolling me several times, and pummelling me as it dumped me onto the shore. Liam put his camera down and ran to help pull me and my board out of the water. Half laughing, half impressed that I'd managed to surf part of the wave, we both stood there a little shocked.

'Holy crap, did you get that on camera?' I asked, thinking that would look great in a promo video.

Liam shook his head. Unfortunately his camera-holding hand had dropped – just like his jaw did – as he'd watched it all unfold.

After double-checking that he did actually know what he was doing and that he'd get the wave count right this time, we tried again. And there was no problem: I was out past the breakers before the next set rolled in, and I felt so much calmer this time round in comparison to my wipeout paddle with Tim. Now, I could stand up (even if very gingerly) and found my momentum, paddling back and forth along the beach. As I went, I kept a close eye on Liam to make sure he was keeping a close eye on me. I knew that I was definitely still nervous and inexperienced – you can tell from the pictures of that day that I'm a bit tense and hunched forward. But this wasn't so surprising. My Durdle Door session was still only the third time I'd actually been paddleboarding on the sea.

No skipper, no boat, no funds

I'd kept in touch with John, my Irish yachtmaster skipper, via email as I worked on pulling everything else together. It transpired that he had a few things booked in for April but could be available from May onwards – perfect! This meant that I just needed to find a skipper to cover from my start date, which would hopefully be in mid-April, until John's arrival in May, then I'd be good to go with my crew.

For me, having no knowledge whatsoever of anything sea-based wasn't a barrier, it simply presented an awesome opportunity to learn. Google could give me some of the basic stuff, but by far the easiest and best way to learn anything new, I think, is to speak to people. There's only so much you can get from a computer, and a person will understand (hopefully) the nuances of what you're trying to achieve. They can also make you feel reassured, give you new connections to other people who may be able to help with a different question and be on call when something unexpected pops up and Google just won't cut it.

So, I reached out – across social media, through my existing network, talking to family friends, and even complete strangers. Every time I met someone (and by this I mean literally anyone I bumped into anywhere), I'd ask if they knew of a skipper or a boat for sale. Plus, having just moved to Bristol and discovered an awesome crowd of adventurously-minded people there, it was wonderful to be among people who saw life in a similar way to me: prioritising time spent outdoors, over time spent trawling town centres gathering more stuff we don't need.

I'd also found Instagram was a brilliant way to connect with people out west. One day I received a message from Janine Doggett, a woman who loves getting outside and wanted to meet to chat about all things adventure. She was thinking about taking on her own Land's End to John O'Groats cycle trip, going via the highest peaks in England, Wales, and Scotland to boot. We met for a coffee: I shared my experience from my previous LEJOGs and she gave me a contact for a skipper she knew, who then put me in touch with a guy called Mike Pickering, based in London, who ran a website helping people to find skippers – what are the chances?

It turned out that Mike actually worked for another friend of mine, Henry Burkitt, who I'd met back in 2015 on that entrepreneurship course with Escape the City. Together, they now run Kraken Travel and had the perfect set of connections to help me source an extra skipper. Over a cuppa – and several hours – Mike poured out all of his experience in sailing. Soaking it up, I seized the opportunity to ask all those basic questions that someone this close to taking on this kind of adventure should have probably already known.

How do tides work? What do I need to think about with finding harbours? How quickly can a boat travel? How much is the expedition likely to cost me in fuel? What kind of insurance will I need?

My usual approach to planning how long an adventure is going to take is simply to figure out how far I can travel each day, then factor in where there are suitable places to stop for food, camping, etc. These two elements then pretty much dictate my schedule. But, given that I'd never SUPed on the sea for a full day before, I really had no concrete idea how far I could travel in that time – just my conservative 12-mile per tide estimate, and the 15-miles per tide I'd pushed my figures up to after John's gentle mocking. I wanted more accurate numbers.

Beyond knowing that the tide comes into the shore over a six-hour window, then goes back out again over the next six hours – giving you both high tide and low tide twice in every twenty-four hours – I really didn't have a clue how they worked. But Mike explained that, essentially, a tide is one big wave that pushes in towards the land over the course of six hours. Starting gently, it gains in pace, becoming its strongest halfway through the tide (typically between hours two and four), before reducing in strength in the final two hours. This start/end of each tide is a period called slack water, when the tide has little, if any, strength.

What determines the direction a tide pushes you is the way it moves around the land. Along the south coast of England, tides will take you east or west as they push in from the Atlantic and then recede six hours later; whereas, along the east coast of Ireland, the tide pushes north and pulls south. Mike described how I would need to look up the time of high water (the end of the incoming tide) at Dover and then the corresponding time at the location I'd be paddling to. From this, I could work out what time of day each of the two tides at any given location would be pushing north.

To make things a little more complicated, the time that the tide comes in and out shifts by around fifty minutes every day. So the time of day that I could paddle north with the tide would actually depend on exactly which day I was paddling and where. For example, if I was thinking of paddling from Land's End to St Ives on the 21st April, I'd need to be on the water at around 1pm (when it was low tide and about to turn, then start pushing north for six hours). However, if there was bad weather and I couldn't start until two days later, my start time would be pushed back to 3pm. Not only would this make a big difference to how many miles I could cover in a tide – get it wrong and I'd go backwards – but it could also be the difference between paddling in daylight or the dark. In the space of just a week, a tide that pushes north from 1–7pm would flow in that direction from 7pm–1am.

In order to make swift progress, I would need to be on the water for the full six hours of each northward tide. I calculated that where both tides in my favour in a twenty-four hour window fell within daylight hours, I could try to paddle both tides. And where one tide fell at night, I would only paddle the other tide. At this point it hadn't occurred to me to paddle at night – I'd never deliberately travelled overnight during any of my previous adventures and, given the increased risk of being on the sea, the last thing I'd have wanted was to be lost out on the water in the dark.

Mike was unbelievably helpful and I was really starting to feel supported on this expedition: I now had several great people who really knew what they were talking about and were really keen to help. During the time that Liam and I had been down in the West Country, I'd initially found another highly experienced skipper who said he was happy to help us get underway once he was back in late April from delivering a boat. But, as the days drew on, he got slower and slower at replying to emails to the point that he stopped responding. Had he just lost signal at sea or was he ghosting me? I gave him the benefit of the doubt and waited for a couple of days. Still nothing. I could only hope he'd get in touch once he reached land.

However, as the days continued to slip away from me, I could see that there was no way we would be ready to go in time for the second week of April. So, I pushed the start date back to late April, hoping a new weather window would open up. In the meantime, I still had none of those ever-so-slightly essential things that I needed to get started...

No boat.

No skipper for the first week or so.

No cash sponsorship.

But, I figured, there's always a way. I'd realised by this point that getting a financial sponsor was not going to work, so I'd started looking at self-funding options. Without a fixed income, I was classed as 'unemployed' in terms of getting a loan, but I was really lucky to be able to borrow against my mum's house – this meant that, with her backing, I could take out a mortgage on the property in order to fund the expedition.

The main expense, still, was buying a boat. I'd briefly considered renting one, but at around £1,000 per week with no fixed end date, that was going to be serious money that I just didn't have. However, I calculated that if I could buy one, then I could sell it after the adventure to help pay off the loan.

So, within about a week I'd secured a loan in principle and set about getting the paperwork sorted. With a lead-time of six to eight weeks, I was not going to actually get access to the money any time soon, so I would have to make do until then with some savings to fund my crew and pay for general expenses once we'd started the adventure.

This was where my amazing friend, Erin Eley, came in. She'd been saving for a house and had enough cash set aside to loan me the money to buy a boat before my mortgage loan came through. Not many people would willingly hand over their house deposit to a friend going on an adventure with no exact date for when the money would come through to pay it back. I was so grateful and, with Erin's support, I could now continue the boat hunt and finally make some more progress towards the start line.

The search for a boat had been going on for months. Based on a little advice, I'd been looking for a sailing yacht rather than a motorboat in order to keep fuel costs down. I was also looking for a swim deck to make getting on and off the board easier and a boat of at least 32 feet to ensure it was big enough for three of us to live relatively comfortably for several months.

I'd seen a variety of boats online, but nothing seemed to be just right. This was a big decision. If I got the wrong boat it could mean the end of the adventure – I had visions of engine failure, horrible conditions that would make my crew leave, or even sinking. Plus, now I was really feeling the pressure of using my friend's house deposit to buy it. I was almost in decision paralysis, but I kept on looking.

As it happened, we had weeks of bad weather throughout April, so realistically I couldn't have paddled anyway, but – just as my financial situation was beginning to improve – so, too, did the forecast. There it was! Two clear days of good weather, low winds, low swell, and not a spot of rain in sight.

My mind was made up. The upcoming weekend was my time to set off and I, at last, had a starting date: Saturday 21st April. I needed to get cracking and find a boat as soon as possible.

Shogun

During our time down in Cornwall and Devon, looking at boats and sorting out logistics, Liam and I had occasionally stayed with my friends from university, Rowan and Amanda Edwards, their springer-cross Douglas, and two-year-old daughter, Pippa. They were in the process of renovating their gorgeous home and turning their coach house into an AirB&B. Nestled on top of a hill in Sticklepath, North Dartmoor, they have stunning views out across the moor and plenty of opportunity for mini adventures right on their doorstep.

Despite having so much on their plate, they always made time to support me and my grand ideas, which I'm very grateful for. In fact, I had stopped in with them during both my LEJOG cycling and walking adventures, so it was great to complete the trio and have them support SUP Britain too.

Before heading down to our second boat viewing, we popped in to chat to Amanda's parents, Susan and Charlie Breach, who live next door to her. A boat owner himself, Charlie was happy to talk about all the various flaws we should be looking out for – for example, signs of osmosis in the hull (which would mean that the boat wasn't watertight) or fraying in the stays (the metal lines that keep everything upright and in the right place on deck) – as these would be expensive to sort out.

With Charlie's invaluable advice in mind, we drove to St Mawes on the south coast of Cornwall near Falmouth. When we pulled into the boatyard there was no-one in the office, but one of the chaps working on another boat stopped to set up a stepladder for us and then went off to find the keys.

With the boat out of the water, we could see the condition of the hull and, once we'd also inspected the inside, it seemed like the best option so far. It was spacious and Liam liked the fact that it had been decked out with surround sound speakers. While Shogun was an old boat, she had had a fair bit of new technology added by the current owner – that would be crucial for easy navigation and tracking my route. So far, so good.

As we continued our survey, I was glad that Liam at least understood any basic terms that chap would refer to, but we were pretty much the blind leading the blind here. This meant we had to go on gut instinct. And our guts told us this that boat was the best one we'd seen and that the agent was trustworthy enough.

Simon Carter from Red Ensign Yacht Brokerage seemed upfront and personable – it's always good when you don't feel like a salesperson is trying to screw you over. He understood what I needed and explained exactly why this was the best boat they had for what I was trying to do.

She was in good condition given her thirty-four years of sailing. The hull looked smooth, with no signs of the osmosis Charlie had told me to look out for, and everything on deck looked like it was in decent shape. Below deck, the stairs led down into a main living area with a tiny kitchen to the left, kitted out with a four-ring hob, oven, fridge, and sink. To the right was the chart table, the all-important controls for the surround sound speakers (including Bluetooth and radio), plus a few bits of navigation technology and the main VHF radio for contacting lockkeepers, other boats, and – should it come to it – the coastguard.

Further forward of the stairs, the living space was made up of a sofa on each side with a fold-out table in the middle. Behind each sofa ran shelves and above those were narrow windows the length of the main space, plus two skylights.

At the front of the boat was the main cabin with a double bed, some hanging space, and shelves. In here was where they'd stored all the sails, and now we just needed to figure out how to rig them up.

Tucked under the stairs to the left, next to the kitchen, was a second double cabin. To the right of the stairs was the toilet and sink. And directly underneath the stairs was the engine that would help us chug our way the length of Britain.

Back up on deck, Shogun had plenty of storage space, perfect for the paddleboards when they weren't being used. Given the boat's small size, she wasn't large enough for a steering wheel, so instead she had a tiller (basically a long handle) – and, luckily, it came with an autohelm, which we'd come to learn meant that you could set a course and the boat would essentially steer itself. You still need to check you're on course every so often and keep an eye out to make sure that you don't run over any lobster pots, hit a paddleboarder, or head into the path of another boat, but for long days on the water an autohelm is a godsend.

Given a lack of space near the tiller, the navigational tech was located *just* out of easy reach above the stairs, meaning that you couldn't check it and steer at the same time. There were four screens in all. From left to right, the first showed the depth of the water below the front of the boat from the water line (the keel was five feet, so we didn't want the depth to drop too close to that, otherwise we'd hit the bottom). The second screen displayed boat speed over water.

Third was the wind speed and direction screen. Wind direction is important for working out which side of the boat you want the sails out on (or whether to get them out at all). For me on a paddleboard, however, the issue with wind direction would be more about a tailwind pushing me forwards or a headwind pushing me backwards. Either way, if the wind was fairly light – well, below 10mph – it wouldn't make too much difference as I could still make ground against a headwind. But anything above this and I'd be struggling to make any progress if it was coming at me head on.

On the final screen was a map, known by seafarers as a chart. This would show us everything we needed to know about approximate depths, potential hazards, harbours, etc. It would be super handy in enabling us to plot a course and track our actual route covered, plus mark an X on the spot where I finished paddling each day so we knew exactly where to head back out to the next day.

This screen also showed our speed over land. We'd use this in conjunction with the boat speed through the water to work out how fast we were travelling. So, for example, if there was no tidal influence on the boat, then both readings would be the same. However, if the boat speed through the water was 3mph and our boat speed over land was 5mph, we would know that the tide was pushing us along at 2mph. Conversely, if the boat speed through the water was 1mph and boat speed over land was 0mph, we would know that the tide was pushing us backwards by 1mph and, in that case, all we'd be doing was holding ground and not moving anywhere at all.

It was fascinating learning all about how the boat moves in water, what the different bits of apparatus could tell us, and what the various readings mean in reality. And, all in, Shogun was in good condition for a boat older than I am...

That is, except for the wall lining. Almost entirely throughout the boat it was peeling off and, ideally, needed replacing. Added to the dark wood finish that is typical for a boat of this age, Shogun's interior was fairly dark and dreary. But, for an adventure boat, it really makes no difference – she'd probably get a little worn during the trip anyway. Even so, Liam and I could both imagine what she might look like renovated: paint the wood white and re-line the walls, plus add some new soft furnishings and she'd look a lot more appealing for resale.

When we met Simon back at his office after the viewing, he told us about the market in general for boats of this age – lots of them were now flooding the market as people prefer to opt for newer boats. This means that it can take a while to shift the older ones and, so, he advised, I would be best off sticking to well-known brands like Jeanneau (who made Shogun) and that I should expect it to take a few months to sell on at the end of my trip. His advice was welcome and left me feeling much more confident about making my decision.

Liam and I headed to another marina to view one more boat, the only boat we'd found that had a twin keel. This means that there are two fins under the boat, which allow it to sit stable on a beach or in a dry harbour without toppling over when the tide goes out. The benefit of this was that it meant we'd be able to seek shelter in more locations if bad weather hit – and this was a serious consideration given that on stretches like the north coast of Cornwall there are very few wet harbours. So, in the event of bad weather, with a single keel like Shogun's, we'd either have to drop anchor in potentially exposed waters, being thrashed about by wind and swell, or make sure we get to Padstow, the only wet harbour along our Cornish section, some 80 miles from Land's End, before the storm hit and before the tide went back out.

That said, we weren't fixated on having either a single keel or twin keel and wanted to weigh up what both boats were like all round. On seeing the twin keel boat we both soon knew –

keels aside – that the first boat of the day had been the better of the two. We just had that gut feeling..

And, so, the decision was finally made – I would try to buy Shogun, a 1984, 32-foot Jeanneau Attalia yacht.

While I'd finally found my expedition support boat, the funding was taking even longer to get sorted than expected and there was no way I'd be able to get it through that week. But, even though I didn't own Shogun yet (I was still to negotiate a price and find a suitable day for her to be lowered into the water), or have a replacement skipper for the one that had ghosted me, I was determined to get going, to make the most of the weather window, and to start covering some miles.

Then the news came through that John could no longer join us in May. He'd had other plans come up (but suggested that he could still help us out with crossing over the Irish Sea). It was disappointing, but I understood that I was asking a lot. It just meant that now I'd have to find a skipper for as much of the rest of the journey as possible.

My first thought was that maybe we could borrow a boat to get me started, to get me out there. I'd spoken to a number of boat owners and skippers who said that, while they couldn't help out themselves, there must be loads of people with boats who would love to get involved in this kind of adventure. Running with this idea, Liam and I visited the major harbours along the Cornish coast, explaining what we were doing, and asking around for contacts. At Newquay harbour I chatted to the harbourmaster to see if he knew anyone he could suggest (and also to give him a heads-up on what we were doing!) – and this proved useful if only to get some advice on the harbour itself. Unfortunately, there was no-one with a boat available.

Next up, we headed to St Ives and, again, chatted to the harbourmaster there. This time we had more luck and he scribbled down some names and numbers of local boat owners who might be up for an adventure. After contacting a couple, one got back to me and said that he was interested in letting me rent his boat with him as the skipper. He'd acted as a support boat for other local sea-based challenges before, so was aware of what was involved and could help for a fee.

His boat was a small motor boat usually used for day trips ferrying tourists out to see the local wildlife. It had a large, covered deck out the back, which would fit a SUP and would be a good spot from which Liam could take photos and yell advice at me while I was out on the water. However, the fee per tide was an eye-watering £500. I realised this was fairly standard for boat hire (including two crew and fuel), but I was fast running out of cash waiting for the loan to come through, so I tried to negotiate some marketing for him in return for a reduced rate, but he was having none of it. Fair enough.

But it was now Thursday the 19th of April, and the good weather window was just two days away. There was no way I was letting this slip past me and I could think of no other option to get me on the water and past the start line, so, I reluctantly agreed and we arranged the logistics for Day One and Day Two.

The relief! I finally had a firm start date — I was about to set off and start a new adventure, at last.

In hindsight, it looks ridiculously hard to have pulled it all together, but, truthfully, I really relished the challenge of it: using my ingenuity to think of different solutions and find people to help us out. I loved making those connections. And I was so proud to have managed to pull enough into place to hit the water — to reach that coveted start line that is often so tricky in itself. There had been plenty of opportunities to go home, to think it wasn't going to work out... but I hadn't doubted myself. Not once had I thought I wasn't going to make this happen. And I was excited we now had the ability to put in some paddle strokes and get down to the business of making miles.

After starting the adventure, my plan was simply to paddle as often as possible. I still had no real idea how frequently that would be when it came to it. The forecast beyond that weekend was not looking great. Spring storms were rolling in and meant that I wouldn't be able to paddle for at least a week after the first two days. In a way, that was lucky. I hoped it would be enough time to sort out the finances and buy Shogun, ready to hit the water again when calm weather next came our way.

3

Starting before I'm ready

Only 800 miles to go

The windscreen wipers were going ten to the dozen as we drove down narrow country lanes towards the sea. The road curved left through the tiny village, perched next to the wide, sandy bay that opened out beyond our foggy windows. I turned into the car park next to the harbour. As we sat waiting for a dry spell, we tried to figure out if it was just the heavy rain spraying the cars parked in front of us, or if it was the sea crashing over the seawall.

Shawn Mendes finished playing on the radio and we reckoned this was as light as the rain was going to get that day — we pulled up the hoods of our raincoats and headed out into the grey to investigate. The stretch of sea leading out from Sennen Cove Harbour to our right and round to Land's End to our left was where I'd be launching my board in just two days' time.

It turned out that it wasn't just rain pelting the cars. The harbour was being battered by a ten-foot high, angry, white swell that crashed violently onto the shore, one wave after the next, unrelenting and unforgiving. The biggest waves of the set roared in, smashing their energy against the huge rocks that lined the bottom of the cliff. They seemed to compete with each other to see which could get the highest — the volcano-like spray from one managing to clear the top of the 50-foot high cliff as I watched.

Liam and I, along with a few other hardy souls who had ventured out for a walk, stood silently in awe of Mother Nature. All we could do was hope for a calm after the storm.

Beep beep! Beep beep! Wriggling in my sleeping bag just enough to grab my phone, I turned off the alarm, and checked the timings for the day ahead. I only had the final, last minute packing to do that morning, ready for the big event. Neither Liam nor I were in any rush to face the day — both anxious of what was to come.

After emerging from our tent and with everything ready to go, we went for a coffee to quell my nerves. We walked down the steep roads into St Ives and sat down outside a lovely café, basking in the warmth of the morning sun, overlooking the harbour. The streets were already bustling with tourists enjoying a relaxing Saturday by the sea. I found it hard to think of anything other than what I was about to confront in a few short hours, but the much-needed normality of hanging out over a coffee helped a little.

Back at the campsite, I walked with my gear to wait for the taxi that would take me to Land's End. As I lingered by the campsite gates I tried to test the radio that would allow me to talk to Liam while I was out on the water, but, after pressing several buttons, it was clear I'd messed up the settings. I started to panic that I wouldn't be able to communicate with him at all, but — just then — he thankfully appeared with the SUP Britain tee shirt that I'd forgotten. We sorted out the radio before the taxi turned up to whisk me away, and the adrenaline burst subsided... a bit. With everything packed in the car, I turned to give Liam a big hug goodbye — both of us on tenterhooks. The next time I'd see him would be in two hours, out on the water.

It was in that moment that I realised Liam had begun to feel like a safety blanket. If he was with me, I felt like I'd be OK; but for the next few hours, I'd have to deal with this on my own. It was an odd feeling. I'd never been so reliant on anyone else before to feel OK. I'd walked and cycled the length of Britain, totally able to steady my own nerves, and make myself feel better. But not now — not when it came to leaving the shore behind. I was truly scared and it felt daunting, particularly the prospect of that stretch I would have to paddle, out from the beach at Sennen Cove Harbour by myself, before I could meet up with Liam and the team on the support boat.

Arriving at Land's End, I went to the hotel to sign their official LEJOG book and asked the lady on reception to sign my own log book. And there it was. My first entry into the book that would record evidence of the adventure from strangers and friends along the route.

Next, I went round to the Land's End signpost where I asked the official signpost photographer to sign my book. He also made the official sign up with 'Fiona's LEJOG' and took a couple of pictures on my phone for me. As I walked away from the sign I spotted a cyclist, fully clad in lycra and on a rather snazzy road bike.

I bounced over excitedly, 'Hi! Are you about to start or finish LEJOG?' I asked, keen to share the start line moment with a fellow adventurous soul.

'Oh, er, I'm actually just out on a local ride! I live down this way,' he said before spotting my huge bag. 'What are you doing on the top of a cliff with a SUP?' he asked, clearly intrigued, but seemingly not surprised — as if he was used to people doing things slightly differently.

Once I'd explained what I was doing with a paddleboard so far from the nearest beach, he asked if I'd heard of the company he worked for, Finisterre.

'Oh, yes! You guys are sponsoring me!' I said.

He looked a tad confused. 'Oh, really? Ha, I didn't know that. I'm surprised I'd not heard about your trip... I'm the head of marketing.'

Sporting a pretty good adventure beard, Oli Culcheth was clearly an outdoorsy kind of guy. It was comforting to meet someone who seemed equally up for a challenge just as I was about to set off on mine. Oli and I swapped details, and he became the third person to sign my book. After doing some live videos on Facebook and Instagram and taking a few pictures, I lugged my heavy board onto my back and hiked the mile down to Sennen Cove harbour.

The path twisted and turned along the top of the cliffs — not the easiest terrain with 20 rather unwieldy kilograms strapped to my back. Plus it was the UK's hottest April day for 70 years. With top temperatures reaching 29°C that day, that hike carrying all my kit took more out of me than I realised. Probably not the best way to start an 800-mile journey...

As I reached the top of the path before it headed down into the harbour, I stopped to look out over the bay that stretched out into the distance. Thankfully, it was a picture of calm; gone was any remnant of the wild storm we'd witnessed two days before. I was utterly relieved.

Down at the harbour, I set about sorting out my kit. Along with my SUP, I had a drybag to keep the other things that I'd either needed during the walk down from Land's End (like the log book and trainers), or that I'd need with me while I was out on the water (like food, drink, and sunscreen). Liam had suggested that after I'd pumped up my board on the shore I could tie the pump and empty SUP bag to the back of my board, and then hand it over to the support boat, once I met up with them. But — nervous about making it unstable — I was keen not to carry more than I absolutely needed to on my board. So, I'd decided that the SUP bag and pump should be left onshore. Hopefully I could find a friendly local who would be willing to look after it for me until I could pick it up the next day.

The first shop I went into was the kind of all-purpose seaside shop you'd expect to see in Cornwall. Crabbing buckets and lilos were stacked up next to postcards, ice cream, and cheap sandwiches. I explained the situation to the guy behind the counter, a tall English man probably in his fifties. He looked at me like I was crazy and said firmly, 'Oh, no!' shaking his head. 'Not in this day and age. It could be a bomb!'

I looked at him quizzically, 'It's an empty SUP bag, with a pump in it. You can look if you like!'

'Well, that's what *you* say,' he snapped back, emphatic that I was a terrorist.

So, I went on to the next shop – a little ice cream counter where Eleanor, a twenty-something woman was serving. I was hesitant to ask, expecting another no, but I figured that maybe if I smiled more I'd look less terrorist-like and she might help. Again, I explained what I needed help with and, to my relief, she couldn't have been more helpful. She grinned immediately. 'Of course!' she said, explaining that while they might not be open the next day (as the weather didn't look good for selling ice cream), the shop was owned by her gran who lived upstairs, so I could just knock and she'd let me grab my bag from the back of the shop.

Relieved, and chuffed to have not been considered a threat to public security for the second time in one day, I headed down to the harbour beach at last, sat next to my board, and attempted to make myself eat half a sandwich. I could see that the support boat with Liam on board had arrived and was bobbing in the bay. They'd got there thirty minutes early, which, while better than being late, made me feel seriously under pressure to get going. My stomach was doing backflips. The moment when I would actually have to leave dry, solid, stable land behind and face my fear was rushing towards me like a train.

But, nonetheless, here it was. The train was almost at the station and I had no choice but to get aboard. I put the uneaten cheese and pickle sandwich back in my SIGG tin, packed up my kit onto my SUP, and got ready.

The calm sea I'd been so relieved to spot on the approach down from the coastal path was even better up close. I'd had visions of wrestling with my board to get out past the breakers, as I'd done when Tim took me out in that raging, brown sea at Clevedon. But there wasn't a single breaker at Sennen Cove Harbour that day, not one. The sea just sat there – still, glistening in the heat from the scorching sun, barely even lapping at the sand – glassy flat all the way out, like a swimming pool. The easiest of launches was a very welcome start, but things were about to get interesting.

I launched at 12.30pm. The cold water around my ankles was a relief from the warm day and I jumped straight up onto my feet, paddling round past the harbour wall and out through a relatively shallow, rocky section. The support boat skirted to the outside of the rocks to meet me on the other side and I waved nervously to Liam and the boat's crew, Mike and

Daisy. I started to make my way south, following the land to my left, to get to the spot where I'd be precisely inline with the Land's End sign from the water. I had thought it would probably take around half an hour to go down to reach it, before turning around and starting to head north. We'd timed it so that I'd paddle out during slack water, and then – hopefully – once I turned around and started to head north, the tide would kick in and be helping me on my way.

As well as the unexpected heat of the day, we were also met with unexpected winds. All the apps and forecasts had been predicting manageable wind speeds, but, as soon as I headed out of the bay, the wind picked up, gusting 20mph offshore... four times what we'd accounted for. I swiftly dropped to my knees for stability and I tried my hardest to paddle round to my left and follow the coast. Almost immediately, I was being blown out towards the Atlantic.

Liam and Mike were repeatedly telling me, with growing concern each time, to go closer to cliffs where I'd be sheltered from the wind. I was trying my hardest, but the wind was just too ferocious. Heading straight into the wind, it took me an hour to travel the mile down to the Land's End sign – twice as long as I'd expected. But, as I drew parallel with the sign Mike sounded the boat's horn and Liam and Daisy cheered. This was it. This was my start line. SUP Britain had officially begun.

I was thrilled to have finally started both on land and at sea, the sign slowly fading into the distance behind me, and the complete unknown lying ahead. I was so thankful to have that little team with me on the water, enabling me to even be there, keeping me safe as I started those very first miles of paddling.

The start line joy was fleeting, though, as I slowly retraced my route back to Sennen Cove Harbour and then onwards north. While I was indeed glad to be underway at long last, the start was far harder going than I'd imagined it would be. Not only was it physically exhausting fighting the wind after having lugged my heavy board for a mile in the heat, but it was also tough mentally.

All morning, Liam had seemed generally nervous and Mike was not hiding his feelings. Even though they had cheered for me as I passed the Land's End sign, the rest of the time they both looked at me like I didn't have a clue what I was doing, like I lacked the skills necessary to do this, like I was an amateur. And yet, while this didn't exactly boost my morale, at the same time I was thinking, *Well, duh! I am an amateur, that's the whole point. If you expected me to be good at this, to not be utterly terrified, clueless and slow, then you've got the wrong end of the stick. This whole expedition is about seeing what happens when I have a go.*

So, there I was. This was me having a go. Yes, I was slow. Yes, I didn't have perfectly honed paddling skills. Yes, I lacked any real experience to speak of. But you know what? I was bloody trying and I would simply *keep* trying until something physically made me stop. *Just wait*, I thought, *I'll get there eventually.*

I had been kneeling for two hours while fighting the blustery wind and my legs had lost any strength and all feeling. Liam goaded me to get to my feet. 'The longer you kneel the harder it'll be to stand,' he shouted across the waves and wind. 'Trust me! It doesn't matter if you fall off – you can get back on again. Come on, stand up now. The wind's not as bad, and you'll go quicker!'

I couldn't disagree. I knew that it would be quicker and easier standing. Reluctantly, I struggled to my feet and I attempted to stand, but in an instant I was in the water. Falling off feet first right next to my board meant that I was back on it as quickly as I'd come off. So quickly, in fact, that Liam and the crew hadn't even noticed that I'd fallen off. I was thankful that I didn't go completely under the water – my face getting wet is the worst bit for me – so I was, at least, spared that. For the rest of that day I stayed on my knees to avoid being constantly in the water.

While I appreciated that you do have to get wet if you want to get better at paddleboarding, I was also very conscious that I wanted to try to get some miles under my belt and the idea of continually falling in was too much to contemplate given how tiring the day had already been. Plus, of course, I was bloody scared.

As I paddled beyond Sennen beach, the rugged Cornish coastline stretched round to the right. I could see old mine workings perched on perilous cliff edges with the waves crashing some one hundred metres below. Out to my left, there was nothing but ocean until it met the horizon.

After four long hours of paddling, I recognised a section of the coastline and suspected it was St Just. I radioed over to the support boat to confirm and decided I was happy to call it a day here. I had hoped to keep going well into the evening and make the most of the tide, but the hike, the heat, the battle with the wind early on, and the hours of kneeling all meant that I was not on good form.

When you kneel, you paddle in a different way to how you do standing. So, unsurprisingly, my shoulder was hurting and, with another day of paddling ahead of me, I was aware that this was just day one of many more to come over the next few months. The last thing I wanted was to get injured.

I called it, marking my spot on the boat tracker, and turning off the two I had on myself. With day one down, I'd managed to cover seven and a half miles in four hours.

A dream scenario would have seen me paddling most of the way round to St Ives, some twenty miles from Land's End – or at the very least half way. But, despite this disappointment, I was still pleased to have set off and to have covered some miles. After all, this was it: I'd actually made it over the start line of this grand adventure. I didn't have my own boat, a skipper for the next week or two, or, indeed, the funds in my account to buy the boat, but I was – nevertheless – underway.

And what's more, I'd actually felt reasonably comfortable out on the sea once I was kneeling. Being lower down had meant that I didn't feel like I was going to fall off in the swell. I didn't care that it was slow or ungraceful or not how you're 'supposed' to do it. This was my way to get going – a way that felt manageable. And at that point I think I was too caught up in the immediate job at hand to feel any danger or let my fear overwhelm me. Instead, it was just really hard work and for that I was glad. The whole point of taking on this expedition was to do something that was totally out of my comfort zone, something that pushed me to face my fear despite the stomach-twisting nausea.

Liam and Mike pulled first me, and then my board, onto the support boat and I wrapped myself into my dryrobe to warm up, pulling on all the layers of other clothes I could find underneath. Although this was the warmest April day in a very long time, the brisk sea breeze felt pretty nippy now that I wasn't paddling.

On the way to St Ives, where the boat was kept, Mike explained the tactics he reckoned I should adopt the following day, taking into account the expected wind and tides. As we motored along the coastline that I was yet to paddle, he tried to manage my expectations... Based on today's lack of progress, he told me that he didn't think I'd make it much past Morvah, just five miles beyond where I'd paddled to that day.

It was funny when people gave me their guidance as to the distance they thought I could cover in a day. I always listened and tried to gauge their knowledge of the water and conditions, taking on board their expertise, because I recognised my own blindspots, knowing relatively little about the sea or the local geography. But, at the same time – based on my own extensive past experience of myself – I know that I can do more. If the conditions allow, I can absolutely crush out the miles. I know the difference between pain and injury: I can push through and push hard. In fact, that's what I love: getting in the zone and driving myself forward by willpower alone. And that's how it seems to be for me – most of the miles I cover on any adventure are down to my will, not my physical ability or my strength.

As I lay in my sleeping bag that night, after Liam and I had stuffed our faces with pizza and beer, I looked at the map. The one thing I'd struggled with that first day – other than the wind and the heat – was not having clear marker points to aim for. Without those I couldn't gauge how far I had come or where I really needed to aim for next. So, I picked out two distinct headlands roughly the same distance apart, and then Seal Island as a third marker point (just before St Ives). Based on my first day's mileage, if I could reach the first headland within two hours, and then the second in another two, even if I didn't actually reach the island itself, I'd be happy. It would be double Mike's prediction and it would mean that I'd cover ten solid miles in the six-hour tidal window.

I can do this

The next morning we drove back over to Sennen Cove Harbour to pick up the SUP bag and pump from Eleanor's nan, before getting more food supplies for the hours ahead. Out on the water the previous day, I'd realised that I needed to drink and eat much more often, so, that morning, I stuffed my life jacket pockets with cereal bars to make sure they were always at hand.

After some lunch, I had an early afternoon nap in the tent for an hour or so, then we packed up and headed down to St Ives harbour to meet the support boat. As we motored our way back round to be in line with St Just, where I'd finished paddling the day before, Mike explained how the swell, tide, and wind should be in my favour that afternoon. This meant that, unlike the previous day (when I'd needed to stick tight to the coastline to be sheltered from the wind), I could instead go out further, away from the coast, to really make the most of the conditions by getting the elements to push me along as much as possible.

On reaching the GPS dot where I needed to jump onto the water, Liam pumped my board up for me – not easy on a swaying boat with limited room for manoeuvre! – while I got kitted up and ready to go. The last thing to do was turn on my SPOT tracker – the GPS device that would feed data into my ZeroSixZero live tracking map on my website.

I pressed the on button, but no yellow flashing lights came on. Nothing. It just wouldn't turn on, but, oddly, the SOS button light was solid green. Initially I thought that this meant I had accidentally triggered the rescue function and soon international rescue (aka the Thunderbirds and co.) would be whizzing to my aid. I tried desperately to turn it off but, no matter what combination of buttons I pressed, the SOS light was determined to stay on. I rang the manufacturers, but to no avail.

They just said it sounded like the unit was faulty and to take it back to the shop I'd bought it from – *slightly* difficult when you're a couple of miles off the coast of England.

After an hour or so of faffing with possible fixes, I gave up and jumped on the water with just an app on my phone to track me. Like the other device, it was linked to ZeroSixZero, so my map would still update live as I went, with a little me on a SUP marking my location. It was a great way for people to follow me on my journey and it turned out that Liam's mum loved reloading the page several times a day to see if we'd made progress or if the wind had sent my line a little wobbly.

With just the one tracker I was worried that it might also stop working and then I'd have no record of my progress that day, but the guys on the boat checked it every now and again throughout the paddle and luckily it kept working.

That day, I was determined to stand up. I'd spent most of Saturday on my knees, trying to limit the impact of the wind, but this had caused blisters on my toes and I didn't want them to get any worse.

As soon as I jumped on the board, though, as much as I wanted to, I knew I couldn't stand. The swell was just too big at around five feet and it felt rough – like it would've knocked me off my board. And I was too scared of falling off. I just couldn't do it.

Still determined to make progress, I decided that, rather than trying to stand and keep falling off, I'd put my head down and get the miles behind me. There was always another day to make more progress with my standing ability in swell. So, off I went, kneeling on the board but driving my paddle hard into the water and getting into a strong rhythm – counting to eight in my head, then changing to paddle on the other side of the board. This seemed to keep me heading relatively straight as I focused hard on the next headland that I'd picked out on the map. Just fifty minutes in and Daisy pulled the boat up close to me. I saw that Liam and Mike had a new look on their faces. Rather than the concerned 'I don't think we're going to get anywhere soon' look, they actually looked impressed and slightly stunned.

'You're doing really well!' Liam yelled, his excitement palpable. 'You're making really good ground – keep going!'

Mike gave me the thumbs-up with a big smile to match. I'd just managed to smash out five miles. I'd already more than doubled my average hourly mileage from day one, and, in just one hour, I'd gotten to where Mike thought I'd reach in six. This was incredible. I felt so much more confident now that I'd proved to myself – and to them – what I could do, even if I wasn't standing yet.

Gosh! What if I could actually get close to Seal Island? I ploughed on, spotting the next headland in the distance and setting my sights on it.

I was generally feeling much stronger that day, but the issue with the tracker earlier on had thrown me a bit, and I had felt really physically sick when I first got on the water, even questioning if I should've gone out at all. But I was so glad I had. The sick feeling eased off slightly the more miles I covered (although it never completely went until right at the end of the day's paddling). It was probably a combination of seasickness from bobbing in the swell while staring down at my tracker as I tried to fix it for nearly an hour, plus the sheer nerves of being out on the water.

Honestly, it had never occurred to me before that I might get seasick. I couldn't think of a time when I'd been on a boat and felt ill, so it just hadn't been on my radar as something to think about. I guess, though, no matter how seaworthy your stomach is, that relentless rock of a boat on water will make you feel queasy at some point.

Two hours in and I had covered around nine miles, making it past my second marker headland and coming into sight of Seal Island. I paused my tracker and got onto the boat for a break and to get some more water. Looking at the map, I could see that I was just four miles from St Ives... *What?* I'd almost made it to St Ives! It was an awesome feeling and the guys on the boat seemed much chirpier than the day before too.

I jumped back on the water after ten minutes or so and the sun began to set behind me. As it got lower in the sky, so did the temperature, and I could see my breath lingering in the air in front of me. Paddling past Seal Island, St Ives came into view and the chill set in. Feeling shattered now, I wondered at what point they'd insist that I get off the water due to the fading light. *Surely they'd think it was dangerous to paddle in the dark*, I thought. But they didn't seem in the slightest bit concerned.

The boat kept pulling round in front of the SUP, giving Liam a pretty good angle from which to take pictures of me against the sunset. He managed to get one of me from about four feet below the board, revealing just how big the swell was. He was keen to get a particular shot and radioed over a couple of times: 'If you fancied standing, now would be a good time!' The cheeky laugh in his voice told me that he knew that I probably wouldn't do it, but he was giving it a try anyway.

My feet were numb with the cold by that point and I was too tired. I'd had such a good day and I didn't fancy ending it with a splash, so I denied him his standing shot and kept paddling until I was in line with the south side of St Ives. The sun had disappeared and, while the crew seemed happy for me to keep going until the end of the tide (around ninety minutes later), I was done. Exhausted, I climbed onto the support boat and we whizzed the short distance back into the harbour. Sitting on the back deck looking out at the water rushing behind us, I wrapped myself up tightly in my dryrobe. I was cold, tired and on the edge of tears from fatigue – a sure-fire sign I was well and truly done for the day.

Back on dry land, after unloading our gear from the boat, Mike congratulated me on how far I'd gotten with a firm handshake. He was astonished at the difference between the two days, and I was glad to show him that I was capable of doing this adventure. I knew that given the right conditions I could do this, despite the fear, and it was nice to have him see that – even if I wasn't standing up much, yet.

Liam and I got a taxi back to the campsite, by which time we were too shattered to cook, and it was too late to go out for food. Instead, we ate leftover sandwiches and a supermarket tiramisu in the tent before falling into a deep, comforting, and well-earned sleep.

Buying a boat

With my paddling timetable completely dictated by the weather, over the next two weeks we kept a close eye on the forecast, but it wasn't looking good. On the one hand this was frustrating as I wanted to keep making progress, but, on the other, it was actually handy to have a break long enough to sort out buying Shogun. So, during that first week of bad weather I negotiated and agreed the price for her, then found a suitable date that worked with the tides to have her put into the water.

Liam and I moved from our tent at the St Ives campsite into YHA hostels. It was only a couple of pounds more per night in exchange for a lot more comfort. We moved from one hostel to another depending on where they had availability and if we needed to visit a particular part of Cornwall or Devon to look at the boat or meet up with friends.

When we got the chance, we also got Liam's slackline out. He had begun slacklining in Dubai, practising not only walking on it, but starting to do drops and spins with the line over soft sand or the sea. Give Liam any new sport that requires balance and he seems to take to it like a duck to water. It was also, of course, a great way for me to work on my own balance, an essential skill when it comes to paddling on the sea, dealing with swell and choppy waters.

We set up Liam's slackline in a forest car park near our hostel on Dartmoor and, after a while, I managed to walk from one end to the other in one go. I could definitely feel my balance improving the more I practised. Once I was done, Liam took the opportunity to raise the line a metre off the ground – twice the height that he'd put it at for me to practise. He was then straight into trick mode, trying to spin every which way, but watching him bounce so high off the ground with only hard gravel to break his fall didn't exactly fill me with confidence. But, he was determined to get a new routine nailed, and wouldn't give up until he'd managed it.

That was until one wrong positioning as Liam came down to bounce on the line saw him flung – head-first – over the line and into the gravel. When I'd picked Liam up from his mum's house a couple of weeks before, his stepdad had waved us off with a stern 'take care of my boy' look in my direction. So I really didn't want to be ringing them after Liam had broken something falling off his slackline... I decided it was time to go and get some food while he was still in one piece.

Having worked on my balance with the slackline, and still being unable to be out at sea due to bad weather, it meant that it was also, according to Liam, a good opportunity for me to work on falling off my board. While I wasn't overly excited by the idea, my friend, Chris Shirley, joined me and Liam down in Dartmouth and the three of us went for a SUP lesson in the harbour. Chris is a tall, adventurous ex-marine. He still keeps in shape and if you follow his Instagram you'll see him going on ridiculously long runs, pushing weights, and climbing. He's had a few adventures of his own, having rowed across the Atlantic and run the Marathon des Sables, although, amusingly – given he's an ex-marine – he's scared of open water too.

In fact, despite all his exploits, Chris had never SUPed before, so this was a great chance for him to have a go. It was also a low pressure way for me to mess around on the SUP, with Liam setting us challenges like seeing who could jump the highest or go furthest back on the board without falling off. While I'm always nervous of falling, it's the rush of water over my face when I fall that makes me panic the most, so being in the calm harbour wasn't as scary as being out at sea, and the camaraderie of having the guys with me made me feel a tiny bit more relaxed.

Towards the end of the session, we spotted a cameraman filming seagulls and it turned out he was shooting some footage for the BBC. Chris explained what I was doing and gave them all my contact details, while I got back on my board so they could film me paddling up and down. I don't know if they ever used the footage, but it was always good to try and get a little coverage – the more support I could get, I figured, the more likely it was that I'd be able to find another skipper or get help with the other things we might need along the way.

Chris stayed with us for two nights at the hostel, eating, drinking, playing board games, and watching crappy films. We also tried to go surfing one day, but – luckily – there was nowhere open to hire boards, so we had to leave the wild and chilly wind-churned waves for a cosy afternoon by the fire instead.

After Chris left, Liam and I headed for a coastal hostel in Treyarnon Bay, north Cornwall. It was good to see the stretch of water that I'd paddle past in a few weeks' time. There was a narrow but very deep beach that stretched far out at low tide between the cliffs that rose up on either side. The gentle gradient of the beach plus the right conditions produced small waves, meaning that it was a great beach to have a go at surfing on. And, with the sun shining this time, Liam convinced me that we should take the SUPs out to have a go at SUP surfing.

Building on my confidence from our 'falling off' session with Chris, I gingerly followed Liam out into the waves. We got past the breakers and, sitting out back on my board, I watched Liam stand and attempt to catch wave after wave. I was keen to catch a wave too – Liam did make it look like loads of fun – so I paddled for a few small waves, although I chickened out of standing and knelt instead. I occasionally slipped off my board as the waves pushed me from an awkward angle, but it was always a minor enough fall to be manageable, and I hopped right back on the board easily enough before paddling out again. The thrill of catching a wave, no matter how little, was instant and I could totally see why people love it.

As I sat bobbing in the sunshine and watching Liam throw himself, quite literally, into catching waves, I was in two minds about how I was feeling. I was still fearful of being wiped out by a wave – as I had been both with Tim at Clevedon and Liam at Durdle Door – but, at the same time, no longer as scared of the big expanse of sea behind me, especially given that I was so close to shore and to Liam. I wanted to let go of my fear completely and throw myself into the surfing, but I also didn't feel the need to prove anything: I was happy bobbing and basking and bodyboarding the odd small wave. After two hours we were both starting to get a little cold, so we dried off and warmed up, watching the sun set over the bay as some bodyboarders made the most of the last light.

With the mortgage loan making slow but steady progress, Erin had been a godsend lending me enough money to buy my boat in the meantime, and Shogun was – at last – almost ready to hit the water. She'd been sitting out of water in the boat yard for over a year, so, while that meant we could check the hull for any signs of osmosis or gaping holes, it also meant that we would be on tenterhooks as she was lowered into the water that evening, not knowing if she would still be floating the next morning.

Before Shogun was put into the water, we went out to buy a tender – a small inflatable boat that you use to get from the shore to the main boat when it's out on a mooring. We'd definitely need one, and Shogun didn't come with one, so I'd been searching eBay for second hand options. I chose one with an outboard engine as it's a lot easier to deal with tides or waves with a motor than with oars.

Overnight, as the sea came high enough on a spring tide, Shogun was lowered into the water with a big crane. The following morning, Liam and I were out the door of our hostel first thing, the car fully loaded and feeling eager to move into our new home. We met Simon, the agent, at his office and checked in with the boat yard, who – thankfully – confirmed that she was indeed still floating. They'd hung around for a while after she'd been lowered in to check for any signs of water ingress, but luckily she'd seemed watertight. It was a relief that Shogun hadn't fallen at the first hurdle!

After making the final payment, we hopped into the agent's rib and they took Liam and I over to get Shogun off her mooring. We climbed on board and Simon was straight at it rummaging around, figuring out where all the controls were. He got the engine started for us and showed Liam the basics of how to drive her before promptly leaving him to take us over to Falmouth Harbour solo while he continued searching around Shogun. Liam steered the boat, manoeuvring around the others dotted about the bay with the sun glistening down on us.

I was now the proud owner of a boat and Liam, after a whole five minutes of instruction, was driving a yacht for the first time – relaxed and clearly capable. I don't think either of us could've been more excited. This was all getting very real and I could feel my energy building. After all those setbacks, all the pushing to keep going, all the attempts to find ways to make this happen, things were starting to slot into place.

Simon got us moored up on the pontoon in Falmouth Harbour and directed me on where to check us in. He'd given Shogun a quick check internally on the way over and was pleased to report that she seemed to be a sturdy little boat. Once we were tied up, they left us to settle in.

'I might pop back tomorrow to check in on you and see if you need any help. Do ring if you have any issues,' Simon said as he left. He was such a brilliant help.

Much like with moving into a new house, we began by pulling out all the junk, figuring out where the storage areas were, and moving our things in from the car. Liam started scrubbing the deck but promptly broke both the bucket and the deck brush, so he resumed rummaging. He was delighted to find a pair of yellow trousers and a yellow jacket, quickly changing into them. He looked exactly like a cartoon fisherman in head-to-toe attire, except I really should've bought him a yellow hat to finish off his outfit.

I popped into the shed by the entrance and one of the guys behind the desk started checking us in to the marina. With a serious tone he began asking me lots of questions about Shogun, like her draft and length, but I could only stand there with a slightly confused look on my face.

'I've only just bought her and have never had a boat before!' I said chirpily, as if being a novice was a suitable and slightly exciting excuse to not have a single bit of information that he'd asked for. But I assured him I'd go back and check through all the paperwork for the answers he needed, and that, given I didn't yet have a skipper, I wouldn't be sailing off in the night without paying my dues.

'Actually,' I began, 'I don't suppose any of you are yachtmaster skippers are you?'

The three of them stood there clutching their cups of tea looking at me like this was a trick question, one that they shouldn't answer in case I was roping them into something. Hesitantly, they nodded.

'You are? Awesome! So, I'm doing this challenge...'

As I explained the rough idea and invited them to become my skipper and follow me inordinately slowly up the length of Britain, it turned out – funnily enough – that they all had other plans. However, one of them, Kris Butler, was intrigued.

'Wait, did you post about this in a Facebook group? I saw that. That's pretty cool what you're doing! I can't skipper you unfortunately, but I'll share it with everyone I know locally and see if we can help you find someone. Have you tried the main harbour office? They love having content to share on their socials and they'll know lots of people in town who might be willing to lend a hand.'

At this point I was asking anyone and everyone I met if they were a yachtmaster skipper, which, while it didn't seem to have been going so well to start with, it had certainly paid off in this instance. Having the support of a local to rally some troops was a wonderful boost. And, after exploring the high street, I headed in to see the harbour team who were delighted to spread the word about SUP Britain, sharing it on Twitter and chatting about it to the locals. I had my fingers well and truly crossed that someone would offer to skipper.

Erm, the boat's a bit sloshy

Over the next two days, we continued clearing out the proverbial loft of the last owner's junk – we delved under the sofas, into the cupboards, into the nooks and crannies all over the boat, under the chart table, behind the toilet mirror, under the floorboards... there were so many little cupboards making use of every single available space aboard Shogun that we didn't actually locate all of them until about two months into the expedition.

As we uncovered the first few, though, we stumbled across some interesting finds. In the first aid box – the contents of which were mostly out of date and pretty dirty – we found two bandages, one still in its factory plastic wrap from 1945. Over seventy years ago! Plus, there was an old nautical brass horn, a retro navigational calculator from the 1970s in its original wooden box, and an old slightly broken glass fishing rod.

While digging around under the sofas, we also found the fresh water storage bag sitting in a fair bit of water. Of course, the fresh water bag should have water *inside* it (not around it!), so this needed seeing to right away and the first question was whether the bag was leaking... or the boat was leaking. Liam did a quick taste test, which revealed that it was fresh water, putting our immediate concerns of the boat sinking at bay. The bag itself didn't seem to have any holes in it, although the connections looked worn. After trying to tighten them every way we could possibly think of, we realised that we needed a new bag – after all, that one had been sitting on the boat for at least twelve months and was probably not a particularly clean place to store our only source of drinking water. Time for a shopping trip.

A chandlery (a shop for boat stuff) is a fascinating place. From wellington boots and toilets, to sparkly silver accessories and two-stroke engine oil (which I knew was very different from four-stroke, although I still have no idea what the stroke count actually refers to). We not only got the fresh water bag, but a floating knife for my life jacket, a new set of flares for the boat, and three life jackets.

It turned out that a lot of the safety gear on Shogun had had its day. Shogun was built two years before I was born, and, while she seemed like a solid boat, she needed her accessories upgrading. There were six fire extinguishers on board, a life raft and a set of flares, but all of them were out of date. The life raft was probably her original one, by the looks of it, and the last service had expired five years previously. I was obviously keen to make sure the boat was safe for my crew, but Simon suggested that it wasn't a necessity to get it serviced or replaced. I calculated that, given that we had the tender pumped up on deck and two inflated SUP boards, we had plenty of escape options should the worst happen.

'Plus, you never know,' he said, 'the raft might work fine.'

Back from our shopping trip, we continued to sort and organise. We successfully fitted the new water bag and filled it up. Liam got the sails out from their storage in the front cabin and looked at how they needed to be attached to the mast. He was confident on how to attach the jib – the sail right at the front of the boat – as it was fairly similar to those he was used to putting on to dinghies. So, together we got it out, linked up ropes and pulley bits, and – hey presto! – it was up. The main sail was another matter entirely though... it was far more complicated, as it needed to be linked to several different ropes.

As Friday evening started to set in, I noticed Kris from the marina office motoring a tender round the harbour. Waving and smiling sweetly, I hoped he would come over and give us a hand.

'I don't suppose you know how to put sails on, do you?' I shouted over.

'I do indeed. I'm just heading to my mate's boat for some beers, so I'll grab him and we'll come over in a bit,' he called back.

Perfect. We got our own beers in the fridge ready as payment and tidied up the boat a bit too. A little while later, Kris came back with his mate, Ben, and his dog. They climbed aboard and Liam showed Kris around the boat, explaining where we'd gotten to with the sails. Meanwhile, I sat with Ben and his dog on the back deck while he played Liam's guitar. It was great to hear someone able to play so well. From what I'd heard of Liam's practising, he wasn't quite at Ben's standard yet, but we had several months ahead of us for Liam to improve.

As more of Kris's friends turned up, they helped Liam put the mainsail on and the beers flowed. A little later, a second dog appeared, followed by some more local sailors. Alex Elsdon, a boat engineer, asked if he could have a nose around Shogun. Given that I hadn't had a survey on the engine, the offer of a quick glance over was more than welcome. I stayed on the pontoon chatting to some of the guys and after he was done Alex popped back up to join us.

'So, when are you staying until?' he asked.

'Until I find a skipper,' I said plainly, not at all expecting what came next.

He turned and looked at the boat. 'How about 8am tomorrow?' he asked, putting out his hand to shake on it.

My eyes lit up. 'Seriously?'

'Yeah, why not? I've only got my day skipper, and I've had the runs from drinking too much last night, so I'll poo in a bucket to avoid blocking your toilet, but I'd be happy to help you out.'

Trying to ignore the toilet issue, I looked at Liam with the biggest grin – *we're off!*

It sounds a bit out there, I know. I'd known Alex all of ten minutes and here I was unquestioningly entrusting him to keep my £17,000 boat and Liam safe, but you just get a feel for some people. He immediately swung into preparation mode, checking through the boat with Liam from front to back – lights, engine, equipment, etc.

Arriving promptly at seven the next morning with his fishing gear, tool box, and day kit, Liam converted Alex from an Italian breakfast – a cigarette and a coffee – to a peanut butter and chocolate spread sandwich with a coffee, as the three of us settled down for a chat. Liam had already easily persuaded me of the merits of these sandwiches over my usual muesli earlier during the trip and they were now a daily standard.

After breakfast we were ready to set sail. The only thing left to do was fuel Shogun up. Just like fuelling a new car for the first time, we had to start by locating the fuel cap, which was on the port side (to the left) of the boat – it was very important to not get this mixed up with the fresh water cap on the starboard side. Then Alex showed us where the fuelling berth was in the marina and, once filled up, I waved Liam and Alex off as they motored into the grey fog that hung over the marina that morning. For the next twelve hours, they motored (and sailed when the wind allowed) Shogun south from Falmouth, round the Land's End peninsula, and up the north coast of Cornwall to St Ives.

While I spent the day running errands on land, the guys enjoyed getting to know Shogun, with Alex sharing as much of his sailing knowledge as possible with Liam. They tried to fish off the back of the boat, rigging the rod and line up, and leaving it for a while, but they soon realised they didn't have a heavy enough weight, meaning the hook was too close to the surface of the water with the speed they were going. No fish for dinner!

Once they made it to St Ives around 9.30pm, they anchored Shogun in the bay and Liam brought Alex ashore in the tender so I could drive him back to Falmouth. I gave Alex a heartfelt hug and a bottle of Kraken rum as a thank you – he had really saved the day. In return, he gifted us his 2018 nautical almanac: an annually printed, several inch thick sailing book, which gives information on harbours and tide times, amongst other things. A very useful bit of navigational equipment! We were so grateful to him for all he was doing to support us.

Returning to St Ives an hour later, I called Liam so he could come out in the tender and pick me up. When he answered, he sounded not only shattered from a long, intense day at sea, but also a little worried.

'I'll meet you at the end of the seawall where the other support boat dropped us off... oh, and just to warn you, the boat's a bit sloshy.'

'Sloshy! What do you mean the boat's a bit sloshy?'

'You'll see when you get here...'

Standing on the end of the seawall, I looked out into the pitch black night and tried to see through the thick fog that sat over the water. I could tell there was a gentle – yet persistent – rock in the sea, as the mast lights of several boats were swaying in the darkness. Searching for a sign of movement, not knowing which one was Shogun, I eventually spotted a smaller light lower down moving towards me as Liam emerged from the fog on the tender.

He was clearly shattered, dejected, and considerably freaked out by the eerie conditions – it was not fun to be out in this, especially on a boat on your own. I really felt for Liam and massively appreciated what he'd done that day. His third ever day sailing on a yacht in his life had been a long one, with more responsibility than he'd probably wanted.

Once back on the boat, the 'sloshiness' Liam had referred to earlier was immediately apparent. Every time the boat rocked in the swell, water would come up from under the floorboards – from one side, then the next – washing across the floor. It seemed like there must be a lot of water in the boat for this to be happening, and the prospect of my boat sinking on the third day that I had owned it was not one I was willing to entertain.

My immediate concern, though, was Liam as he'd had a splitting headache for the last five hours, so I dug out some codeine. I then asked him, cringing, if Alex had pooped in the bucket. He dismissively shook his head. To be fair, I couldn't imagine how you'd poop into a bucket up on deck with a boat swaying beneath you in the swell. Well, rather uncomfortably, I'd guess! And, despite Liam's initial concern for the water spilling over the floor, he was soon falling asleep, saying we'd fix the water issue in the morning.

Now, for the past year or so I'd been running Adventure Book Club, and the previous month's read was *Last Man Off* by Matt Lewis – a harrowing tale of a boat sinking in the Southern Ocean and how it was the most inexperienced crew member on board, Matt himself, who called abandon ship and was the last man off the doomed vessel. The moral of this story for me had been to not ignore small problems and think you'd deal with them later. So, with this tale fresh in my mind, the idea that Liam and I would sleep on a boat that clearly had water coming in, and tackle the issue in eight hours' time, was not one that sat comfortably.

Luckily, Alex was still up and he replied immediately to my text. On his advice I checked some screws that held the packing tight in the stern gland, usually creating a watertight seal around the rotating shaft. But, now, water was pouring in as if someone had left a tap on. Ideally, the packing would be replaced, but that's something that needs to be done with the boat out of the water; as it was, with compacted packing, there was more room for everything to move around, as the screws that should have held it tight had wiggled loose when the engine was running. Thankfully, having identified the source of the water, I just needed to tighten them up with a spanner to stop the flow. Immensely relieved that no more water was coming in, I lifted a floorboard so I could bail some of the water out, then – reassured by the success of my efforts – I curled up to get a little sleep.

Learning to skipper

Come the next morning, Sunday the 6th of May, two weeks after I'd last paddled, the fog didn't burn off with the sunrise. Despite being just half a mile from the harbour, we couldn't see St Ives. However, the lack of visibility at that point didn't feel ominous: the sun was bright, making it feel more like we were in a *Truman Show* bubble than anything else.

As the sun fought through the enveloping mist, Liam suddenly yelled for me to come quick. I climbed on deck to see him excitedly pointing towards the water. *What was it?* Then I saw... four or five fins glided beneath the surface, before popping up further down the side of the boat, and finally disappearing – a pod of dolphins had come to say hello as they swam south for breakfast.

This was to be day three of paddling, and Liam and I were alone on the sea. The tide pushing north was due to start around 3pm, giving us time to prepare the boat in the morning, before raising the anchor and motoring slightly south of St Ives to pick up my last paddle point. As I still couldn't find a skipper – and Liam had had a crash course from Alex the previous day – there was only really one option. It was Liam's time to shine. Excited and daunted in equal measure, he threw himself into his new role, checking weather conditions and planning our route.

Wrapped in thick mist the whole day, we never saw land or any other boat after leaving the harbour. In fact, it was so foggy that our top priority was simply to not lose sight of each other – just ten metres of visibility at points meant that it wouldn't take long for me to be completely lost.

Liam spent the next six hours carefully mapping our course along the coast using the GPS and paper maps on board the boat. For most of the day, the sea was glassy flat and there wasn't much wind to speak of, which made tracking a straight course relatively easy with Shogun's autohelm keeping her roughly on a set course. The biggest danger, though, was rocks. We knew there was a rocky outcrop north of St Ives bay, and Liam initially said that we should go around them on their far side as he wasn't sure it would be wise to take Shogun through that stretch for fear of hitting the rocks – after all, it's far better to have lots of sea between you and them. But, as we approached, still surrounded by fog, he changed his mind.

'Let's go through,' he said. 'I think it'll be fine. It's such a still day and I think I was being overly cautious.'

Given that this was Liam's second day ever skippering a yacht – and his first solo – I was more than happy to go with an overcautious approach. He was adamant, however, that we could go through. He had way more experience than me at sea and he had all the information in front of him, so, through the rocky outcrop we went.

After around half an hour or so, Liam radioed over to me as I paddled behind the boat. 'That's it, we're through,' he said, relieved and chuffed at making a good call. And, in fairness, we hadn't seen a single rock as we passed through.

On my board, the flat water had made me feel comfortable enough to stand. Fear to one side, this was awesome. I was actually doing it – I was standing up on the sea – and it felt ridiculous, exciting, and terrifying all at the same time. This was what it was supposed to be like: manageable sea conditions (though minus the fog would've been preferable), me standing and paddling, and making miles. Plus, my very own support boat to make sure that I didn't die (OK, an experienced skipper would've been good too). But, issues aside, this was really happening!

After about five hours, I was starting to get tired and my legs were turning to jelly after standing still for so long. We'd made it seven miles round to a sheltered bay that Liam had spotted as a suitable overnight stop and we dropped anchor. Other than the night before, Liam had never dropped anchor on a yacht before and neither had I. It was now 7.30pm and dusk had set in, making it hard to see exactly how far away from the shore we were.

It was a small bay with a beach in the middle and surrounded by high, craggy cliffs on either side. As darkness fell around us, we started to see lights from houses on top of the cliffs and it became apparent just how close we were to the rocks. It's one thing locating your position on a map and reading a chart to understand how the terrain sits around you, but seeing it is another – and it's a far better indication of your location and the conditions.

We were both nervous, but Liam was particularly so. This was the first night that it was purely his decision where to anchor. I didn't have a clue about what to consider so he was feeling the pressure. His nervousness made me nervous: *what if the anchor slipped along the seafloor in the night and we drifted onto the rocks along the shore?*

We lifted the anchor and moved further out of the bay. But, even in deeper water and further away from the rocks, it was another tense night sleeping on the boat. We had an anchor drift alarm on, and Liam set his phone alarm to wake him every two hours to check on our position.

Come morning we were both pretty shattered, but luckily everything had been fine throughout the night. It was still gloomy and damp outside – and, when we checked the weather forecast, we could see that worse weather was on its way. As we'd learnt at the planning stage, the north coast of Cornwall has only one option when it comes to wet harbours: Padstow. This was some thirty miles away from our current position, meaning it would take us seven hours to motor there in good weather, but that we also had to be mindful of when they would close the gate to the harbour before the next low tide.

Located about halfway up the north coast of Cornwall and three miles into the River Camel, Padstow is protected from the worst of the Atlantic weather. Its approach is infamous, with the Doom Bar sands providing plenty of opportunity to get caught out and run aground if you're not careful, so it's best to arrive before any strong westerlies kick in. The town is centred around the inner harbour, in which the waterline sits two metres below street level. There's a huge, solid metal gate that rises up out of the harbour floor two hours before low tide, in order to prevent the harbour from drying out and providing a safe haven for all manner of boats. However, this means that if you miss the window you'll be forced to sit out the low tide on a mooring in the middle of the river instead. No biggie in good weather, but far from ideal if bad weather is bearing down on you.

The initial plan that day was to paddle two tides. The first was 6.30am to 12.30pm, and the second was 7pm until after dark. We'd woken at 6am, ready to hit the water, but the prospect of putting on a cold, sodden wetsuit and getting back out on the board – versus heading for the safety of the harbour before the stormy weather hit – was too easy a call to make. The added stress and lack of sleep from worrying about the anchor had really taken it out of us and we really needed some proper rest. It was bad enough having to deal with my fear of the sea, but our fear of crashing into the rocks while we were sleeping had added an unneeded extra layer. I knew that this was exactly where a skipper would have really come into their own. They would've been confident about whether or not this had indeed been a good spot to anchor, plus they could have shared checking duties throughout the night with Liam, so we'd all have had a better night's sleep.

I find that making the call on whether to push on and make miles or to head for shelter is often a tricky balance. Sometimes, it's actually really rewarding to graft onwards in challenging weather, and other times it's just utterly miserable. Invariably, I'd always rather err on the side of caution if it's looking more extreme. I wasn't willing to regret my decision later, particularly given that I had someone else's safety to consider.

In this instance though, with the magic of hindsight, it ultimately transpired that we had had plenty of time before the bad weather hit and I should have paddled that first tide. Such is life...

We got to the harbour just in the nick of time before the harbourmaster pulled up the gate to close it off from the receding tide. Once inside, all Liam had to do was park the boat against a ten foot stone wall with a crowd of tourists looking on.

The small, square harbour in the heart of Padstow draws crowds throughout the summer months – people come down to sit on the high wall and go crabbing with a Cornish pasty in one hand and an ice cream in the other. It's such a tiny harbour that there's only one pontoon in the middle, enough for around ten boats. Any extra boats need to tie up on the edge of the harbour against that tall stone wall.

Now, the skill it takes to park a boat shouldn't be underestimated. There are no brakes, just forward and reverse. Imagine if every time you parked your car you had to time the angle and speed precisely, so that you'd just roll to a stop in exactly the right place in one go. Oh, and with a car already parked in the space in front and a brick wall to your right... It's kind of the same with a boat, except the 'ground' is moving and the wind or tide might push you off course – tricky, to say the least.

You also have to judge how any movement in the water, such as tides or rips, and the impact of any wind, will affect where you end up. Where you can, you want to use these forces to act as a brake, so a head wind or going against the tide is helpful sometimes. But when they're with you, pushing you towards the wall, you have to make sure you nail that parking first time.

After you've figured out how to account for wind and tide, you have to approach your parking space at forty-five degrees – so it looks like you're going to plough straight into the wall – then hold your nerve until the last moment, when you turn the boat parallel and, ideally, just drift gently right into the spot you were aiming for.

Luckily, on this occasion there was no tide or wind to affect the boat and, amazingly, with our full crowd of onlookers, Liam bossed it. First approach and he was spot on. Slow and steady worked a dream. We got Shogun tied up to the wall and set about finding the showers and laundry room.

Despite the warning of bad weather, by the time we'd got into harbour the fog of the last forty-eight hours had cleared to bright sunshine. The next day the weather in harbour was still gorgeous, but we knew it was a different story out at sea – strong winds and big swell meant it would be a couple of days before I could paddle again.

Finding space

It was the first night on my own in four weeks. Pottering around the boat, I almost don't know what to do with myself. Liam and I had been in each other's pockets for the past month, hopping around Cornwall and Devon, getting everything sorted, and making progress over the first three days of paddling. It'd been intense to spend so much time with someone I'd never met before and, while we were getting on well, this was very different to what I was used to on an adventure.

Usually solo and self-supported, I have a lot of freedom out on the road. I decide when to stop or when to keep moving. I seek out company when I want it, but love the ability to be completely alone in the wild too. Looking back to that first walk the length of the River Cam, it was the thinking space that I loved the most, and I'd not had that yet on SUP Britain. It's such a key part of why I adventure: I crave time to think things through, to process my life, and to see things differently.

Liam's girlfriend, Amy had driven down to spend some time with him while we were stuck in the harbour waiting for good weather out at sea. With him away for the night, I pulled on my trainers, locked up the boat, and headed for the trails that led west out from St Ives. Running gently with the sea to my right, I noticed the tension I'd been holding in my body, and tried to shake it free. I let my mind wander and my feet feel the solid ground beneath me.

As I ran, I began to realise that each time I had been out on the sea, it took every ounce of my concentration and, as much as I tried, I couldn't lose myself in the motion of moving forwards. My mind was constantly buzzing, assessing the conditions, trying not to fall, wondering how far I'd cover that tide, brainstorming where else I could look for a skipper, calculating Shogun's fuel levels, reflecting on how Liam was holding up, checking and double checking that we were safe out there. It never stopped.

The fear of falling off my board was constantly there and the challenging weather conditions so far had kept me focused on what I was doing – the high winds of day one, the big swell of day two, and the fog of day three. Of course, I had to keep my guard up if I wanted to avoid any unnecessary situations. It was the sea after all. I was acutely aware that, out there, things can change in an instant.

As I turned and headed back along the beaches, I realised just how much I'd missed my own company. I also realised that for this expedition to not drive me insane, I would have to learn to relinquish control over my progress to the weather and to those around me. Having a crew is obviously different to going solo. On the face of it, it looks like a holiday, right? People to ferry me to and from my paddle points, someone to make me lunch, someone to do the navigation and safety. But I couldn't push myself hard without pushing any crew hard too. And, so far, I knew that I was putting a lot on Liam's shoulders – especially given that he'd technically signed up as my photographer.

Resolved to find a way to get more crew on board, I got back to the boat and dived into dinner, before trying to find a new strategy. But first, finances – the loan was taking a ridiculous amount of time to come through. My financial advisor kept telling me it should come through the next week. Then the next.

By this time Erin had found a house she wanted to buy. She'd put down an offer that'd been accepted and the estate agents were asking her for proof of her deposit – which, at that point, meant explaining that she did have the cash, but that she'd just leant it to a friend to buy a boat for an expedition, and that she'd have it back in her bank account in a few days. Panicking that she'd lose the house if she didn't have the money back as soon as possible, all I could do was keep putting pressure on the bank to hurry up while reassuring Erin.

Then, the following day, after weeks and weeks of waiting, I was officially in debt to the bank and Erin had her cash back. Very glad to have the finances for Shogun and the whole expedition finally sorted, it was a huge relief and meant I had one less thing to occupy my mind.

We still couldn't paddle due to the weather, so we decided to use the time to make Shogun some signs to promote the adventure and potentially help us garner some support along the way. With Liam and Amy back, they headed to a local sail merchant, Freeman Sails, who generously let us have some big offcuts for free – perfect for making up signs for both sides of the boat, covering the sea spray protectors that we already had, and an additional sign to tie onto the main sail when it was folded away. This was particularly great in Padstow as the boom sat at the height of the wall so people looking at our boat could see it easily, whereas signs on the side of the boat were five feet below them and not visible.

Liam and Amy set about making up the signs, writing my social media handles and my SUP Britain mission on them. They spent most of the day writing out one sign, only to realise that the pen they'd been using was far too fine and couldn't be read from further than a metre away. But, with bigger pens borrowed from a local shop, the signs soon fitted the bill. Perfect timing – the weather forecast was improving, Amy said her goodbyes, and Liam and I got ready to leave the next morning, Sunday the 13th of May, and start paddling again.

My alarm rang at 3am. Not expecting to be back in the harbour for a few days, I went to settle the bill with the harbourmaster. As I put my pin number into the machine, he explained that the swell had picked up that morning more than expected. Noting the number of lobster pots that we'd have to pass on our way out to sea, and conscious that it was still pitch black, he said he'd be happier if we waited until 4.15am when the sun would start to come up. The last thing that anyone wanted was for us to get caught on a lobster pot and need rescuing. So, we heeded his advice and flopped back to sleep for another hour.

At 4.30am we were out of the harbour. As we came out of the River Camel, turning out of the lee of the headland and into less sheltered water, it wasn't nearly as choppy as Liam had expected after the harbourmaster's warning. I wasn't so sure, though. It was more boisterous than I'd have liked. Nonetheless, we made it down to my last paddle point at Portreath and I jumped on my board. With around three feet of swell, I was far too nervous to stand, but the lovely morning sunshine warmed me up and set a lighter mood that helped me focus less on the fear that surrounded me.

The plan for the end of that day had been to tie up to a mooring buoy in Newquay bay and head ashore to find somewhere to sleep, as it would be far too rocky on the buoy for a good night's rest. But, after several callouts on social media and some cheeky requests at expensive-looking local hotels, no-one could help us out and I was concerned that the idea of sleeping in Newquay wouldn't pan out.

However, by mid-tide we'd already covered eleven miles up from Portreath and were sitting just four miles south of Newquay, so it seemed like we'd potentially make it past Newquay before the end of the tide. Liam put the kettle on for a short break and I hopped aboard for a cuppa. I'd started to flag a bit by this point, having been kneeling a lot and feeling anxious in the swell, but tea and biscuits worked a treat.

Jumping back on the board, I felt revived and managed to stand. Better still, I felt stronger as the hours passed and was pushing to see how far I could get before the tide turned. Recognising a hotel and some bays on the coast, I used them as target points. *Just push on until you reach the first bay.*

This was a strategy I'd developed during the JOGLE walk – using points I could see up ahead as targets to reach to keep pushing forwards. I'd make myself get to the bend in the road, then once I got there I'd set my sights on the next target. Small, manageable chunks of distance were what worked best: something that seemed achievable, something that I could tick off in my mind as having done.

Endurance adventure is all a mental game really, just like, well, achieving anything in life. Having a big goal is great, but if I don't focus on what I'm doing right now, in the next hour or so, time can easily slip by. If I keep stopping for cake too often and lingering just another thirty minutes, the day is soon gone and fewer miles have been covered than were possible. Of course, it's a balance. I want to make enough miles today to feel satisfied with my progress, but not so many that it hampers my ability to go again tomorrow.

Milestone by milestone, that day I made it well past Newquay and was roughly in line with Trevarrian. By that point we were just as far from Padstow as we were from Newquay, so we opted for an easy night's sleep back in the harbour we'd come to know well.

Talking is better than buying burgers

The weather was set to be good for a few days at that point in mid-May, so the next morning we were out paddling again. Now with a much shorter commute of just a few hours, we could leave a little later and catch the north-going tide at slack water around 11am. The sea was much calmer and I was determined to stand for more of that day's paddle. Tentative at first, I felt out of practice and wobbly. The previous day had been the first time I'd paddled on the sea in 6 days since leaving St Ives and I was still trying to figure out how to balance the fear of falling off, with the need to make progress with standing rather than kneeling. As I relaxed into it, though, I felt a bit more confident with each hour that passed and enjoyed making progress north.

Using my milestone technique, the Trevose Head lighthouse on the cliff south of the entrance to the River Camel was a great first target of the day. As I began to pass the lighthouse, I thought I could see long, wide strips of seaweed weaving up through the water and brushing the surface beneath my board. It was almost hypnotising. *Was it really seaweed or was it something else?* This was dangerous though, where you look is usually where you end up, so the last place I should have been staring was into the water beneath me. In an instant, I felt myself caught off balance and quickly resumed looking at the horizon, trying to ignore what I thought was lurking underneath my board.

As I paddled on, I realised it wasn't seaweed at all, but in fact it was the water around me changing. With the smoother sea behind me, it had now begun to shift and flow differently; the seaweed effect was from the way the light now refracted through the water in a new way. It made it look like there was something lurking down below me, but, when I caught it from a different angle, the sea looked jet black.

Then it changed again. The sea became more choppy and rough, so I dropped to my knees through this section. Once out the other side, Liam lined up the support boat so he could get a picture of me with the lighthouse behind.

'Stand up, this is a great shot,' he called through the radio.

'I can't, my legs are shot from kneeling and I'll definitely fall in – it's still choppy,' I said wearily. The mind tricks from the light and tackling the choppy waters had exhausted me mentally as well as physically. I didn't care how great Liam's shot would be. This was me, doing this adventure. *Capture this. This is reality.*

'Oh, come on,' he insisted, 'just for a second. I'm ready and I'll get the shot in less than a minute, then you can kneel again.'

'Oh, for god's sake! You better be bloody ready.'

Liam laughed, pleased he'd pushed me to stand. I gingerly rose to my feet, barely balancing. I began to try to paddle. He got his shot, sure enough, but I look uneasy and unstable, slightly hunched, rather than gracefully gliding past the lighthouse, which is what I think he thought the shot would be. But this was real life: I was scared and tired and we needed pictures that showed the reality of what I was going through. Not more in front of lighthouses or sunsets.

Despite the fatigue, I wasn't done for the day and pushed on for the same distance again, making Trevose Head lighthouse the halfway point for the twenty-five miles I covered that day. At each rest stop every couple of hours, Liam would explain how far we'd come, how much tide we had pushing us along, and how much longer he thought we had left before the tide turned. I found it really useful and reassuring to get all this information – it allowed me to focus on the positives of how far I'd come and set a target for what was still left to cover. I could manage my effort levels based on either needing to conserve energy or going for it and pushing through to the end of the tide. And it kept me motivated.

I was also fascinated as I built up my understanding of what the tides were doing, what was happening around me and, specifically, beneath me. The idea of travelling over a moving element seemed like an odd one to such a land-lover. Imagine walking along the pavement only to find after ten minutes that you're still in the same spot you started from – it's weird. But of course there are the benefits too and, like freewheeling down a hill, having the tide push you along is a wonderful feeling. It's like nature wants to help you out.

I made it to roughly in line with Tintagel at the end of those twenty five miles and, even though I was tired and kneeling for most of it, it felt like a good, substantial day. The sun had been shining and I'd made solid progress along the coast, having finally made it past Padstow, where we'd spent so long waiting to get back out on the water during the bad weather.

That day I'd started to see more wildlife too, counting five barrel jellyfish in all. They were pretty big as far as jellyfish go – hence the name – and they can grow up to 90cm across and weigh up to 35kg. Apparently, they have eight frilly arms, which contain their small, stinging tentacles, surrounded by hundreds of little mouths! Luckily the ones I saw were only half the size of fully-grown ones and their sting isn't usually harmful to humans, but that didn't make me feel any better. In fact, seeing them pass by made me even more conscious that I absolutely did not want to fall off...

Once the day's paddling was finished, we had to motor back to Padstow as it was still the closest harbour. After getting changed I joined Liam on deck and we soaked up the afternoon sunshine with a celebratory beer in hand. With Shogun's motor gently chugging away, the four-hour journey back with the tide in our favour was a relaxed and fun one: we chatted away and enjoyed the view over the ocean and coast. The cliffs were rugged, having been battered by the Atlantic swell, but not nearly as high as those round at Land's End. Topped with green grass and small villages that rose out of the sandy beaches that dotted the coastline, there were few trees or tall buildings to puncture the outline of the land.

Day 25 of the expedition and day six of paddling was another early morning and we were out of the harbour at 7.30am, ready for the five-hour motor back to my paddle point opposite Tintagel. Where I was paddling at that point was so far away from Padstow that, including the motor out there then back (plus needing to leave the harbour once the gate had opened and be back before it closed again for low tide that night), we had to motor for twelve hours, which allowed me only two and a half hours of paddling time. It almost felt pointless. But harbours and anchorages were so few and far between along that northern stretch of the Cornish coastline, and the next safe haven was much further away in the opposite direction – well over a tide's worth of paddling.

This was a major downside of having a support boat. While I might've been able to hop off the water for tea and cake breaks and ensure I didn't drown, it was much more involved and time-consuming than if I'd just tried to paddle solo from beach to beach along the coast. Of course, while it's slower in this respect, it did also allow me to take routes which I wouldn't otherwise have been able to, and we were about to reach some rather lengthy open water crossings. From the north western tip of Cornwall I'd cross the Bristol Channel – which has one of the world's biggest tidal differences – then after reaching Wales, I'd set off to cross over the Irish Sea.

That day turned out to be one of the shortest paddles of the trip, but the long commute definitely caused something to change. Liam seemed to pay little attention to me on the water – gone was the useful information on what the tide was doing or the encouragement. Instead, he spent forty-five minutes on the phone, only glancing at me occasionally. At times the boat got too far away for me to feel safe.

'Liam, are you there? Pick up.' He didn't seem to have noticed how far away he was, but I got no response. Either the radios weren't working or he couldn't hear it.

I looked at my phone – no signal. I shouted as loud as I could, but Liam didn't flinch. He just sat with his back to me, watching the front of the boat as he motored on ahead. I glared at his back, willing him to hear my thoughts as I screamed at him in my mind to turn around, to see how far he was, to not leave me behind. He seemed intent on leaving me at sea.

It was a foggy day and though the fog didn't envelop us, instead clinging to the horizon, it added an eerie feel to being out – ignored – on the water. Eventually Liam turned around and noticed how far away I was. He kicked the boat into neutral and returned to his phone call while waiting for me to catch up. As I got closer, he put the boat back into gear and sped off again. *What the hell was he doing?*

The second time I got close, I yelled at him to wait and stay with me. He was clearly pissed off about something, but I wanted him to voice his frustration rather than leave me to the mercy of the sea. It felt like he was punishing me for going too slowly, but I was exhausted after having covered nearly forty miles in two days. I slept for a lot of the journey as we motored out that morning, and being tired made me feel less stable on the board so I was spending a lot of time on my knees.

It's often easy to assume when someone's mad at you that it's because of the thing you feel like you're failing at in that moment. I felt rubbish that I couldn't stand. I knew it would make me quicker if I did and that the pictures would be better and that I wouldn't hurt so much. But I was still really scared of falling and being fatigued only made the fear worse.

Looking back, I don't think Liam cared in the slightest about me kneeling or not. In fact, thinking about it afterwards, I realised he was probably pissed off at me because I had slept on the way out, while he'd had to stay awake and motor us to the paddle point, alone. Liam had told me fairly early on that he likes to be with people and that he doesn't like being on his own all that much. He craves social interaction. But I'd never had someone else's morale so squarely in my hands before. This adventure was intense. Just the two of us cooped up on a small boat, and the actions of one immediately impacting the other.

I think Liam was missing Amy. That's why he'd been on the phone for so long. Plus, this was not what he'd signed up for as an adventure photographer – the days were long and lonely.

Rather than voice his feelings, and rather than me asking him about them, we spent that day on the water mad at each other for different reasons.

We got back into harbour after another six hours of motoring around 7.30pm. Not liking the tension in the air, I wanted to make peace and fix the situation – but I didn't grow up in a household where we had tough conversations and talked about our emotions. I should've simply asked Liam how he was feeling and what was up. But I didn't and the only way I knew how to fix it was with food. I took us for a burger in a fancy local restaurant. We had a nice chat, but still avoided talking about the actual issues between us.

Again, bad weather meant that we were going to be off the water for a few days, so, as we sat eating lunch in the boat the following afternoon, I tried to bring up the topic of how far away Liam had got on the water the day before – plus the safety element of not being able to communicate with broken radios and no phone signal.

'Well, what specific distance do you want me to be, then?' he snarked back, pushing for me to name an exact figure.

'Shouting distance, Liam,' I replied, exasperated. 'If the conditions are good, that'll be slightly further, if they're bad, you'll need to stick close.'

He didn't appreciate the idea that I was giving him feedback on his skippering. He was so defensive that we couldn't have a proper conversation, which left me feeling nervous about it being just the two of us out at sea. I now knew I absolutely had to find a skipper to join us for the first crossing over from the Cornish coast to Lundy Island and then Wales.

Liam had previously flagged that his navigation skills were the aspect of skippering that he was worried about most, so I continued to put the call out for a skipper that could help us. I was adamant we wouldn't start the sea crossings until we had another pair of hands, both for general safety and because I was worried about Liam. I was well aware of how long the days were for him – it was a lot for anyone to take on and I wanted to spread the load. Plus, I knew that I would feel safer and like there was less tension between us with someone else on board.

Even still, no matter the cause of Liam's unhappiness, I should have asked him about it and been more willing to simply say, 'tell me more about how you're feeling.' This was a big lesson learnt for me about managing a team:

communication is the single most important thing. I really think that if we'd have sat down and talked it through, we would both have been a lot happier pressing on and would have understood each other better.

I asked around the Padstow marina office and again with Chris, Alex, and the others I'd met at Falmouth Marina. There was brief hope that one new contact might come through, but in the end they couldn't make it during the weather window that was coming up. Despite Liam's concerns about the crossing, and after struggling and failing to find another skipper, the prospect of us not making progress at all made him keen to push on regardless. So, he took the reins on the navigation front and planned it all out, pushing for us to go ahead despite not having a more experienced person on board.

It was a tough decision given the safety aspects involved. We'd be crossing the entrance to the Bristol Channel – with all the tidal issues that came with that – but I too was keen to make miles while the sun shone so, following careful thought, I decided we could go for it, with the first crossing over to Lundy Island as a kind of test. After all, if anything went wrong we wouldn't be too far from shore and there would be people on the island who could help us, with the option to turn back as our safety net. And, if all went well, then we could press on to Wales.

Over the next couple of days we both cracked on with getting the boat ready for the final time we would leave Padstow harbour and the first big crossing of the journey.

4

Tears before Ireland

Paddling with dolphins

The alarm went off at 7.30am on Friday the 18th of May, three days since I'd last paddled. I pulled on a large pair of black sailing trousers and the old jacket that I'd found on the boat when we first came aboard. I didn't even look in a mirror. Barely opening my eyes, I grabbed the toilet block key and my purse, climbed off the boat and up Padstow harbour wall for the last time. The light was just starting to brush the horizon and there was a quiet stillness hanging in the air before the day began. Under streetlight, I briskly walked round to the harbourmaster's office to pay for our two-week mooring and thank them for their help. By the time I was back on the boat, Liam had already disconnected the water and electricity and we were all packed up and ready to go.

Mornings were always about getting underway swiftly. Given the frequent early rises and long days, we favoured more time asleep than spent dilly-dallying. That day we had a lot of progress to make as we started heading up into the Bristol Channel, aiming for an anchorage near Clovelly, a village tucked around the top of the Hartland peninsula. To get there, we'd cross over the border from Cornwall into Devon, and have our first county behind us.

After three and a half hours of motoring, we arrived earlier than expected to the paddle point from Tuesday's session which, unfortunately, meant the tide was still pushing south and there was no point getting on my board just yet. Instead, we'd have to wait until it slackened off enough for me to not be paddling just to stay in the same spot.

Now that the sun was up, it was a bright day and the sea was alive – but, luckily, not too bouncy. We turned the engine off and let Shogun bob in the tide with land just a mile or two off to our right. I hate bobbing – it makes me nervous. As I don't like the sea at the best of times, it just means that my anxiety at getting off the boat and onto the board has time to build. So sitting there while we swayed in the water for ninety minutes did nothing to help.

Then, just before I was about to get onto the water, Liam suddenly stood up, intently focused on a spot in the distance.

'What are you looking at?' I asked, trying to see what he was staring at.

'I'm pretty sure I just saw a fin.'

'Shut up, are you kidding?'

'Ha, I don't know what it was, but I definitely saw something. There, look!' He pointed north of the boat and, coming straight for us, were several fins gliding above the surface before sinking out of sight again.

'It's dolphins!' I shouted excitedly.

Liam ran inside the boat to look for his long lens, while I quickly hopped on my board. They reached us just as I unclipped from Shogun.

'Liam! Liaaam! They're here! Liaaammm, forget your lens!' I yelled from the water. They were all around us.

He finally came out and started photographing and filming as we sat with them. Swimming all around me on my board and the boat, they were incredible. Beyond that glimpse of their fins in St Ives, I'd never seen dolphins properly before and their inquisitive nature was a joy. They were so gentle and playful – it was amazing to watch them pop up again and again, darting around, clearly having a great time. They got so close: one swam up just two feet to my left and almost seemed to slow down as it came up to the surface to get a really good look. I wonder what it made of me.

Eventually, they headed off and we finally got paddling. It had been awesome. The dolphins were such majestic animals and instantly calming – I never once felt like they would knock me off my board. They were a brilliant and welcome distraction that meant I lost all nervousness, leaving me with a massive smile across my face, the perfect antidote to my bobbing anxiety.

Elated, we cracked on and it was only a little while later that Liam noticed that in all the excitement I'd forgotten to put my leash on. I was usually so cautious about getting on the water – double checking I had everything: tracker, phone in its waterproof case, insulated water bottle, snacks in my life jacket, hat and sunglasses on. With this same routine of getting onto the board each time, I'd do my leash up on my right ankle immediately once on the board, then clip my insulated water bottle onto the bungee cords at the front, before, lastly, unclipping myself from the boat and turning my tracker on. Now, the lack of leash caught me off guard and I was pulled back to how quickly things can go wrong. Not that they had of course, nothing had happened while my leash was off, but if I had fallen in, my board would probably have drifted away from me and Liam would've had a double rescue on his hands if I couldn't get myself back to it.

It was funny how each day on the water felt so different to the last. The weather conditions and sea state both had such an impact on morale. That day the going only felt slow. The sea wasn't overly choppy and I was able to stand, but it really felt like I was on a treadmill, getting nowhere fast. We could see the land off to the right as we tracked north but, with no particularly discernible headlands or features to aim for, it was hard to tell if I'd travelled far as the minutes turned to hours.

One tea break down, somewhere between getting back on the water and the second break, it honestly felt like I'd gone backwards. I couldn't work out what it was about that day that seemed to make it drag. According to the boat's trackers and gauges the tide was with us, the wind was calm, and we should've been making more progress.

After the second break I hopped back on my board, by then neither of us expected to get up to the tip of Hartland, my planned paddle point for the day. We felt pretty dejected.

But, as I pushed on, nearing the last couple of hours of the northerly tide, incredibly, we felt a shift in the water and it was like something weighing us down had lifted. There was an odd push that seemed to come with the end of the tide and it began taking us along at four knots. This shouldn't have been happening. The end of the tide is when it's usually at its weakest, but there must've been a last minute kick caused by some aspect of the lay of the land around us there that we weren't aware of. Both astounded, we were excited to make the most of this unexpected tidal push and to keep paddling for as long as the tide kept pushing us north.

Liam also took another look at my route and figured it made sense for me to start paddling away from the Devon coastline that we'd been tracking, and instead make ground out towards Lundy Island, twelve miles offshore to our left.

Despite the long day and early start I kept paddling until sunset, happy to make the most of the tide and have miles passing beneath my board after such slow-going progress for much of the day. As the light faded, it was peaceful on the water, the darkness starting to touch the horizon a welcome signal that paddling would soon come to an end. In my last hour on the water, Liam had realised that we actually had another anchorage option: Lundy itself. At that stage, Lundy Island was the same distance from us as Clovelly, our original destination. While Lundy's anchorage was more exposed than Clovelly's, the weather overnight was looking calm and it felt better to head in the direction we actually wanted to go, rather than motor away from our route.

As we set course for Lundy Island, the sun disappeared and an incredible night's sky stretched out above us, pitch black and filled to the brim with stars. Lying on the back deck, with Liam on the other side keeping an eye out for lobster pots, I gazed up in wonder, tired, but deeply satisfied with our progress.

It's always calming and reassuring to stargaze. It reminds me just how insignificant we all are, of course, but it also reminds me that what we do each day, how we choose to spend our time, the things we worry about, and the things we celebrate are all fleeting, so we should remember to embrace it all. If our time here is short, then we have no reason not to live boldly, to chase dreams, to come up with wild ideas, and to make them happen. Ultimately, today will pass no matter how we spend those precious twenty-four little hours. And when the sun returns once more, I know it's time to make a start, to begin from where I am and dare to see how far I can get.

We approached Lundy in utter darkness, unable to see the terrain in front of us and figure out the exact anchorage spot. It was difficult to translate a digital map to what little we could make out through the black, but we spotted the mast light from another boat that was anchored nearby and figured that this must be roughly the right area. We used the depth gauge to find a decent point to drop the anchor and hoped for the best.

Lundy Island

Having gone to sleep unsure of our exact surroundings, but confident enough that the anchor was holding, we woke refreshed around 10am to bright sunshine filling the boat. Liam was up first and, as I climbed onto the deck, I was greeted by what looked like a deserted island. The water was utterly still in the bay; barely a ripple touched the surface as far as the eye could see. Endless blue reached up and touched the sky, all caressed by a golden light and the warmth of the full morning sun. Towering above us were the cliffs of a beautiful, lush, green island waiting to be explored. It was like a dream. It was as if we'd been washed up the night before and woken to find that we, and the two other boats anchored here, had this whole island to ourselves.

Liam was already sunning himself, using the upturned tender on Shogun's front like a sunbed. But, soon enough, he decided the water looked far too inviting to not go for a swim, even though we knew it was Baltic. Thinking it best to acclimatise himself, Liam-style, to the chill before he dived in, he started pouring several buckets of icy seawater over his head. As you do! Having reduced the chances of cold shock, he enthusiastically somersaulted off Shogun and into the blue. Instantly gasping for air, he didn't hang around, clambering up the swim ladder back out of the freezing water. In a way, I wanted to go swimming too, it did look incredibly inviting and the weather was so deceiving. It felt like a waste not to make the most of the dreamy setting and calm waters. I changed into my bikini and shimmied down the swim ladder to knee depth...

'Oh my god,' I laughed, 'it's freezing!'

'Come on, you have to go in properly. You'll warm up as soon as you get out.' Liam insisted.

But I wasn't convinced and hopped back onto the deck.

Aware that there was no shower on board Shogun and that some days we'd be anchored up rather than in a marina, back in Cornwall I'd bought a solar-heated shower. That is, a black bag with a hose on it. You leave it in the sun to heat up the water then, Bob's your uncle, you've got a lovely, warm shower no matter where you are. I'd left it out on deck the day before and it was now ready to go, so Liam rigged it up on one of the ropes and hoisted it above the deck. He tested it out first, then I popped underneath still in my bikini, letting the warm water flow over my back and using the hose to rinse off my legs and feet. It was a pretty idyllic setting for a shower.

As I stood watching, a large boat packed full with tourists approached the island from the mainland (the first one of many to come that Saturday as it turned out). Liam suggested I might want to put some more clothes on. Not sure whether to be offended or think it was cute that he didn't want people gawking at me, I wrapped a towel around myself just as the wake of the tourist boat hit us. As Shogun went from being perfectly still to rocking rapidly, the shower began to swing out of sync with the boat, snagged itself on something, and ripped as Liam tried to get it down. Well, no more showers on deck then!

After brunch we decided we'd better head off to do some paddling, so we motored over to the last paddle point, just eight miles southeast of Lundy. We both sunned ourselves on the motor over – those spots we'd missed with sunscreen turning red in the heat of the day.

Arriving early again, we bobbed for about an hour waiting for the tide to turn. In such calm, idyllic waters there was no sense of foreboding and I was almost looking forward to getting onto my board. Jumping on around 3pm, I was hoping for more dolphins, but they only briefly showed up, keeping to a distance. With such still conditions, Liam risked getting his drone out – without a spare pair of hands to help him launch and catch it from the moving boat – and he captured some awesome photos and videos of me paddling in the vast expanse of sea that day.

The water and weather were so calm that it felt surreal. I stood up all the way over to the island, enjoying the stillness and peacefulness that smooth seas allowed. It was only once I reached a choppy bit of water just before Lundy that I dropped to my knees. At both the southern and northern ends of the island, as the tide whips around the rock, the sea swirls and pulls strongly into eddies that I knew I would find it hard to fight. To get through that tidal race, I followed Liam's instructions on angling my approach so that the water pulled me in the direction I wanted.

Getting through the tidal race south of Lundy some time after 6pm, I was pretty shattered, having not had a proper rest since starting to paddle hours earlier. I'd usually break every two to three hours to stretch out my feet, have a cup of tea, eat some cake, and refill my water bottle – but the dreamy conditions had meant I'd just paddled on, trying to make the most of it and cover as much ground as possible.

Hunger stirring, I asked Liam to check what time the pub on the island stopped serving food, hoping that we could grab a proper meal and Wi-Fi that evening. Disappointingly, it was not meant to be though: food orders stopped at 8.30pm and we'd never make it back in time. As I paddled onwards, a little head popped up from beneath the surface – a seal! It was inquisitive, but too shy to come say hello and soon slipped off to explore elsewhere.

Shouting over, Liam suggested we pause for a little while. He turned off Shogun's engine. We sat and took in the silence, enjoying the calm of the island in the sleepy sunlight. Far above us over the island's cliffs, seabirds and puffins swooped and dived; the day was finishing as blissfully still as it had begun that morning. I lay down on my back on the board and lazily took a stab at a new type of paddle stroke. I don't think lay-down paddleboarding will take off any time soon.

Eventually we started moving again and made it to the north end of the island at around 8pm. The day had gone well. Liam's navigational skills had held up and I'd felt safe on the water with him being more attentive again as we'd moved through the slightly scary eddies, directing me and encouraging me when I'd looked petrified. We anchored closer to the island this time, amongst some other boats that had arrived during the day, and fell fast asleep.

The next morning, we got up at 5am to motor to the last paddle point on the northern edge of Lundy Island. We calculated that if I jumped on the water at 6am, we should have plenty of time to get to Wales within a day. Liam pulled up the anchor while I made breakfast for us both, then got changed into my wetsuit. The sea was choppier than the day before, which was always a let-down and made me wish that I'd pushed on further when waters were calmer.

As I paddled away from the island, I stayed kneeling to start with as I tackled some gentle tidal flows that edged along the north of the island. The plan in my head was to stand afterwards, as I was well aware of the long distance we had to cover before we hit land again.

Liam had taken the navigational planning in his stride. He explained, considering that I was now to cross the Bristol Channel, we had to take into account the fact that I was no longer going with or against the tide. Instead, I would be going across it. This, in theory, meant that I could paddle all day as I'd never be pulled backwards, but in practice it would still make more sense to avoid the strongest points in each tide, in order to limit the distance I would be pulled from west to east and allowing me to put more energy into paddling as far north as possible. The straighter the line north I could track, and the less S-shaped my route, the shorter the distance I would have to paddle overall would be.

Watching Lundy get smaller in the distance behind me, but with no sight of Wales yet to aim towards, it was hard to judge my progress. As I got back on the board after my first big rest of the day, three hours in, I was so happy to be joined by our friends again. This time, Liam didn't bother looking for his long lens and was ready to take some great pictures of the dolphins jumping in the water around me. Their presence was just magical and really helped me to refocus my mind on why I was doing this. There truly are wonderful experiences to be had if we dare to go places we've not been before, to see the world from a different perspective, and to try something new.

After thirty minutes of joyful dolphin watching, Liam and I both simultaneously realised that we couldn't just sit here with them forever – we had to make ground at some point. So, we slowly started to move forwards, wondering if they would stay with us and play in the wake of the boat. They did for fifteen minutes or so, until they too eventually had to get moving towards their destination.

Later in the day, the chop and the wind that had been preventing me from standing died down a little. But rather than flattening out altogether, it turned into even bigger swell, reaching around three feet. However, we were now able to glimpse Wales on the horizon – just the faintest of dark grey smudges coming out of the sea. It was still too far away to enable me to judge any noticeable progress, but it felt reassuring nonetheless.

Our destination of Milford Haven marina was to the north west of Lundy Island, so our heading was a little off due north. As such, when the tide was pulling into the Bristol Channel it was actually pushing slightly against the direction I wanted to go in, even with me cutting directly across it. But then, once the tide turned to head back out, it was moving much more in my favour and I began to make some real progress with my overall speed upping to a heady three miles per hour.

After twelve hours on the water, with a few breaks along the way, Liam decided it was time to call it a day. The tide had dropped off again and was no longer pulling me out west towards our destination and, soon enough, it would start pulling us back in to the east, the opposite of what we needed. But we could now see the Welsh coast clearly and it was a great feeling to have made it most of the way over my first big crossing – twenty-nine miles that day – even if I was still around seven miles from shore.

Concerningly, my left ankle had been hurting since lunchtime that day, no doubt caused by having spent so long on the board, and I was worried that the tendonitis I'd suffered from during my JOGLE walk had come back. With a niggling pain resurfacing, I'd spent the afternoon trying to find different ways of sitting on the board to lessen it or at least avoid aggravating it any more. I'd tried cross-legged or seated with my legs straight out in front of me, the latter of the two seemed the most comfortable, although I imagine I looked rather ridiculous

▲ At Land's End ready to start on 21 April 2018, which turned out to be the hottest April day in 70 years.

▲ Sennen Cove Harbour beach just before I left land for the first time. I was relieved at the stillness of the sea.

▼ Padstow harbour with *Shogun* and my SUP board in the background.

▼ Alex and Liam sailing *Shogun* around Longships lighthouse on route to St Ives.

▲ A cake and milkshake break.

▼ Ged watching over me as I paddled at night across the Irish Sea to Scotland.

▲ Liam taking photos and our unreadable boat sign.

▼ Stepping off Shogun on to my board on the east coast of Scotland.

▲ Liam and Sally sailing to Ardglass.

▼ Liam route planning.

▲ Paddling alongside Shogun as we
  made our way up the north
  Cornish coast.

▼ Paddling over to Lundy Island.

◄ Bristol Channel.

▼ The Cornish coast
as I paddled
towards Lundy
Island.

▼ Laying alongside
Lundy Island.

▲ A huge passenger ferry emerged from the mist as I paddled 40 miles across the Irish Sea on 31 May 2018.

▼ I started paddling at 6am and around 11 hours later was joined by a pod of dolphins, which provided the perfect morale boost.

▲ Liam, Eithne and I in Skerries.

▲ John, Aileen and I in Scotland.

▼ Aileen skippering *Shogun*.

▲ Amy's dog, Bear.

▲ Aileen's dad, Alisdair bringing us cake.

▼ Sally, Liam and I in Ardglass, NI.

◄ A tea and cake break on my board part way down Loch Ness.

► Meeting the locals as I got back on to *Shogun* at Fort Augustus in the Caledonian Canal.

▼ Paddling down Loch Ness before my crew left me to go through the locks.

◄ The final paddle strokes.

◄ Running up the ramp to the sign.

◄ John O'Groats.
10 July 2018,
81 days after leaving
Land's End.

paddling in this position. That is, if anyone other than Liam had actually seen me... There weren't many boats out in the Bristol Channel!

Again, as the day wore on, Liam had taken to motoring away from me. Combined with the big swell – when I was at the bottom of one trough and Liam was at the bottom of another on the other side of the peak – this meant that we often lost sight of each other. It worried me how casual he was becoming about keeping an eye on me while I was paddling. It didn't matter how frustrated we might become with one another, safety had to be our top concern.

Once back on the boat, I changed out of my wetsuit into warm, dry clothes and almost immediately fell asleep on the sofa. On waking, my left side was all tight and sore, from my fingers and wrist to my shoulder and ankle. My body was clearly protesting at having covered so many miles. I had woken to find us coming up to the marina, Liam having navigated us all that way on his own – *whoops*. I was aware that he needed me to stay with him while we were motoring, for his own sanity, but the sheer exhaustion from paddling meant it was hard for me to stay awake. I apologised for falling asleep and got the kettle on.

During the journey towards the marina, Liam looked a bit uncomfortable.

'Are you OK?' I asked. 'You look like you're in a lot of pain, what's wrong?'

'I really need a poo!' he whimpered.

'Oh, well, I'll take over, we've got long enough before we reach the marina, right?'

'No, I don't use the boat toilet. I've heard that they block really easily – and plus, whoever blocks in, unblocks it.'

I had to laugh at his predicament. 'You mean you've not pooed since we got on board because you're afraid your big, manly poos will block the toilet?'

'Well, strictly speaking I have pooed on the boat...'

'What do you mean?'

It was at this point that Liam sheepishly confessed. Back in St Ives harbour, when I'd asked if Alex had pooped in the bucket, Liam had told the truth that *Alex* hadn't... But he'd somehow neglected to mention that, up on the back deck of Shogun, he himself had squatted over a bright yellow bucket as the boat bobbed just half a mile out from the harbour beach. It had been late at night when it was pitch black and he had been shrouded in fog, which, while incredibly creepy, also meant that no-one had been able to see him. Even still, I'd never look at that bucket in the same way again.

Milford Haven Waterway is an estuary forming a natural harbour that has been used as a port since the Middle Ages. It flows out of Pembrokeshire to the south west and has ports dotted along the south and north edges of the water, specially designed to take huge, 1,000-foot container ships that come from all over the world – that's thirty times bigger than Shogun! The ships are so enormous that they have a captain who steers them out at sea and then they need especially trained skippers to park them at the docks. From talking to a few people since, it seems I might have been the only person who didn't already know this, but nonetheless I was enjoying learning new things about the marine industry.

Milford Haven Marina, where we were heading, is nestled around a mile into the waterway on the north side and, given the capacity for international trade in the area, we'd expected the waterway leading up to it to be busy throughout the night. But as we motored with a dark sky above us and bright lights dotted along the water's edge marking various ports and buoys, we seemed to be the only ones around.

Rather than a single tidal gate like the one at Padstow, Milford Haven has its own lock at the entrance, enabling boats to come and go no matter what the tide is doing. As we approached the entrance to the marina, we saw that the outer gate was already open. The guy operating the lock radioed over and directed us to tie up on the pontoon inside it. He then closed the big gate behind us. At a squeeze, there was probably room for six boats our size in the lock at any one time, but this time it was just us. Once the water level matched that of the marina, the second gate opened in front of us and we made our way in.

The marina stretched out to our right, and we passed row after row of pontoons as we searched in the darkness for our allotted row, D. About halfway down we spotted it. The marina was deadly quiet at this time of night and, while there was a fair number of boats tied up, it wasn't full, which luckily meant that there was an empty space next to us, making parking a little easier. As ever, Liam negotiated the new parking situation like an old hand.

The pontoons made an 'L' shape around us – so tying up at the front and down the side of the boat would keep us more stable in any wind and make it easier to get on and off Shogun.

As soon as we were tied up, Liam jumped off and walked awkwardly towards the nearest toilet. On returning, he had the marina codes and everything we needed to settle in. We had dinner around midnight and slept in the next day, glad to finally be in Wales and have our longest crossing yet behind us. Liam had done a great job navigating us over and I think he was feeling a lot more confident about his abilities as skipper. Understanding the timings of tides, the protocol of coming into new marinas, and parking the boat in a range of difficult situations – it was all brilliant experience that he took in his stride. What was still concerning, though, was his attitude towards keeping an eye on me when I was on my board. Perhaps this was just because he was tired and nervous of the crossing – but, either way, I needed him to keep his focus on me while I was on the water.

Looking ahead at the weather for the coming week, it was just too windy for me to head back out. My route would now be taking us west and almost directly into the prevailing winds. Ideal weather would be gusts below 10mph and an easterly to push me along, but anything higher and it would be: a) hard for me to maintain a straight line, having to paddle solely on the opposite side to the wind in order to counter it, and b) more likely I'd fall off. When the swell picks up it gets choppier too.... Altogether, this was not a recipe for fun or progress.

Two days later we headed into town to stock up with food. I'd been conscious that perhaps I should be thinking a little bit more about what I was eating to help me when I'm paddling. So far on all my adventures I'd just basically stuffed my face at every opportunity. All the major food groups were involved: pizza, fry ups, and cake. But, having heard that protein might be important for actual athletes, I thought I'd try to follow suit and found that the cheapest way to get protein would be in milk. At the start of SUP Britain, Liam had bought a two-litre bottle of chocolate milk and necked the whole thing, which had looked disgusting to me. But now with nutrition in mind, I thought he might be onto something. However, I'm not a massive chocolate fan, so I opted for strawberry, keen to see if milkshakes would make any difference.

As we wandered round the local supermarket I spotted a huge triple chocolate cake. Surprisingly, this wasn't a cake I was planning on eating myself. Since Liam liked to profess that he would always win eating contests when his mates dared him to eat a ridiculous amount of food, I figured I couldn't not stop and point out the cake. 'Sure!' Liam said without hesitation and with a confident shrug, as if to say I hadn't chosen a big enough cake to present him with any kind of real challenge. *The cake was bigger than his head though, surely he'd feel sick if he tried to eat it in one go?*

Back at the boat he immediately started to tuck in and, in no time at all, it was gone. Every last crumb.

'I could definitely eat another one,' he said with a massive grin on his face.

Now, I know I'm a serious fan of cake, but it was ridiculous. It made me feel sick just watching him eat it – and, no, I didn't buy him a second one!

Over the next few days I updated my log. I kept an Excel spreadsheet of each time I got on the water: the longitude and latitude of my start and end points for the day, distances covered, plus time spent on the water. So far, I'd covered one hundred and thirty-eight miles in fifty hours and twenty-eight minutes – spread over nine days on the water (and thirty-three days of the expedition). I reviewed the different possible schedules I'd worked out, from the overly ambitious one (two and a half months) to the one John had laughed at for being drifting pace (a full six months). In the most ambitious version of my estimate plan, I'd have crossed over the Irish Sea two weeks ago and be halfway up the Irish coast by now. But, truthfully this really wasn't based on a whole lot and the two things that had held me back most had been bad weather conditions and a lack of crew.

All in all, there'd been far more bad weather than I'd predicted. I had thought that perhaps there'd be two or three bad days per week, but in reality it was much more intense than that, with storm systems blowing in and hanging around for a week at a time. In fact, over two thirds of the expedition time so far had been written off due to the weather.

Plus, I was spending most of my time off the water trying to find another skipper to help us. With just Liam and I on the boat, we could only go for a maximum of one tide each day, automatically halving the possible distance I was able to cover. I knew how much this was slowing us down and putting pressure on Liam, but so far I seemed to be out of options. For neither love nor money, I couldn't find another skipper.

It's always a nice way to start the day: getting up while it's still dark and cracking on with things before everyone else is up. It feels like I'm creating extra time, making more of that one most precious resource that we all have in equal measure, except that those willing to get up before the sun are allowed to eke out a little more, it seems.

The alarm had gone off at 4am on Day 38 as a break in the weather had promised to allow a little more progress. As we headed out to sea while watching the sun rise above the horizon, the fresh morning chill began to dissipate and the warmth of the day gave us the energy to start pushing out some miles. Amy had come to visit us again, this time bringing her dog, Bear, with her – a young, bouncy, toffee brown cocker whippet cross – both of whom would be coming with us out on the water for the first time while I paddled. As we got underway, Amy joined Liam and I up on deck, clearly not loving the early start. Going through the harbour lock and out into the channel, she and Bear sat in the cockpit watching our morning routine. I moved around them, trying to sort out bowlines and fenders without tripping over the dog or the huge duvet Amy had brought up on deck.

Once out into the channel and with the fenders back in their storage area, I left Liam to motor us out with Amy by his side and I went back into bed to catch a few more hours' sleep. A little while later, he knocked on my door to tell me we were almost at the last paddle point, seven miles off the Welsh coast. I limbered up and changed into my wetsuit as Amy made Liam and I some breakfast sandwiches. I peeked my head out of the cabin and was delighted to see the calmest of conditions – just as glassy flat as we'd had back south of Lundy Island, it was a truly gorgeous day.

I jumped on the board and was pleased to be able to confidently paddle along looking like a natural, given we had a guest. It was rare that I felt this at ease and it always made me feel less of an amateur. Not that I really cared what Amy thought – after all, she had been the one to suggest that Liam should apply to come in the first place and she'd visited us during the expedition before, so she already knew how crazy I was. So, I guess it was maybe for my own self confidence than to prove anything to her and, like back down near St Ives on those first two days with Mike and Daisy, it really helps when those watching believe in me, rather than look on, worried.

As the sun beamed down, the water stayed flat and birds swooped around us, settling on the sea for a short while before moving on. Bear loved it, staring at them as they flew close by to check us out, clearly wishing he was allowed to jump in and swim after them.

I kept a close eye on Liam that morning to see how he would cope with having his girlfriend along. I had initially been concerned that his attention would be diverted even more but, actually, I think Amy's presence had the opposite effect. He wanted to show her how capable he was, so he was very much on the ball and far chirpier than he had been for days.

We were making good progress and, when it was time for me to have a break, Liam explained that we were about to come up to a funny-looking bit on the map. He reckoned it was hard to tell exactly what the tide was going to do: there might be some overfalls ahead or the tide could pull round in an odd way as we got closer to the Welsh coast – he wasn't sure. So, we just needed to keep an eye out and be ready to adjust course if needs be.

As I hopped back on to my board after a cup of tea, I was still able to confidently stand and paddle, thrilled to be making progress. Then, ten minutes later, Liam announced that the tide had turned earlier than expected – a full two hours earlier, in fact. He was confident that we weren't making any progress and that there was no point carrying on, as I'd only end up paddling to maintain ground rather than move forwards. I have to admit I was totally unconvinced. *How could he have got his calculations so wrong that the tide was a full two hours early?*

While Amy had been having a good impact on Liam, the sea and early start had not had a good impact on her. She'd been wrapped up in her duvet on deck ever since we left harbour and was now hurling in the toilet. The sea literally couldn't have been any flatter – there was no wind or swell or chop. *How was this making her sick?*

It was disappointing not to make more progress with such amazing weather, but I knew that this expedition wasn't just about me. I wanted my crew to be happy too – we were doing this as a team – so, we motored back.

When it all gets a bit too peaky

'Knock, knock,' came a voice from the pontoon as we sat tied up again in Milford Haven at the very end of May.

'John!' I bounced up the stairs. 'Welcome aboard,' I said, proudly standing atop my successful purchase.

After months of me emailing John with links to boats and asking for his opinion, he was now getting to see in person what I'd ended up with. I was excited to show him around and find out what he thought – the only acceptable response, of course, at this point, having spent a considerable amount of money, was a positive one. John obliged. After a quick snoop he genuinely seemed to think that Shogun was a good buy and I was happy to have his approval.

I don't really know what I had been expecting John to be like but, whatever that was, he was exactly it – Irish (obviously), in his fifties, smiley and happy-go-lucky. During our initial discussions back in January, John had seemed pretty keen to join for the whole trip, even talking out loud about the idea of lending me his own boat that he lived on, so I wouldn't have to buy one. I was relieved when he was happy to still help us across to Ireland, but he added that, unfortunately, he would only be able to stay for a couple of days before heading back home. With a new girlfriend on the scene, for some odd reason he wanted to spend more time with her rather than following a weird woman he'd never met very slowly the length of Britain.

Other than trying to butter him up with lashings of food and hope that he enjoyed the pace of adventure life, there was not much else I could do. So, Amy having gone home that morning, Liam, John, and I headed into town to get the boat stocked up and ready to set sail later that night after dinner.

Since discovering the old fishing rod on board, I'd been keen to kit it out with a line and reel to see if we could catch anything while I was paddling. But I had no idea about fishing, what kit I needed, or whether this old rod would actually be any use. The last and only time I'd fished on the sea was about seven years ago with my school friend, Nicola Malet, and her dad, Barry. We'd gone out in a charter boat with a couple of other people and, using his sonar, the skipper had located a shoal of mackerel. It was probably the easiest way to fish ever – we all caught plenty and had a lovely barbeque that night with Nicola's mum, Anne, filleting and cooking our catch for us.

Nicola's parents are great. They've always supported her to get outside, to try new things, and have been happy to teach her all they can. My dad, on the other hand, was never so forthcoming. I remember being down in Cornwall with my parents when I was a teenager and, having never done it before, I asked my dad if we could go fishing. His immediate response was, 'no, you won't like it. You'll just moan.'

Dad was often like this – blaming me for him not teaching me stuff. He'd trained as a carpenter and spent ten years converting a small cottage into a big, five-bedroom house when I was really young, meaning that my brother and I effectively grew up on a building site. Mum was not best pleased at how long it took.

Given his experience with wood, you'd think that when I asked him to help me build a wooden box for a compost heap in our back garden with some scrap wood (yes, I was that cool when I was eleven years old), he'd have been well up for showing me how. Instead he just said, 'you're doing it wrong. But I'm not going to help you, because you'll get bored and won't finish it.' Thanks, Dad.

So, with only one fishing trip under my belt and no carpentry skills to speak of, we headed for Angler's Choice on Charles Street. I'd popped in for a browse a few days before and Malcolm, the owner, was so taken by my adventure that he'd immediately offered to sponsor the expedition and kit me out with everything I'd need to catch dinner. So, we brought along Shogun's old, blue, glass rod to see what else we needed to go with it. Upon seeing my slightly broken rod, Malcolm and his customers laughed at the thought of me using it and he quickly equipped me with a brand new rod, a reel, line, hooks and weights. I was delighted!

I got chatting to two of Malcolm's customers, a father and son. They told me about how they'd go fishing together off the coast nearby and the big whopper of a fish they'd caught recently. I couldn't wait to see if I could catch something too, although I doubted my ability to catch anything quite as big as they had. Distracted by the Robson Green-esque story of this young fisherman's big catch, I hoped that Liam and John had somehow gleaned all the information that they needed from Malcolm to get the most from the shiny new kit.

Stopping in at the supermarket on the way back, we stocked up on food for a few days at sea. We'd need at least two days' worth, plus extras just in case, so we got all the essentials, including pizza, beer, and cake. I was obviously particularly keen for John to enjoy his time with us and, knowing how much food influences my own enjoyment of an adventure, I shopped strategically. Liam and I were really hoping that he would change his mind and stay with us after the Irish crossing, so Operation Make John Stay was on.

After a dinner of high-end pepperoni pizza and garlic bread, washed down with bottles of Doom Bar (bought to celebrate not getting stuck on its namesake on the way into Padstow), we fuelled Shogun up, as well as a spare jerry can, and left Milford Haven. The plan was to moor up closer to the mouth of the estuary with the aim of making the next day's commute an hour shorter.

Motoring over as the light faded, we spotted the floating concrete pontoon in Dale Bay that we were aiming for. I'd been told about it by a local and, after a quick Google search, I'd read that it's a local authority-owned pontoon offering a safe overnight stay for visiting boats. It was a welcome safe haven that meant we could get a relatively good night's sleep, without worrying about the anchor drifting.

As had become the custom, the next morning, Liam got up early to motor us to the paddle point, waking me half an hour before we arrived with a cup of tea. His mum and Amy found this hilarious as he'd never woken anyone with a cup of tea at home, but I massively appreciated Liam's kindness in that first month we were at sea together. For the most part, it had been just the two of us relying exclusively on each other, which – it turned out – is a good way to get to know someone quickly and serves as a great test of character.

And now John was getting to see what life was like on an expedition of this sort. Clearly effortlessly comfortable with the whole sailing part, I think the experience of throwing me overboard at Skomer Island, then watching as I paddled very, very slowly for hours on end while having to match the boat's speed to mine, was a weird one for him.

Usually on a boat delivery, a gig John does a fair bit these days, one tends to want to get to the destination as quickly as possible. If the wind allows, you'd put the sails up to save fuel and add speed. But there was no sailing while I was paddling. In fact, not only would the boat have left me behind in minutes, but if there was enough wind to sail, then it was probably too windy to paddle.

At 6.20am, I hopped on the board, determined that John wouldn't think I was completely inept at paddling. I was particularly worried that he'd start to wonder if I'd actually be able to paddle across the Irish Sea and therefore question even more what the hell was he doing here with me. This bravado for guests generally meant standing when I didn't feel comfortable, being terrified of falling off into the sea, and trying to look effortlessly comfortable all at the same time.

On most days when the sea was a little choppy and I felt like I might fall off, I tried to embody a steely determination to keep going anyway. *There's only one way to get to the end of anything,* I would tell myself, *and that's to keep paddling. Succumbing to fear and stopping won't get me anywhere.* But that day, I think it was safe to say I looked anything but comfortable. The paddling felt different. The fear was different. And the brave face wasn't convincing anyone, least of all myself.

My fear had always been about being *in* the water. So, as long as I stayed on my board, I found that I could manage that feeling thumping away in my chest. The vastness of it all, on the other hand, oddly didn't bother me that much. On the crossing over the Bristol Channel, from Lundy to Pembrokeshire, we'd lost sight of land in five-foot swell – meaning that I'd lost sight of the boat for a second too, every time I sunk into a trough of the rolling waves. But I had known that the boat was there and that Liam was there, and despite him being slightly distracted, that he could help me if something went wrong.

The crossing from St David's Head in Wales over to Rosslare in Ireland, to my mind, was no different. We'd choose a good weather day, I'd paddle for a few hours more than normal, and keep going until we hit our destination. Looking at it strategy-wise, crossing the Irish Sea made perfect sense. The east coast of Ireland is more sheltered from the weather rolling in off the Atlantic than the Welsh coast is – plus, Ireland also has more harbours for overnights and it was effectively a straight line north, once I'd crossed the sea, whereas Wales' wiggly coastline would mean more miles of paddling.

From the moment I decided to take on this whole adventure, the Irish Sea had never stood out to me as anything I should be worried about. But, as the weeks before the crossing became days, things started to change. In order to drum up publicity, one of my sponsors asked me how many species of shark and whale there are in the Irish Sea. Obviously sharks and whales aren't confined to that one stretch of water, in fact, they could well have been swimming beneath me the whole time since Land's End without me knowing. But when she pulled it to the forefront of my mind – the answer being twelve species of whale and thirty types of shark (she checked) – and specifically highlighted the Irish Sea as a big potential danger on this front, it suddenly seemed like something I should be scared of.

On top of that, we would be crossing some very busy shipping lanes with huge ferries. Over towards the Irish side there's a traffic separation zone, which means my crew would have to be on high alert for bigger boats as it's up to us to get out of their way. A bit like a motorway, marine traffic heads north on one side and south on the other – separated in imaginary lanes. Any boats crossing this stretch should do so at a ninety degree angle to ensure as quick a crossing as possible.

And, of course, there's the one huge thing that I'd totally underestimated – the fact that it's the Irish Sea. A sea! This isn't the same as paddling along a coastline. A stretch of water notorious for changing in an instant – the Irish Sea is vast, it's unpredictable, and it can get dangerously rough. It's forty miles across, so if we were caught out in the middle of the sea and needed to get to land, Shogun would take between four and ten hours to get to safety, depending on the conditions. Just imagine it... ten hours being thrown around on a small boat in a storm. Plus, with Shogun having all the driving bits (technical term!) outside completely exposed to the elements, someone would have to be outside at all times, no matter what the weather. Even if you don't usually get seasick, you probably would in those conditions and you'd be soon wishing you'd never left dry land.

All this began to sink in just twenty-four hours before I left Welsh waters. I was feeling overwhelmed. The fear felt like it was physically swelling up inside of me, pushing on my stomach, and making me feel sick. I also felt nervous and a touch shaky, with a lot of emotion being pushed back down so that I could get on with the task at hand. After all, I still had to paddle to the western edge of Wales before I could even start my crossing over the Irish Sea the following day.

I don't remember much of the next three and a half hours, other than that it was a cold, grey day with choppy, uncomfortable conditions. As I progressed along the last of Wales' south-west coast, fog hung over the land off to my right, allowing just an outline to punch through. By the time I'd paddled to St David's Head, I was feeling seriously fragile.

As I continued to paddle west past the headland and slightly out into the Irish Sea, the northerly wind swept down the coastline, whipping up the water into short, sharp chop, making it rougher than it had been so far that day. Coming side on, the forceful waves pushed at the edge of my board in never-ending succession. It instantly reminded me of being out with Tim back at Clevedon before I'd left. All I could think about was how, at any moment, the chop could flip me off my board. As each wave rolled and peaked under me, it felt like my SUP was teetering on a knife-edge. If I got my balance wrong or misread a wave now, that would be it – I'd be thrown into the freezing water.

Cowering on my knees, my face was a picture of pure panic and worry, but the guys were oblivious. Paddling up to the back of the boat as they sat talking, I looked at them and then back at the sea as if to say, 'look, this is too rough, I need to come in'. But they both just smiled back, almost with a shrug of dismissal, and then turned to look again at the sailing instruments, eat biscuits, and chat.

Liam was usually pretty intuitive by this point, picking up on how I was feeling and offering me reassurance when I needed it – if I looked like I was on the edge, he usually saw it.

But, I think unlike with Amy, having John on board pulled his attention away from me, particularly given that Liam wanted to learn as much as possible from John while we had him with us. John's knowledge, and influence on Liam's skippering skills, was hugely welcomed by both of us but, in that moment, I desperately wanted Liam to hear me shouting at him from inside my head.

I pushed on a little more: hoping it would get better, hoping that maybe I could deal with this, hoping that I could rationalise it in my mind and try to relax. But I couldn't. It was draining being so hyper alert. I'd had enough and was on the edge of tears. It was all too much to deal with.

I called to Liam that I wanted to come on board. He initially refused, saying that I'd had much worse and that the conditions were fine. I was taken aback... I didn't think he'd ever done that before – not letting me get on board. Usually, he'd chat with me about why I wanted to stop, give me information about our position, how much the tide was pushing us or anything else useful, and gently encourage me to stay out. Putting my foot down, I reiterated my request and, this time, Liam took note. They killed the engine, lowered the swim ladder, and I climbed aboard Shogun. Liam then started talking me through the conditions, trying to explain that everything was fine and there was no need to stop, given we still had a couple of hours of tide with us.

'Look, the waves physically can't tip your board over at this height. It's too low. You might as well carry on and get some more miles done. Just keep going another hour, then we can call it a day.'

'Liam,' I pleaded, 'I don't like it. When it's coming from the side like this, I don't feel safe. It's too... too peaky. I don't like it when it's peaky!'

I sat on the back deck, tightly wrapped up in my dryrobe. As my lip began quivering and a tear ran down from under my sunglasses, he quickly realised *I* was the problem, not the sea conditions.

John suggested a cup of tea and some biscuits, which is always the answer to everything in my book. Gently trying to reason, Liam began thinking of ways to help me cover a few more miles, but even the thought of going back out there was too much. I headed downstairs clutching my cup of tea to get some space.

A little while later, Liam came to me for a chat. He explained that he didn't think it was a good idea to end the last paddle before I crossed the Irish Sea on a bad note. He suggested that he could jump on the other board and paddle alongside me, or that we could just jump in the water together to try to get me used to it a bit more. But, again, the idea of being out there made me well up.

Accepting that I wasn't in the right headspace, he went to go back up to the top deck, but as he reached the bottom of the stairs he hesitated for a second. I looked over, expecting him to have thought of another reason for me to go back out, but – instead – he silently turned around and purposefully walked straight towards me with his arms out. Jumping up, I grabbed him tight. A hug was the one thing I had needed more than anything else.

Finishing my tea, I realised that spending a little time in the water with Liam right by my side might be a good idea. If I could face a bit of my fear, it might help me to rest my nerves a little. Liam excitedly popped his wetsuit on and, in the typical fashion of a twenty-two-year-old guy, he backflipped off the boat, giving no thought to the fact that we were bobbing on the edge of the Irish Sea over a mile from land. His carefree silliness was a great benefit to the expedition, most of the time. It calmed and distracted me whenever my fear began to get too much and made for lots of laughter during our downtime in harbours.

Obviously, though, I wasn't going to backflip into the chop; instead, I gingerly stepped down the ladder and into the ice cold water. With the board's leash on his wrist, Liam swam away from it and the boat and encouraged me to join him. As the swell threw me around it only reinforced the sense of a complete lack of control that scares me so much. But, at the same time, I could see that I wasn't drowning. Nothing bad was happening, it was just uncomfortable.

As I made my way over to Liam, he reminded me to breathe – something you can easily forget to do when the water is so cold. We bobbed around for a little while and he tried to make it fun for me... getting on the board and falling off, then even doing a headstand on it, which was impressive given the chop!

Meanwhile, I clung to either Liam's hand or the leash the whole time, panicky and nervous.

We finally got back on the boat and, as Liam and I dried off, John motored us to an anchorage near Whitesands Bay. It was a lovely little spot, close enough to the beach for us all to hop on the tender and go ashore in search of some phone signal, each heading in a different direction to make our calls.

Back on the boat, John went for a nap as he'd been up since 5am and it was now nearing 7pm. Meanwhile, Liam and I put our new fishing gear to the test for the first time. It turned out Liam was actually quite into fishing (or at least he had been until a few years previously when he had sold on all his kit). Once he'd rigged up the rod, we sat with it out the back of the boat for an hour or so as we chatted under the setting sun. Unsuccessful with the fishing, it was time for dinner and I rustled up a pea and bacon risotto – not our usual boat fare, but the second dinner of Operation Make John Stay. It seemed to go down well and we headed to bed to get some rest, before our Irish Sea adventure the next day.

Crossing the Irish Sea

Having monitored the Windy app almost by the hour, we were pretty sure the weather that Thursday (31st May) would be perfect for paddling the forty miles across the great, open expanse of water that is the Irish Sea. When I got onto my board at 6.30am, the forecast seemed correct.

'Liam's been up all night ironing out the sea for you,' John joked.

While dense fog meant that I couldn't see Wales just a mile or so behind me, the water had indeed smoothed out overnight and was almost glassy. The relief of having good conditions, and most importantly no peakiness, was definitely felt all round but a long day lay ahead.

Deciding on the timing of the crossing was far less straightforward than for a typical paddle along the coastline. Usually I'd be going with the tide, letting it carry me north, then stopping when it turned south. But heading west meant that I'd be paddling across both incoming and outgoing tides, just like I had on the crossing over to Wales from Lundy Island. Given my pace and the amount of daylight we had, I reckoned I could make forty to fifty miles in the one day. I felt strongly that, given we now had John on board, we could push our time on the water as much as possible and really maximise the distance covered.

Liam and I had initially been looking at going from St Davids in Wales to Rosslare in Ireland, but I was now keen, with a more northerly trajectory, to see if I could make it most of the way to the next harbour along, Courtown, some twenty-five miles further north. However, John was less inclined to push things and we seemed to butt heads about my ability to paddle for such a huge number of hours, and therefore what was a realistic distance to aim for. To be fair, I think his concern – having seen me buck at the idea of peakiness the day before – was based on a mixture of what he'd seen of my ability and his own experience with what is a changeable and dangerous stretch of water.

The other problem with my suggested route was that if we didn't make it, Liam and I would have to start from fairly far out in the Irish Sea the next day without John, who had now made it clear that he couldn't stay and would have to leave first thing the next morning. Liam and I were disappointed but hopeful that John would return later in the trip.

Our mismatch in feelings had only been aggravated by my teary exit from the water the day before. I realised that while I knew myself – and had known that this was a one-off which would pass overnight – John, on the other hand, didn't know me. He had no knowledge of my endurance abilities or how I'd cope so far from land. But his expertise was sailing and he had had lots of experience being out in the Irish Sea, having experienced rough conditions many times.

Eventually, we resolved to take it as it came, going for a middle ground on the course we were going to take. However, I ultimately had no control: I couldn't navigate on my own and had to rely on my crew to stick as much as possible to the goal that I had, while keeping us safe, and making sure we got over to Ireland in one go.

As he would now finally have the time to do what he'd signed up for, I really wanted Liam to embrace the Irish crossing from a filming perspective, in order to be able to pull together a short film about it afterwards. After my previous expeditions, I'd always looked back and wished I'd recorded more – more video diaries, more shots of me doing the basic stuff (like getting kitted up and sorting out my gear), as well as more of the big, dramatic shots. And this was the massive benefit of having a photographer this time round. I wanted him to lurk in the background, taking pictures without me noticing, recording those small, intimate details that seem like nothing in the moment, but actually really capture the mood of the experience. In hindsight, he had needed much more guidance on this, particularly given that the role had been somewhat sidelined since he'd become skipper.

Around halfway into the crossing, I asked Liam to film me again while I paddled. I think initially he didn't see the point as I'd been enveloped in fog all day, so one patch of fog looked just like any other. But, as he started recording, a huge passenger ferry appeared out of the mist in the distance. *A perfect shot!* I knew that it would capture the vastness of the ocean and the potential danger that lurked out there. We didn't have any kind of radar or equipment on board that would alert us to nearby ships, meaning that, if we didn't see them coming, they could be on top of us fairly quickly – bearing in mind the added time needed to get me back on board Shogun before we could change course and motor out of the way. Thankfully, the bigger ships had their own radar so they would be able to see Shogun and radio over in plenty of time if our course would bring us too close. Hypothetically anyway...

At 1pm I took an hour's break to let my feet properly warm back up and to get my first dose of strawberry milkshake. I preferred to paddle barefoot as it gave me better feedback from the board about how it was playing in the water. Plus I felt like I could move around more freely meaning I was less likely to fall off – if a wave caught me off guard, I could rebalance more naturally without soles over-gripping on the board's surface. But my feet were just too cold out on the Irish Sea that day and I was so thankful to have my NRS neoprene booties at hand once the feeling had finally returned to my toes.

I went back at it for two hours more and the miles flowed under me, clocking up around thirty in all, before breaking for lunch at 3pm. Through my experience of suffering tendonitis, I'd learnt how my rest strategy needs to change when I'm looking at months, rather than hours, to reach my target. If my SUP challenge was to just paddle over the Irish Sea (I say 'just' – that's a milestone achievement in itself!) then I'd probably go all out, paddling as many hours as possible, on as straight a course as possible to get over in the quickest time. For SUP Britain however, with weeks of paddling ahead of me, my goal was not speed, but rather to get across while preserving my body as best as possible to paddle again the next day. And the day after that. And the day after that...

When I stayed with Sean Conway during my walk, after I'd been off for a week on crutches recovering from the tendonitis, he explained that he'd used long lunch breaks to great effect during his Running Britain adventure. I'd taken his advice during the remaining miles of my walk and it had worked much better from an injury prevention perspective than trying to rush through the day's miles and finish in the early afternoon. So, I adopted a similar endurance approach during the Irish Sea crossing too. Having paddled for around seven hours, I stopped for an hour's lunch break followed by an hour's nap. Then, suitably re-energised, I got back on the water to make some more miles.

To be honest, hours and hours of paddling – particularly when the only two things I could see were the back of the boat and walls of fog – got pretty monotonous. All I could focus on was making miles, hoping that if I paddled for long enough and relentlessly enough, we'd make it not only over to Ireland, but as far north of Rosslare as possible. Then the shout came...

'Dolphins!'

I don't remember which one of us shouted it, but we all scrambled to grab a camera of some sort. I had my phone in an Aquapac dry case on a string around my neck and was quickly poised ready to capture them. The guys, on the other hand, were hilarious – running from one side of the boat to the other, trying to catch a glimpse of the dolphins.

From my vantage point behind the boat, I could see them swimming around it.

'They're on the other side,' I'd shout and point.

John and Liam would run across the boat and lean over, just as the dolphins would pop back up on the opposite side once more, almost as if deliberately tormenting them.

Continuing to paddle, I moved further behind Shogun so Liam could get some good photos of the dolphins playing all around my board, swimming right next to and under me. It honestly never gets old. Then Liam had the bright idea of strapping my GoPro to the end of the swim ladder and lowering it into the water. It came out as a brilliant bit of video – you can see me paddling on top of the water, then as the camera ducks under the surface and, through the churning, murky depths, shapes begin to appear. Difficult to work out at first, they move across the screen heading straight for the camera and then there they are! Four dolphins coming to check out what on earth has just appeared in their world.

Buoyed up by a visit from our friends, I settled back into my rhythm – paddling westwards. However, working across the tides rather than with them, the usual tidal help was simply pushing me from side to side, rather than forwards. On the one hand, this meant that I could paddle all day without facing any serious resistance, but, on the other hand, it meant moving at a much slower pace – around 2mph. I pushed on nonetheless.

After fifteen hours on the water, we got to within a few miles of Rosslare harbour on the south eastern coast of Ireland that night. Although it wouldn't be completely dark for another hour or so, we were all very tired and ready for some dinner and sleep. Still, five miles from land and surrounded by fog, I clipped my board onto the safety line, stepped aboard and announced, 'Woo hoo – we made it to Ireland!'

After 12 hours of paddling over a 15-hour day, I'd made it across the Irish Sea and was one giant step closer to Scotland.

Rosslare harbour is actually a commercial port. This means that it doesn't have the capacity to take private leisure craft, except in certain circumstances. Luckily, they allowed us to moor overnight on one of the fishing boat spots. Unlike a leisure mooring (usually a nice pontoon with electricity and water), it was a ten-foot stone wall with a metal ladder that we tied up to, plus no amenities. This didn't bother us in the slightest, though, as the boat was stocked up with everything we needed for the night and we were just grateful to have somewhere safe to get some sleep after a quick dinner.

The next morning, John left before dawn as we needed to get out of the harbour before the big ferries and other marine traffic started for the day. Then Liam motored us back to the point where I'd finished paddling the day before. Another flat, foggy start cleared to an endless expanse of gorgeous glassy water. Wispy clouds streaked the sky as the sun warmed my face and our spirits. We were still shattered from crossing over the Irish Sea but couldn't have asked for better conditions. The rolling, lush green hills edged our horizon to the left and – for the first time since leaving Lundy Island – really made me want to stop and linger. *If only I had more time.* Needless to say, Ireland is now officially on my To Do list.

When the sun shines, you can't help but smile. And it seemed that we weren't the only ones out exploring that day. A little, round, black head popped up about fifteen metres away from me. Making seal noises and talking encouragingly, I hoped it would come closer to say hello. I stopped paddling so it could come and investigate, but it kept its distance. As I continued on, it followed curiously.

Meanwhile, Liam had received a call from the BBC requesting a live chat on *BBC Breakfast* the following morning. He talked through the details of the expedition with the contact and arranged for me to call back later, once I was off the water for the day, to go through the main points to be covered in the interview and to sort out any video and photos that we could get over to them.

As the tide turned after the morning's paddle, we waited out the southerly tide by anchoring on a sandbank a couple of miles from shore. When anchored, the best place to be on a boat is in the middle, as it rocks in the swell from the chain that runs out the front. Keen to catch up on some sleep, we brought our sleeping bags through from Shogun's fore and rear cabins, taking a sofa each. It was a bit like a sleepover, chatting to each other and munching on some snacks before drifting off to sleep. When Liam's alarm went off three hours later, we had both had the best sleep we'd had in a long time and, feeling refreshed, I jumped back on the board and we covered a further eleven miles up to Arklow to moor for the night.

Coming past the sea wall into the Avoca River channel, we spotted Arklow commercial marina off the left and, in the river channel itself, a pontoon with mooring buoys down the centre. We radioed the harbour master – who directed us to moor up anywhere we liked as he was off to the pub and would catch us in the morning – then opted for a space on the channel pontoon.

In stark contrast to the efficient control of British harbours, we came to find this indicative of the relaxed approach (and level of drinking) in Ireland.

The next morning we had the live call with *BBC Breakfast* – all about my paddle across the Irish Sea, having just become the first woman in history to do so on a SUP. With Liam holding my phone as the camera, I Skyped into the programme and shared my story to date, live on air. They also showed Liam's footage of me paddling with the dolphins, plus the pictures from the crossing itself, as well as the earlier material he had shot around Lundy Island. We were both pleased to get this kind of exposure for his work so early on in his career, and Liam was really chuffed to have his work shown on television.

My phone pinged later that day with a message from David, the friend who had taken my promotional photos before I left:

'Have to admit, I wasn't sure you'd make it to the start line when you told me you didn't have a boat. But am so impressed and inspired that you did and have done all this so far, and that your courage and faith in putting yourself out there, saying that you're going to do it, has been rewarded.'

My initial reaction was to question what on earth he had meant... I felt berated by my own friends. It seemed for some reason that lots of people I knew didn't think this whole thing was possible. They might've smiled and said what a nice idea it was, but they also clearly thought that I was just talking up an idea I wasn't actually going to make happen. Given I'd already walked and cycled LEJOG, I found this was incredibly annoying. *Why weren't they taking me seriously? Why weren't they supporting me?*

But then, after David's message sank in, I realised what I'd actually achieved. They all thought I couldn't do it because it seemed impossible. But in my mind, that was a solid reason to forge ahead and to make it happen – not to stop. On the other hand, they just saw what I was up against: they saw the absurdity of not having a boat or a skipper or a clue what I was doing. So I was beginning to realise that it wasn't that they thought *I* couldn't do it necessarily, but that they simply thought that it couldn't be done at all.

The Emerald Isle

My food strategy clearly hadn't been enough to make John want to stay and I guess this was all just too different to what he was used to, too frustratingly slow perhaps. So now I was back to crew issues. As it had proven difficult – impossible, actually – to get a skipper just for those first few weeks or even for the crossing over the Bristol Channel, the idea of being able to find someone for the remaining month seemed hopeless. But it was absolutely clear that we needed another pair of hands. Liam was shattered and the relentlessness of being at sea was obviously getting to him.

I was fully aware that this was turning out more and more to not be what he'd signed up for. At first, when it was sunny and the days weren't that long, it had been fun for him to learn to skipper a boat – plus, the idea that, at the end of it all, he'd be able to say that he'd skippered a sailing yacht the length of Britain on just two days' experience seemed cool. However, the reality of it was somewhat different. As the days got longer and longer, the days off fewer and fewer, and the expectation that a skipper would come onboard fell by the wayside, being shattered most of the time soon lost its appeal.

So, rather than looking for a more experienced skipper, I decided to go in another direction and put a call out for deckhands. Appreciating that most of us don't have a month spare, I asked for people who could come for at least a week, thereby saving me money by not having to pay for someone's travel if they were only available for a couple of days, and also making sure Liam didn't spend more time teaching new people than he was getting the rest he needed.

'Anyone who is keen to get stuck in, doesn't get seasick, and wants the opportunity to learn about boats and sailing, please get in touch.'

Facebook came to my aid again. Friends shared my post and one of the first to get back to me was Sally. A friend of a friend, she had no experience on boats but had just left her job in London so the timing was perfect and she arranged a flight out to Dublin for that Friday.

Ready to push on, we started to pack up in order to catch as much of the tide as possible. Before we left, the harbourmaster wandered over with his little Jack Russell tottering behind him. Speaking from behind dark glasses on what was a dull, misty morning, he immediately apologised for his shabby appearance, as he'd had one too many in the pub the night before. Having read the sign on the side of Shogun, he was curious to know about SUP Britain, then – upon hearing what I was up to – he waved us off with a free night's mooring.

I was back paddling on the water by 10am: the sun was shining and it was a glorious day. With glassy, dark blue water, white clouds streaked across the pale blue sky, and rolling, green hills along the coastline to my left it was set to be another day of incredible paddling. *How could I be scared of this?*

That morning, given the good conditions and miles under my belt, Liam had decided it was time to swap boards. I'd been paddling on a 12'6 x 32" board up until that point and had been thankful for the extra stability. However, he suggested that I'd gained more confidence and experience on the water over the past month, so should be fine on my faster 13'2 x 30" board. I could see his point, but I was reluctant to give up the security of the board I had come to know. *What if the conditions suddenly change?* I thought. *Surely I'll need a more stable board.* But even so, going faster did sound like a smart idea.

The going was good in these conditions, and the sleeker board actually felt relatively stable – and ever so slightly quicker in the water. With around three miles an hour of tide plus my two and a half miles an hour of paddling speed, I was making good progress. We'd originally planned to meet Sally late that afternoon at Wicklow, just an hour or so's bus ride south of

Dublin, but with such favourable conditions we'd managed to get there early.

As we approached, we could see that there were no visitor moorings, simply wide-open seawalls offering little protection against the weather. The only option was to moor against the seawall itself, which was already full with boats double parked along most of it. We decided to risk it: going into the shallower end of the harbour to sit directly against the wall, but the locals soon popped over and advised us to move back as the tide was still going out. After a quick chat, Liam calculated that we had enough depth to last us around two hours... just enough time for me to walk to the other side of town and load up our bags with all the food I could carry, as there would be little time to stop and restock for a few days. Once Sally joined us, the plan was to paddle every tide to get as close to Belfast as possible before she left.

Restocked, we hit the water once more – Liam and I were both glad to be out of Wicklow and free from the worry of being beached by a receding tide. A quick two and a half hours of paddling and we had Greystones harbour in sight as our new overnight mooring and meeting point for Sally. We pulled around the much more protective harbour wall and were greeted by row after row of pontoons and expensive looking boats. Clearly this was the better harbour to overnight in!

Sally was waiting for us on the pontoon, backpack and pillow in hand, her beaming smile and bubbly personality the first thing I noticed. Excited to have our first deckhand, we welcomed her aboard and she immediately got stuck in, taking the bins out for us as I put the dinner on, then helping me prepare it once she was back. Sally told us about her change in career – she'd decided that estate agency wasn't for her any more and was on a break between that and her next job. Despite having never sailed before, her fresh enthusiasm and willingness to help us out was much welcomed.

The next morning it was day 44 of the expedition: Sunday the 3rd of June. In a month and a half we'd made much more progress than my 'reasonable' estimate plan, despite several fortnights of bad weather along the way. It had been interesting to note the changes in sea conditions as we travelled north. Along the west coast of Cornwall and the southern tip of Wales we had been much more exposed to storms that rolled in from the Atlantic. Then, as we started up the east coast of Ireland, there had been a marked increase in tide strength, adding a welcome boost to my speed and overall progress, and – crucially – far calmer weather given the shelter Ireland offered from the Atlantic weather. However, as we neared Dublin, the power of each tide was starting to drop off and my progress dropped by a third.

In all, I managed to paddle fifteen miles in four hours by the end of the first tide that day. Not only was the tide slower, but also the wind had picked up a little, adding chop to the water beneath my board. All day, Liam had been showing Sally the ropes, talking her through tides, how the sails worked, and our routine on the water. As the tide started to turn against us, they needed to get ready to pick me up and bring us into Dublin marina. Sally began putting the fenders out along the side of the boat when one slipped through her fingers and into the sea. So Liam swung the boat around for our first rescue mission of the trip and instructed me to keep paddling on. I seized this as an opportunity to see how far away from them I could get before they caught up with me – I was paddling past the mouth to Dublin bay at that point, not far from land at all. I got just thirty metres away from them. They did have an engine after all...

After having dinner and waiting out the southerly tide, we headed back out for the evening northerly tide. We went to fuel Shogun up before we left and were chuffed to find that fuel was much cheaper in the Republic of Ireland than in England. Rather than splitting the fuel 60/40, propulsion to domestic use, with a reduced tax rate being only applied to the non-propulsion element, there was a reduced tax rate applied across the full amount of fuel.

Making the most of it, we filled up the spare can too to ensure we had all we needed, then motored out again. Back on the water, as I paddled north of the entrance to Dublin bay, the water became calmer and less choppy. And, as the sun fell from the sky we got incredible views across the silhouetted coastline, backlit in orange with planes flying overhead into Dublin airport.

Heading between the small islands that sit just north of the bay, birds started to flock together on the water. We wondered if they were feeding or getting ready to sleep out there, but as I paddled past I noticed that they were actually pecking at the water, and as I got closer still I could see a shoal of tiny fish just beneath the surface. I guess sundown is feeding time.

The decision of when to finish each day was always a balance between Liam's gauge of the tide and my own willingness to push on. As we approached the next harbour, Liam said I had thirty minutes left of paddling then we'd need to call it a day. But as we approached that point, I was still going strong. The water was so glassy flat and I felt like I still had more to give that day. Having Sally with us had taken a lot of pressure off Liam, which meant that I felt more relaxed too. I was hungry for miles and for as long as the tide wasn't pushing me backwards, I was determined to keep going. I put my game face on and got into a strong rhythm, looking ahead and noting particular buoys to aim for. Then, once I'd reached them, I'd aim for the next one and the next one and the next...

Back down along the Cornish coast, Liam's main concern about skippering had seemed to be his lack of navigation theory and experience, but by now I could see that he had a great grasp of this sailing malarkey. He soon realised that I could keep going for a few more hours and so looked for other overnight options beyond the harbour we'd just passed. While we wouldn't make the next harbour some ten miles up the coast, he managed to spot a suitable anchorage off an island up ahead: it was sheltered enough for the expected weather conditions and was right on our route.

As the sun disappeared from my left, a slight, warm glow remained on the horizon in front of me, illuminating just enough of an outline of the islands to see which direction I needed to paddle in. As I turned to look at the boat behind me, it was pitch black – just the small lights from the boat making it visible. Good job I wasn't heading south, otherwise I wouldn't have been able to see where I was going!

We made it up to the last of the little islands by around 11pm, having been paddling on and off for well over twelve hours. I wasn't tired so much as numb. I couldn't really feel my feet any more. The cold had burned into them after the sunset which, combined with standing still for so long on the board, made for an uncomfortable sensation. Also conscious that my crew need food and sleep, I called it a day right next to Lambay Island. From my marker at the end of paddling, we motored just ten minutes to reach a point with a good depth for dropping the anchor. I downed a glass of strawberry milkshake in a way that was now becoming something of an addiction and, after getting changed, we settled down for dinner.

The next morning, we all woke in unison. As the tide had swung in the other direction and the wind had increased, it was interesting how our states of subconscious had each picked up that something was different in how the boat was moving. Gone was the glassy water and in its place was chop.

Initially, we were all in a good mood. Buoyed by the previous day's mileage and beautiful sunset, we even had the shortest commute of the whole trip – just ten minutes from anchor point to paddling point was a novelty, and meant that we'd managed to get more sleep than normal.

But, back out paddling at 9.30am, it was clear to me that this was going to be a very different day to the one before. The wind and choppier conditions made paddling slow and hard going. Added to this, the tide had dropped off even further. There was very little flow pulling me north which, while it had meant I could paddle so late the night before, it now meant I was having to battle the wind without my usual tidal assistance. We covered just seven miles in three hours to make it alongside the Skerries lighthouse – at which point the wind picked up further and I was barely making any ground at all.

We had known that this section of water might be tricky and had been told that the tide doesn't really do anything in this stretch between Dublin and Belfast, effectively creating an area of permanent slack water. We could see that we were getting nowhere fast, so, rather than roughing it out, we headed for shore and into Skerries to meet Eithne Hynes, a friend of Liam's parents. A keen rower, Eithne was the perfect person to help us figure out what was going on with the tide and how best to approach it.

Hooking up to a buoy in Skerries bay, we left Sally to have a nap on board while Liam and I headed ashore to meet up with Eithne who introduced us to Stephen Sherwin. It turned out that Stephen was slightly more qualified than your average local paddler to help out with SUP Britain. In August 2017, he and his friend, Peter, had been the first people to SUP across the Irish Sea. *What are the chances?* Back in the day, Peter's grandfather had been a keen windsurfer and had been a real pioneer of the sport. Demonstrating its ability to travel distance, he had also become the first person to windsurf across the Irish Sea. So, sixty years later, when Peter, Stephen, and two other paddleboarders wanted to take on a challenge, they had naturally sought inspiration from Peter's grandfather and helped him to continue the family tradition of setting world firsts.

A friendly, straight-talking guy, Stephen chatted to us between getting his guests ready to go out on the kayaks and SUPs that he rents out from Skerries harbour slipway. He advised us to stay well away from the coast, going out wide to pick up what little tide there was. Just like crossing the Irish Sea further south, if we got caught out here it wouldn't be fun as we'd be fifteen miles from land at our furthest point – but it was very useful advice and reassuring to hear it directly from a local with excellent knowledge of the water around there.

Letting Stephen get back to his customers, Liam and I headed to the local café to get our cake fix with a little chocolate cheesecake. It was nice spending time with him again, just the two of us. It felt like our relationship was ebbing and flowing, as you would expect with anyone, albeit in very intense circumstances. Having crew on board meant that the dynamic on the boat had shifted. It felt, on the one hand, that things were easier for Liam – he wasn't so exhausted and there was less pressure on him. But, on the other, I'm not sure how he felt about having help. I think, perhaps, that Shogun had become his domain, so having other hands on deck giving him assistance shifted his perspective. From initially feeling out of his depth, then learning as much as he could, Liam seemed to have come through the frustration that he had felt during long days down in the Bristol channel and along the coast of Wales, now enjoying sharing his new-found knowledge with a crewmember less experienced than himself.

A couple of hours later Liam, Sally, and I met up with Eithne again, this time with her husband and son. She was excited to have us there and proudly paraded us around the town, introducing us to everyone. It was lovely to spend time on land meeting folk. It was something that I had been missing on this adventure compared to my previous land-based escapades. There was little opportunity to meet people while out at sea for hours or curled up in bed in the harbour, so this was a refreshing change of pace.

Naturally, we headed for the local pub on the waterfront. Eithne and her husband kindly bought us a couple of pints of Guinness and had even brought us some of their son's birthday cake to take back to the boat. After chatting for some time and enjoying the local brew, with the evening tide fast approaching, we decided that we should probably get back to Shogun and sort out some food before setting out again.

But with the rough conditions continuing into that evening – and feeling the effects of a few pints of the strong stuff – we opted to anchor in Skerries bay rather than hit the water. Being a fairly wide, open bay with just a short seawall on the town end, it's exposed to the swell and chop that rolls in during windy conditions. Unfortunately, this made for a rough night's sleep.

The plan for crossing this long area of slack water was to paddle the sixty miles straight across from where we were in Skerries, just north of Dublin, over to Ardglass, a small marina in Northern Ireland. We couldn't tell how much tidal momentum we'd be able to pick up on this route and, as such, planned to go with the timings of the tides just in case. The last thing we wanted to do was assume no tide and end up paddling against it.

Doing this in one big push would mean that I'd have to paddle as far as I could in one day, then we'd bob out at sea for a few hours overnight to get some sleep, before continuing on the following northerly tide and making it to Ardglass marina.

The conditions had settled slightly as we left Skerries the next morning, but they were still far from ideal. The wind was making itself known as a nice, gusty tail wind, giving me the push I needed to cover twenty-three miles to our bobbing spot in the middle of the route from Skerries to Ardglass. We set an alarm and headed to sleep.

Sally and I woke with a jolt at 4am. As the weak tide changed, we felt the boat moving differently and our subconscious pulled us back into the here and now. The winds were picking up far higher than we had been expecting. Raging at over twenty miles per hour, the sea was in a dramatic state and we were beginning to drift further away from my last paddle spot. As we hadn't needed to go anywhere overnight, we'd allowed

Shogun to drift with the engine off, saving fuel – with one of us always on watch, the key poised in the ignition should we have needed to move for any reason. The first job was to get the engine on and in control of the boat, in order to stop us being stuck at the mercy of the wind and the waves. Clearly exhausted, Liam went to start the engine, turned the key to the left, and pushed the big, red button. Nothing.

He tried again. Wiggled the key, pulled it out, then put it back in. Still nothing. Liam went below deck to look at the engine and see if he could spot anything that looked different. *Maybe he'd forgotten to open the valve that lets water in to cool the engine?* But, nope, nothing looked out of place.

He tried yet again, but still not a sound. Shogun's engine sat silent.

As the sea roared outside, he came back down the stairs, clinging to the rail so as to not fall over as the boat rolled and crashed in the choppy swell.

'I can't start the engine. I have no idea what's wrong with it,' Liam said, looking completely out of ideas and completely out of his depth.

My approach had very much been one of letting Liam get on with the task of skippering. If he needed me I was there to help, but I wanted him to own it and to learn, both about the boat and skippering, and also about team management once we had other people on board. But, up until that point, I'd only ever seen his worried face once before – at the St Ives campsite as we'd hugged goodbye before I headed off to Land's End in a taxi.

If Liam didn't have a clue, I knew who would. Alex had been a godsend, both at the beginning when he had skippered Shogun round to St Ives and showed Liam the ropes en route, as well as when the boat had been a bit sloshy during that first night on anchor. I was hoping he could do his thing again, as we drifted in the Irish Sea without a working engine early in the morning. I texted to explain the situation and, while it was impossible for Alex to accurately diagnose the issue from over the phone, he immediately suggested a couple of options – the last of which was to essentially hotwire the engine. It would mean potentially damaging it, but if we could get the engine going then we could get back to harbour more easily and safely. Alex explained to us what we'd need to do, but Liam was hesitant to do anything that might cause damage, particularly given that we didn't know exactly what was causing the problem.

'Of course, there is one obvious alternative,' Liam suggested. 'We could get the sails out.' Shogun was a sailing yacht after all and he knew what he was doing far better with sails than he did with motors. Loosening off one rope, he pulled hard on another and the mainsail lifted up, the wind filling it aggressively. Very quickly we were being pushed hard in the right direction, Shogun transforming from falling in every direction at the mercy of the waves to forcefully carving her way through the water, harnessing the power of the wind in her sail.

She was soon heeling hard – the edge of the deck that would usually be three feet above the water skimming the surface of the waves and the far side of the boat was some six feet in the air. Balancing on my usual perch on the steps, with the boat racing along at that steep angle, it looked to me as though you could easily fall off...

Liam tried to reassure me that people rarely fall into the water when boats are heeling. He told me that there was also the option of clipping my life jacket to the boat with a safety rope, so no matter which way I fell off the boat, I'd still be attached as Shogun dragged me along in the water. Needless to say, I didn't feel reassured.

Despite it being so early in the morning, the sun was up. The raging, dark sea and howling wind contrasted with the clear, pale blue sky and dusky pink hues that rested gently on the horizon. I really hated these conditions: rough seas, a sideways boat, and the feeling of being unable to control the situation. On the other hand, Liam seemed far more relaxed – rigging up my GoPro to capture some video of himself sailing. I wasn't entirely sure how Sally was holding up. She had a big smile on her face when I looked over, but she was holding on tight and wasn't talking much.

I decided to hide inside the boat, initially clinging to the kitchen worktop as it felt much safer down there. Plus, that was where the cake was, so I could use the heel as an opportunity to dip into the snacks early. Everyone else was too distracted to notice the crumbs around my mouth. After the sugar calmed my nerves, I perched myself on the stairs again. This was my preferred spot when sailing: I could see what was going on above deck, but felt secure by being inside the boat, and comforted by being within an arm's reach of food.

Our plan was to sail to Ardglass harbour, our original destination for the end of the paddle that day. Once nearby we'd have to call the harbour and ask for another boat to come pick us up, then tow us in and onto a mooring – you're not allowed to go into a harbour under sail as you just wouldn't have enough control in the tight space.

An hour into our sail and Liam had obviously been trying to rack his brain as to why the motor hadn't started.

'I'll just give it another go,' he said, moving towards the red button, curious to see if anything would have changed.

We all looked at each other, stunned and laughing. There it was... the reassuring sound of a working motor as it kicked into life! Thank God for that. With our power back, we wouldn't have to make that embarrassing call to the harbour to say we had no working engine.

Given we were already out there and, by this stage, nearing my last paddle point from the previous tide, Liam was keen to not motor all the way to the harbour only to have to come right the way back out on the next good weather day. If I could paddle now and make at least some ground towards Ardglass, he was keen for me to do it.

While understanding the hassle of such a long, twelve-hour round commute, I was more safety focused. The wind was still gusting over twenty miles per hour and the sea was rough far beyond peakiness. As we were driving through the waves, under both motor and sail, I could see that Shogun was still being knocked around. However, I relented to at least try and paddle, if only to prove to Liam that it wasn't possible. When we dropped both the sails and put the engine into neutral to see if I could get onto my board, the boat was at the mercy of the thrashing sea.

I couldn't see how this would work or be safe. Just getting from Shogun onto the board was dangerous – moving quickly, I unclipped and pushed myself a little away from the boat, as it bucked unpredictably in all directions, so as to not be crushed by it. At the same time, I was desperately trying to stay close enough to not be blown away, unable to get back.

Usually Liam would set a course on the boat's GPS and the autohelm would mostly keep Shogun on that bearing, Liam adjusting by a couple of degrees here and there every so often. But in these extreme conditions and at such a slow paddling speed – probably just two miles per hour including any tide – the autohelm didn't work. There wasn't enough force at low speed to cut through the power of the water and stay on track. Liam had to manually steer the boat as it rocked violently in all directions. I tried to follow as best I could, but I too was fighting the hazardous conditions – I had to use all my strength to keep the board pointing in the direction of the violently rocking boat as Liam fought to keep the course straight.

After fifteen minutes the conditions hadn't improved and we were both struggling to stay on track and to stay together. Plus, we'd barely covered any ground, making this inordinate effort pointless. As much as it pained Liam to give in to the idea of heading for harbour, the situation was unsafe for everyone involved and I called an end to the paddle session. A bumpy, six-hour sail and motor later and we got safely into Ardglass marina. The relief to be back on solid land after conditions like that never gets old.

Liam and Sally were both shattered, so the evening was spent having a relaxing dinner followed by a gentle walk to explore the area around the town. It definitely did us good to stretch our legs and walk through green fields, feeling the firm ground beneath our feet.

Liam leaves the expedition

The only section of the route that I wasn't totally sure of in terms of which way to go was whether I would cut across from Northern Ireland to the southern tip of the Mull of Kintyre then go through the Crinan Canal, a much more sheltered route, or head northwards along a quicker – but more exposed – route, avoiding the slow canal section. I'd figured I could leave this to the advice from my skipper once we got closer, given that the weather conditions at the time would probably have a big impact on the decision too.

Enjoying a day off after our treacherous sail to Ardglass, we took the time to recoup. Sally and I went for a paddle with the marina seal in the afternoon before she headed off. It had been wonderful having her on board – she had got stuck in when needed, never complained and was always chirpy, despite the seriously rough conditions we'd had to deal with.

Frustratingly though, the weather that day was perfect to paddle. The forecast said it was to be the calmest day of the whole week, but after the last forty-eight hours, Liam was in no state to skipper – so, I had no option but to defer by a day.

Looking forward, the crossing back over the Irish Sea was coming up. Just ten-odd miles this time, whichever route we took, but it was then followed by the most challenging stretch of water: between Crinan and Oban along the south western edge of Scotland. As we discussed how we'd navigate this stretch, though, I could tell Liam had had enough. It was two and a half weeks until his planned family holiday when he'd get a week off to sun himself in Spain. No depth gauges or scared paddleboarders to worry about... Indeed, as we talked through our options for crossing points, how long we thought it'd take to paddle, and how we'd approach Scotland's deadly western waters, he said outright that he didn't want to skipper that part. It was fair enough – I appreciated that he was tired and that the novelty of skippering had fully worn off.

But I felt pretty powerless to change the situation for Liam. I'd tried for seven months to find a skipper and my only hope was that John would re-join us. He'd said he was keen to catch up with us once we got round into Bangor Marina, just outside of Belfast and across the water from Carrickfergus Marina, where his own boat was moored. I was hoping that he would be up for at least the crossing back over the Irish Sea and getting us past the dangerous waters. Only time would tell.

Liam and I headed off at 4am, facing a six-hour motor back to the last paddle point. As he went up on deck to start getting us ready to leave harbour I overheard him saying 'morning.' Poking my head up, I looked around but there was no-one there.

'Who were you saying morning to?' I asked, confused.

'Oh, er... to Steve,' he said, as if I'd caught him doing something he shouldn't be.

'And who is Steve?'

'Er, well, you know! Steve the spider!' he said, trying to hold back the laughter as he peered down the metal flag holder fixed to the stern of the boat.

'What? Not only is there a spider onboard – that you've failed to get rid of, despite our deal – but you've actually named it?' I shot back.

'Yeah, I say hi to him every morning. Well, you're usually asleep so I don't have anyone else to say good morning to. Steve's cool. He just stays in his corner. Sometimes I chat to him when we're motoring along and you're paddling, too.' Liam was almost crying with laughter at that point and I jokingly punched him in the arm to remind him how uncool this was.

I gingerly got closer to have a look. 'Is Steve big? I can't see him.'

'Yeah, I can't actually see him this morning either. Maybe he's gone for a walk.'

'Well, when he comes back from his walk you can help him to take a hike! And, of course, our deal's off. If we ever find a snake onboard, you're screwed!' I laughed and headed downstairs.

The sea was calm enough to cook en route that morning, so I made us a fry up before having a nap and leaving Liam to catch up with Steve after his morning walk. A few hours later, we arrived at our GPS X. The winds were higher than we'd have liked, although at just fifteen miles per hour, nowhere near as high as before. We bobbed for about twenty minutes in the chop, both with our eyes fixed on the wind dial and waiting for a lull. As soon as it dropped to eleven miles per hour, I was on the board.

It was slightly tricky going to start with, but – happily – calm enough for the autohelm to work on the boat and therefore Liam was able to hold a steady course for me to follow. With the wind behind me, we made good ground and just five and a half hours later, as we got closer to Ardglass, the wind died down until the sea was completely flat. As we approached our destination, Liam briefly seemed to be enjoying himself again, giving me updates on how far away we were, encouraging me to keep going, getting his playlists lined up, and laughing with me. Plus, it was a beautiful spot.

The smooth seas were a relief and a joy to be on, the stress of the turbulent weather behind us. The sun lowering in the sky cast a golden light across the seascape with the odd bird flying above us to check us out, before settling a little distance away on the water and watching from afar. We made it to just outside the marina at around 9.30pm and Liam counted me down to the point he'd marked on Shogun's GPS.

'Just one mile to go!' he exclaimed, with Radio 1 pumping out in the background.

'Just half a mile now – whoop whoop whoop!'

We were both so glad that this section of water was coming to an end. Jubilant, excited, and completely knackered...

Back on dry land, we enjoyed a quick shower before heading out for a celebratory Chinese. That vast, slack area of the Irish Sea was finally behind us and we were back to following the coast, an altogether far less stressful and more motivating prospect as we would be able to see the land pass by as we pushed north. And, of course, marking off the route we'd covered on the map back at the boat was a great sign of just how far we'd come: we were officially well over half way, into our fourth country, and the weather was looking good the following day too.

Come morning – on the fiftieth day of the expedition – we motored back to just outside the marina and I jumped onto calm seas. I paddled off, trying to take a more direct route than Liam, although I was quite sure that his was more direct given he had a GPS and was literally following a straight line on it. An hour or two later, as I jumped on the boat for a break before gearing up to approach the small islands ahead, Liam suggested that he'd need to go round the outside with Shogun, while I could take the more direct, inside route once we'd passed the lighthouse up ahead. This south eastern section of Northern Ireland was peppered with shallow, rocky outcrops for us to manoeuvre around.

As I took the inside route between the rocks, I wondered just how shallow it would get. In no time at all, I could see seaweed waving at me from below the water's surface and realised that it had become super shallow, super quick. The kelp swayed beneath me, brushing my board, and it almost felt like it was trying to reach up and pull me in. It was mesmerising, but dangerously so. If I lost concentration I'd soon be swimming with it. Plus, there were moon jellyfish out here too – at first just a couple as I approached the rocks, then more and more as I moved into the sheltered area. *Don't fall in. Don't fall in.*

It was amazing how quickly it went from deep, dark waters to this clear, kelpy scenery. It really was a demonstration of exactly why understanding charts is so important. One second it looked deep enough to get Shogun through, the next it was most definitely not. The rocks that jutted out of the sea on both sides of me were havens for wildlife, and a weird, screeching sound that had been audible for a while was getting louder and louder as I got closer. Seals!

There was a long, large rock to my right (between Liam and I) and a small set of rocks to my left (between me and the beach). As I looked ahead, there was a line of rocks that stretched all the way into shore, not breaking the surface by much. I tried to figure out a route through, but it was difficult from a distance to make out whether this was a long ridgeline that skimmed the surface or whether it dipped lower at any point, which would allow me to paddle through. The fin on my board was only a foot deep so I didn't need much clearance, and as I got closer I spotted what looked like a low section with a break in the rocks and aimed for that.

This slight change in course took me left, closer to the small island. It was a still and sheltered stretch of water and – if you ignored all the screeching – a gentle scene. That was until all the seals jumped off their rocks with a big groan, clearly not happy with my slight change of course into their territory. They started swimming towards me, almost as a 'what the hell are you doing here?' kind of gesture.

I paddled quickly to the gap, keen to get out of their path, handling the shallows as best I could... I ran aground. Jumping off my board – without a second's thought for the hundreds of moon jellyfish that had been passing beneath me just moments before – I walked my board forwards about three metres, my bare feet slipping on the seaweed-covered rocks, then climbed back on and paddled away as fast as I could from the angry seals who were still in hot pursuit.

There was another set of rocks up ahead, and again I took the inside line, this time managing to avoid upsetting any wildlife. Looking down through the clear waters, I could see what must've been a moon jellyfish nursery because there were thousands of them, of all sizes, swarming in that sheltered section of water. I paused to record a video, thinking it was a shame I didn't have my GoPro with me, as the view from under the surface would have been incredible. The water was almost thick with them.

I knelt down through these shallower, jellyfish-infested sections, both because of the 'don't fall in, don't fall in' mantra that was on repeat through my head, and also for fear of running aground again and being thrown from my board.

The third rocky outcrop ahead had a red cardinal on top. Liam went along the outside to avoid a sandbank and I continued with my inside line. As I paddled on, I noticed that Liam wasn't going very fast. *Is he alright?* But then he sped up and came inline with me at the next buoy. Suddenly, the boat swung forty-five degrees to the right. *Has he hit the sand bank?*

Liam sat there for a while and I stopped paddling to watch him from my board. I checked my phone, but he'd not called or texted to say there was a problem. Figuring Liam would wave or call if there was an issue, I started paddling. Then eventually he set off again. Only a little while later, though, he swung right – this time turning a complete one-eighty back on himself, before righting his course and heading towards me.

It turned out that the first time Liam had stopped, the depth beneath the boat had dropped off so sharply that he'd had to take evasive action, although he hadn't actually beached. It had just taken him a little while to figure out why it had dropped off that quickly and how he could get around that very, very shallow section. The second time, he'd stopped to go back and pick up some balloons floating in the water.

We didn't come across much rubbish in the sea along the whole way, but for some reason the bits we did find were predominantly in the Irish Sea. A few balloons, a glove, a boot, the odd plastic bottle. In comparison to my other length of Britain journeys, this was far less rubbish than I'd encountered cycling and walking. On those routes, roadsides had been strewn with years of accumulated rubbish discarded from cars – unfortunately, often next to roads are ditches with streams that run into rivers, which run into the sea, where most of it ends up beneath the surface...

I had been paddling for almost nine hours with only one or two short breaks by this point, as the tide hadn't felt like it had much effect on us. But, thinking that we could just try to push on and cover the miles, I'd neglected to build in enough rest.

Just as I was coming round the next rocky outcrop, my left arm began to get tight around the wrist. Not painful, just an odd feeling – then, within minutes of the tightness starting – ping! As I'd pulled through the stroke I'd definitely felt the tendon in my left wrist go. *What the hell? This was not good.* Hesitating for a second, I looked at my arm. *Well, it doesn't look like anything's out of place.* I gave it a gentle rub and found that it was sore, as I'd thought it would be, having been paddling for so long that day, but it wasn't as excruciating as I'd expected given the ping I'd just felt.

I went to very gently take another stroke to test out my wrist. *Ha – nope!* I could feel the tension on the tendon begin to build up again as I came through the stroke. 'That wrist has gone,' I thought, quite pragmatically.

Unable to paddle on my left and only very gently on the right, I radioed over to Shogun and Liam said he would come pick me up, but that I'd need to move out away from the rocks, as it was too shallow for him to navigate all the way in to where I was. With just my right hand, I paddled slowly and awkwardly towards him. Luckily, the conditions were calm and gentle, enabling me to do so with relative ease. On board the boat we were both concerned as I described what I'd felt. So, I decided it best to take a solid break and drink two glasses of milkshake to see if my wrist would ease enough to keep on paddling.

After a two-hour nap, I got back on the board and paddled for about ten minutes to check how my left wrist felt. Although the tide still wasn't too strong, the wind had picked up, and my arm was just too sore to keep pushing against it. The last thing I wanted to do was cause serious or permanent damage. Even though we'd not made it round to our desired end point for that day, Bangor, it was essential that I rested up if I was to have any chance another day. I stopped paddling and we headed for harbour.

Bangor marina is just across the Belfast channel from Carrickfergus marina, where John has his boat, and he popped round to meet us there with his girlfriend, Marlene. She was lovely, if a bit more timid than I'd expected. We took the opportunity to ask John about a warning light on the engine and about the voltage reading – plus he had brought us a new gas tank, which was very sweet of him but turned out to be too big for our storage cupboard unfortunately.

They asked when we'd head off next and I explained that Liam was leaving me the following week for his family holiday, meaning that I'd be stuck until he got back. At this point, Marlene piped up and volunteered John's services – just as I was hoping she might. I really needed John, and I think he was still intrigued enough to want to rejoin, for a little bit at least. So John, Marlene, Liam, and I walked back through the harbour, said goodbye, and agreed that I would let John know when I planned to leave again.

Saturday morning rolled around and, having been in harbour for a week, I was keen to get paddling again. It was now the middle of June and two months since we'd begun, back down on the tip of Cornwall. The winds were still a little stronger than I'd have liked but they were at least blowing in from the west, which meant that they'd push me over to Scotland.

We'd looked at Portpatrick over on Scotland's westerly shore as an option to aim for, but our main concern about this plan was getting into the harbour there. It was described in the almanac as having a very narrow, shallow, rocky entrance, not to be attempted with a strong crosswind and dangerous at night or with a low tide. A call over to the harbourmaster confirmed it was not a good idea. Even if we got in alright, they'd had a boat damaged in the past week just while it was sitting in the harbour exposed to those harsh westerly winds. So, we decided against it, which was frustrating, but there was no point risking damaging Shogun or ourselves and then being stuck, unable to keep going. We needed a different plan.

The weather forecast was looking up and John confirmed that he could join me in a week's time for a good few days. With Liam due to leave the coming Wednesday, I wondered if there was any way to get back out on the water for a final paddle, pulling a few more miles closer to Bangor before he left. A break in the forecast appeared to be coming in three days' time, on the Tuesday, which would allow me to paddle with Liam still skippering from Millisle, where my tendon had given up, to the channel into Bangor and Belfast beyond.

So, I hit the water on my board that Tuesday. The tide didn't help as it eddied in and around the channel, but I knew that even one mile was progress and, after three and a half hours, I'd covered nine – lining me up in a good position to leave with John and head straight for Scotland, as soon as the next weather window allowed.

Early the next morning, I handed Liam a thank you card and a big slab of chocolate cake – I was so grateful he'd gotten me this far. I just hoped I could make good ground with John while he was away, and that he would actually return after his holiday, given how hard this all had been for him... If Liam didn't come back, I hadn't a clue how I'd make the final stretch through Scotland up to John O'Groats. *Would I have come all this way and be stranded at the last hurdle?*

5

Whirlpool Monday

Chasing time

The moon shone bright in the night sky, illuminating Shogun a couple of metres in front of me, but the swell and low light made it hard to balance. I started to feel a bit dizzy. Dropping to my knees, I paddled on, following the boat's line as we headed back over the Irish Sea towards the Mull of Kintyre on the west coast of Scotland. John was getting some sleep and it was just our newest crew member, my friend Ged, who was keeping an eye on our progress, making sure she didn't lose me in the darkness.

I paddled twenty-two miles that night and somewhere before dawn, it occurred to me that I'd never seen the moon set before. We were making good progress, and the slim possibility of reaching John O'Groats in the next seven days sat squarely in my mind.

I've never wanted to race anyone. That's the reason I don't compete in any kind of sport. It's not about them, it's about me – it's about my pace, my goals, and my experience of it all. I don't want the gold; I want the memories and the stories, which can be missed if I rush too fast.

But, at the same time, I love pushing myself. And, having had two weeks off due to my injury then bad weather in Bangor, I was keen to drive hard and push on, to see if I could go any faster. Plus, lingering in the back of my mind, was the thought that one of my kit sponsors was keen for me to push harder too.

I'd had nine sponsors in all and their support as brands – as well as individuals – was invaluable. They loved what I was doing, the story of possibility that was unfolding before me, and they pledged to support me no matter how long it took me to get there. However, Red Paddle had made it clear that they wanted me to set as fast a time as possible...

With this in the back of my mind and the finish line just three hundred miles away, I decided to set myself a challenge to see just how quickly I could progress, given the constraints of my team changing over the week ahead. *Maybe this is an opportunity to push harder*, I thought. *If I double down, keep going with two crew on board and paddle every tide possible, could I make up ground I've lost to bad weather?*

Up to this point, Cal Major and I had been pretty much neck and neck with each other the whole way. I'd had long delays waiting for good weather, but when I was actually out paddling, my sea-based route was more direct than her path through England's canals. At the start, it had seemed highly unlikely that I could finish before her, given her huge amount of experience and my utter fear. But, as we each got closer to John O'Groats, I started to wonder if it might just be possible for me to get there first...

When Liam left, I settled to pour over plans and tide times. Up until that point, I'd really not been pushing as hard as I could on the paddling side – other than general fatigue, I'd not yet reached the point where I felt like I had nothing more to give. And I desperately wanted to feel like that, to really push myself to the very edge. I needed more hands on deck.

If I'd had two crew from the start, I worked out I could probably have paddled at least an extra six tides up until that point in Bangor. That would have been an additional 36 hours on the water and up to 120 miles further along. That could have potentially put me in Oban.

Clearly this was frustrating, and totally my own fault. Focusing on trying to get a more experienced skipper had seemed like the sensible and safest thing to do during the first half of the expedition, given Liam's and my own lack of experience. But spending so much time on this had left me blind to the need simply for extra hands and how this could have helped us progress, taking some of the weight of Liam's shoulders. We all live and learn. *So, how could I switch up our approach to make ground more quickly?*

Having comfortably managed fifteen miles per tide so far, with extra crew I reckoned I could push that to twenty miles per tide and do two tides a day. This gave me a new target of forty miles a day. It was ambitious: it was twice as far as I'd covered in a day before that point, but I was excited. *What if the conditions were really in my favour – tail wind, plenty of tide – could I even push more than that?* So, that was it. Three hundred miles, forty odd miles per day... If this went to plan, I could potentially finish at John O'Groats in just seven days of paddling from Bangor.

Luckily, my friend Ged McFaul, a bubbly Glaswegian in her early fifties, was keen to join the expedition. Having met in a field somewhere near London, we'd known each other for a couple of years. When she's not off on her own brilliant adventures, Ged enthusiastically welcomes adventurers – including myself on my JOGLE walk! – into her home, offering a warm shower, comfortable bed, and lots of encouragement to those passing through. Plus, she has a day skipper qualification – the perfect fit for SUP Britain, as I was really keen to have female skippers and deckhands on my team. If they were keen to step up and have a go, I wanted to give them the opportunity that I'd given to Liam.

With Ged lined up as my deckhand for that weekend, John was happy to skipper from the Saturday after Liam left until the following Thursday. By then I'd also arranged for Aileen, a friend of a friend I hadn't met before, to swap in when Ged left us on the Sunday afternoon. So, I'd managed to find myself two new crew and I was raring to get going and put my forty mile per day plan into action. Full of energy, I busied myself, getting the boat ready and stocked up with the food and any extra bits we'd need so that we didn't have to stop en route north. Beyond what was in the engine, we didn't have any spare oil for the boat and with the amount of motoring we were doing, John had mentioned that it would be a good idea to try to get some 10/40 mineral oil on board. I started off in the nearest marine supply store, looking at the oils but none of them seemed to be what I needed. I noticed a pair of binoculars on a shelf and got them out of the box to have a look. Liam had suggested a couple of weeks ago that a pair might be a good idea for the boat, but given how I was always close to the boat I didn't see the need for them so put them back.

I asked the manager for advice, but he admitted he didn't know much about oil either. He phoned around some other stores in town who might stock what I was after, to no avail. Luckily later that day John found some spare that he could bring with him.

Ged made it to the marina around 9pm on the Friday night, giving us time for a good catch up over some dinner. I was so glad to have her with us. Come Saturday morning, we were up and ready to set sail for 7.30am when John arrived with his 10/40 oil for Shogun. We waved goodbye to Marlene and were out of the harbour within ten minutes of his arrival. I was relieved to be on the move again and it was great to have John back – his calm demeanour and obvious experience felt very reassuring. We discussed the best route over the Irish Sea to Scotland and decided that, with good weather on the cards, the quickest option would be to head to the northern edge of the Mull of Kintyre, avoiding the slow Crinan Canal. We'd simply aim to take a fairly straight line diagonally across the North Channel where the Irish Sea meets the Atlantic.

It was brilliant to be back on my board – the miles clocking up beneath me. Making good progress with the tide, we angled our route towards Scotland. At the six-hour mark I was still keen to paddle, full of energy, and the tide not yet fully against me. However, it was clear that John wanted to stop, pulling Shogun into neutral and directing Ged to lower the swim ladder. But I had other plans and shot past them while they were looking down at the map, gunning it as far as I could. My cheeky ploy to get a few extra metres in got them laughing and they soon caught up, overtaking my board, and swinging in front of me so I couldn't paddle off again.

Aboard once more, I changed into warm clothes, had something to eat and went to sleep until we pulled into Glenarm harbour further up the Irish coast. I could hear Ged chatting to people outside about the expedition but I didn't get up, wanting to get maximum rest for my first full night paddle in five hours' time.

I got back on the water at 7pm, with a few hours until darkness would descend. It might have felt rather different had I gotten onto the board when it was already dark, but starting while I still had daylight made the idea of paddling at night less intimidating. It gave me time to become comfortable at each stage of dusk, as blackness crept ever closer.

Once the light had gone from the sky, I stuck close to Shogun as we dodged huge container ships lit up like Christmas trees shuttling their cargo across the Irish Sea. Taking two-hour shifts, Ged and John alternately slept and kept watch, steering Shogun towards Scotland and making sure not to lose me in the darkness. So long as I could see my crew and they could see me, I started to realise that I didn't actually feel too scared paddling at night. Perhaps it was because I couldn't see the sea...

As the moon hovered above me behind wispy clouds, it was almost like stealing extra hours from the day, making progress while most people would be in bed. I was surprised to see that a glimmer of warm, orange light didn't leave the horizon all night long – a literal reminder that there would always be a light at the end of the tunnel and, if I just kept paddling long enough, the sun would slowly rise again.

On the Sunday, I paddled another two tides, each one inching us further along the Sound of Jura towards the Caledonian Canal. It was a beautiful stretch to paddle: like Lundy Island, it was remote, wild, and endless greens and blues glistened in the midday sun, just calling out to be explored. Sea otters, and sometimes the odd seal, played in the kelp, curious as to who was passing by. Another time perhaps, I'll go back, but in that moment I was truly enjoying making miles and having the crew I needed by my side.

Alone at sea

In planning this route, I'd been cross-checking the Windy app and the almanac to see what the tides were doing in this narrow section. Initially, I thought it looked like we'd have strong, quick tides that would pull me through. But, as I examined this section coming up past the easterly point of the Isle of Jura then Crinan, the tide seemed to me like it was doing something weird. It appeared to show a northerly tide from 8am to 2pm in the first half of the channel and, at a certain point near Crinan, it switched to show the northerly tide from midday to 6pm. *Would this mean the northerly tide would run from 8am to 6pm as I paddled up through from one section to the next? A full ten hours of northerly tide – or had I got that wrong?*

While John had grown up on the east coast of Ireland and was extremely familiar with those waters, he hadn't actually sailed through the western islands of Scotland before, just twenty miles away across the sea. But, based on his years of general experience at sea, he dismissed my ten-hour tide theory and instead thought that there wouldn't be much tide at all to worry about. There would just be some overfalls further north from Crinan and – of course – the minor issue of the whirlpools.

During the planning stages of the expedition I'd been chatting with my friend, Chris, the ex-marine who had joined Liam and I for a SUP session down in Dartmouth. He'd pointed out that while, yes, the west coast of Scotland has beautiful islands, I should be sure to avoid the whirlpool.

'I'm, sorry – the *what* now? There's a whirlpool in Scotland?'

'Yup, Google 'Corryvreckan,'' he said.

As I watched YouTube videos of boats being thrown around in a swirling vortex of water, I read up on what creates this unique stretch of sea. The Gulf of Corryvreckan is a strait situated between the islands of Jura and Scarba, off the west coast of mainland Scotland. According to Wikipedia, the name comes from the Gaelic phrase Coire Bhreacain, meaning cauldron of the speckled seas. Strong Atlantic currents push through this channel, which, combined with the unusual underwater topography, creates the world's third largest whirlpool. As water floods into the strait, the waters of Corryvreckan can be driven to create waves of more than thirty feet and the roar of the ensuing maelstrom can be heard up to ten miles away.

My route would take me northeast up the Sound of Jura, putting the Isle of Jura to my left – between me and Corryvreckan. The stretch of water leading along the sound and up towards the area where Corryvreckan and Crinan sit across from each other, was calm and gentle. Sheltered by the islands, I felt protected from the sea and my fear of it. On what was a gloriously sunny, still day the blue sky stretched out overhead, just the odd wispy cloud hung around.

John and I planned to do a crew change and refuel the boat at Crinan harbour. This was the best place for Ged to leave and for our new deckhand, Aileen McKay, to join us. I'd been put in touch with Aileen by a mutual friend, Rory Southworth, who I'd met the year before when our paths crossed in Edinburgh as we both cycled towards John O'Groats.

Given that we wanted to make the most of all tides available at this point, John suggested that – to save time – the support boat could leave me to paddle the sound alone. They would motor on ahead, do the crew change, and refuel then be back out of the harbour within ninety minutes tops. I agreed, comforted by the knowledge that, at this point, I was still fifteen miles south of Crinan and its whirlpool neighbour across the water. Plus, there was no way I'd paddle fifteen miles in an hour and a half (and I was so far into the western isles that I wouldn't be pulled out to sea). *So what could go wrong?* Plus, with such ideal weather conditions, I didn't feel like I'd fall off my board so I was actually feeling surprisingly comfortable with the idea of being out on the water on my own, knowing that John and Aileen would be back out to me within no time.

Before he left me behind, John and I looked at the map and he showed me where I should paddle.

'Keep to the right of the channel,' he said, pointing up ahead, as we bobbed on my last paddle point, 'but don't go any closer to the mainland otherwise you'll paddle further than you need to.'

'OK, cool.' This seemed fine for as far as we could see right now, but I was slightly concerned about getting closer to Crinan and therefore in the region of the Corryvreckan strait.

He continued, 'We won't be more than an hour, 90 minutes tops. We'll almost certainly be back out before you get anywhere close to Crinan. But, if for whatever reason you get in line with that harbour before we come out, just bob near these smaller islands in the middle of the channel, keeping to the right of them. That way, if you do get pulled anywhere by the tide from there, it'll just be further east and away from Corryvreckan.'

All happy, we loaded my board with a day bag, including lunch and my back-up technology, then Ged waved goodbye. I could hear Shogun's engine chugging away for miles into the distance until I lost sight of them, almost as if the noise was reverberating off the mountains.

I was pleased that I felt calm and confident on the water, a far cry from those nervous miles paddling along the Cornish coast. Here, I felt much more in control. I wasn't worried about the tide pulling me out into the ocean and being lost at sea, like I had been back then. Plus, these conditions felt like a dream.

The sun beamed down as I maintained a steady pace and soaked up the scenery. *This* was what adventure is all about. My competitive streak was definitely on full – I rather liked the idea of surpassing my crew's expectations for how quickly I could paddle and wanted to see if I could get to the islands before they came back out. Sure, I thought it was unrealistic but I always love a target.

Soon enough, I started to approach the first of the small islands with a white marker on it. Overly pleased with myself at having paddled so quickly, it didn't occur to me that it might have been because the tide was far stronger than we'd anticipated. I'd not clocked that the distance I'd just paddled to that point was ten miles in one hour, double my fastest pace, which if I'd known, would've been a clear warning sign about the tide. Passing that first island I could see Crinan off to my right and then I realised how quickly I'd covered ground. I decided to aim for the next, much larger island, which sat between Crinan, two and a half miles to my right and Corryvreckan five miles off to the left. I'd beach myself or hook onto a buoy, eat my lunch, and wait for my crew there.

It was then that I suddenly noticed I was *between* the two islands, rather than off to the right of them as I'd planned out with John. I set about trying to correct my course, turning my board to be at a thirty-degree angle to the tide, hoping to ferry glide my way across to land. I paddled hard for ten minutes. Nothing. In fact, I seemed to be getting pushed further and further to the left.

Slightly concerned that the tide seemed to be getting stronger and the water around me more turbulent, I dropped to my knees for stability. Knowing I couldn't fight the tide, and clearly couldn't get over to the islands, I simply wanted to maintain my current position. I figured that the most streamlined position for my board, so as to have as little force acting on it as possible, would be directly into the tide. I turned to face Crinan on my right, the direction the tide seemed to be coming from, and paddled hard.

There was still no sign of Shogun coming back to get me. *How long would I be able to maintain position before I'd be pulled closer to Corryvreckan?*

I decided to text John. 'Pls hurry the tides really strong'.

As I quickly started paddling again, unbeknownst to me, they were already on their way out and heading to a position where they could see down the Sound of Jura, where they thought I'd be.

But once they got there, they couldn't see me. John was instantly worried. He knew that if I wasn't coming up the channel and I'd text because I was in trouble... the obvious and worst-case scenario started to run through his mind: I must be heading towards a deadly whirlpool.

John and Aileen carefully scanned the horizon. They looked for binoculars but couldn't find any, so had to squint in to the distance. Being just a few minutes into her SUP Britain stint, Aileen wasn't entirely sure what she was looking for, but she kept watch.

By this time, small whirlpools had started to form around me. Every time I hit one, my board was thrown from side to side with the swirling water. I couldn't hold it together any longer. I was terrified of where this might lead and tears flooded down my face. 'Where are they?' I cried out in desperation, sobbing. I tried waving to a boat that was off in the distance, but they couldn't see me and didn't change course.

Then I felt my phone vibrate. I knew that it must be John calling.

If you've ever been in a situation when there's someone you're supposed to be looking after and, not only have you lost them, but there's an increasing possibility they're in real danger of being killed, you can imagine how much John's heart was in his mouth.

I then proceeded to answer the phone in the worst way possible – crying my heart out and screaming into the phone: 'I'm being pulled towards Corryvreckan! I'm going to die! Where are you?!'

'Calm down, calm down. What's happened? Where are you?' John's voice sounded far away.

'I went past the first little island like you said, but then I started to be pulled towards Corryvreckan. I can't fight the tide, it's too strong. What's taking you so long?'

'Don't worry about fighting the tide! Just beach yourself on an island and we'll come pick you up.'

'I can't! I've been trying that for half an hour and I can't go anywhere. The tide is too strong.'

'That's OK, don't worry—'

'I'm being pulled towards Corryvreckan, I'm going to die!'

'No, you're not, you're going to be fine. Are there any boats around you?'

'There was one, but it couldn't see me waving. It's over by the coast and heading towards Crinan. I can't see you.'

'Can you describe what's around you? What can you see?'

I tried to pull myself together and speak more clearly and logically, but seconds later all the water around me shifted again. Gone were the small swirls – instead, they'd merged into one huge circle of water – and I was slap bang in the centre of it.

'Oh my god,' I gasped. 'All the water has just moved. I'm right in the middle of a whirlpool. I have to go. I have to keep paddling, I have to keep paddling...'

I was still out here on my own and at the forefront of my mind was that I had to deal with what was happening around me. I couldn't paddle with one hand while I was on the phone and that was the one thing I needed to start doing.

I sucked up my fear, gave John a quick description of the landmarks I could see, and hung up. Paddling ferociously, I pushed as hard as I could to get out of that circle. There was no use in crying.

I paddled and paddled and paddled. Thankfully, I reached a section of calmer water at the edge of the swirling circle, and that's when I saw them heading straight for me.

Hurry up! Why aren't they going any faster? And then I remembered that I'd bought a boat older than myself – Shogun was an amazing boat, but speed under motor was not one of her top qualities.

As they drew alongside, I collapsed onto my board, my steely determination replaced by utter relief and the floodgates opened again. Crying uncontrollably, I clipped my board onto the safety rope, and the relief all round was palpable.

Climbing aboard, I thanked John, then met Aileen for the first time. What an introduction! We had a big hug which set me off crying again. I was shaken. Needing something to take my mind off what had just happened, I went down below deck to make a cup of tea for everyone.

In reality, it turned out that I had still been four miles away from Corryvreckan when they picked me up, but John said that if I'd been any closer he would have called the coast guard. Far better to call them off later if you get the situation under control, than to call them out too late and have them searching for a body – to put it bluntly.

I certainly wasn't as cool and calm as I'd liked to have been under that sort of pressure, but the idea of drowning just was not something I was ever going to face well. Despite that, later on Aileen told me that she had been impressed how, just an hour after being rescued, I'd brushed it off as if nothing had happened and was ready to re-strategise. Onwards and upwards...

Neptune's Staircase

I decided that a shower, some proper food, and a beer or two back in Crinan harbour was in order, so, with that, I called an end to not only the paddling for that day, but to the chase itself. I had never intended this to be a race against time. The world record I wanted was supposed to be by default of merely getting to the end, an extra bit of icing on the cake. I didn't care about setting a super-fast time or about beating Cal. Instead, I wanted to make calls about when we stopped to explore interesting parts of this incredible island we call home, and when we pushed on through long nights on the water; and I did not want to feel dictated to by time pressures. So, from then on, the goal to complete the expedition in the next seven days was off, I'd just paddle as much as I felt comfortable with.

After dinner in a local pub, we headed back to the boat to watch one of the most glorious sunsets we'd had on the whole trip – the silhouetted mountains sat against golden hues and rich pinks, reflected in the glassy, still waters around the quiet harbour.

Back on the water the next day, Aileen was a breath of fresh air. Her incredible enthusiasm almost knocked me for six – as soon as I was on my board paddling, she was whooping and cheering me on with the biggest smile on her face: 'You're doing amazingly! Whoo hoo, keep going! You're totally smashing it!'

I laughed. It felt like she might have peaked too early and that I'd need that encouragement after five hours not five minutes. But, nonetheless, it was very welcome and her positive attitude and support for me never once waned in all the time she was with us.

An avid feminist, researcher, tutor, and editor by trade, Aileen can hold her own in a debate and has an incredible way with words... particularly in any situation where – most often – men make silly, misogynistic comments. She can instantly show them the error of their ways. As well as her energy and general gusto for life, her other top teammate quality was her ability to cook – she transformed our meals into healthy and varied affairs, adding hugely to the fun of it all.

As we approached Oban later that day, I spotted an enormous, 100ft sailing ketch pass us. I was almost certain that it was Irene: the boat owned by Glen Gorman, someone I'd spoken to back at the start of it all when I was still looking for a support boat. Although it hadn't worked out with teaming up for SUP Britain, Glen had been keen for me to visit the boat if our paths crossed en route, so I was glad they finally had.

After I finished paddling for the day, we motored back into Oban harbour on Shogun, then tied up alongside Irene and hopped aboard to meet the crew, guests, and explore. This historic boat had once been burned down to the waterline and, having since been completely rebuilt, she's now host to week-long sailing trips around the British Isles. Unfortunately Glen wasn't on board, but everyone made us feel very welcome. We were shown all around the cabins, including the captain's cabin, with its double bed, leather-topped writing desk, and spiral staircase. It was full of character and, amazingly, the twenty-something year old skipper said they'd sailed her with just two crew in the past. From what we saw, I should imagine the opportunity to spend a week aboard as a guest, helping to hoist the sails and exploring the Western Isles, would be an incredible holiday.

As the wine flowed, it turned out that the skipper and his first mate had never paddleboarded before, so, while we got our first experience on a tall ship, we gave them their first experience on a SUP. Most people gingerly step onto the board on their first go, kneeling at first and then getting to their feet once they feel comfortable. Not these two! They both simply stepped straight onto the boards and paddled off. Bar the occasional wobble, it was almost as if they'd done it a hundred times, so it truly goes to show what boyish bravado can do!

As I paddled north along the inner coastline towards Fort William through Loch Linnhe, the still water lapped at the stony, seaweed-covered shore from which the sun-soaked hills rolled out beyond. For the first time on the whole route, I was able to properly relax while on my board without the fear of being on the open sea. Plus, the wildlife was out in the sun too. We were joined by a sea otter and her cub, carefree and playing in the water. It was wonderful to have them come so close to me. The mum seemed to be teaching her baby about boats and paddleboarders, letting it explore and then calling it back to her.

It was a fairly long, straight stretch on the map, but in reality Loch Linnhe has enough gentle curves to mean that I couldn't see all the way to the end, and, as the Nevis mountain range began to rise up from the lower hills in front of me, I could tell that the scenery was about to get anything but boring as we made our way towards the mouth of the Caledonian Canal.

On previous adventures, I'd loathed the canals that connect up central England. There's something about their isolation that makes me feel deeply uneasy: tucked away behind bushes and trees, with few other people around. It's not that I'm worried that there will be dangerous people lurking that want to attack me – though this is what I think my mum instantly thinks of when I say I've had to walk or cycle a stretch of one – but it's the lack of people combined with the proximity to the water that worries me. As the paths often reduce to not much more than a narrow, muddy bank, images flash through my mind of how I might lose my footing or balance and fall in. With no-one around for miles, my fear of drowning feels legitimate.

But, as we left Oban long behind and approached Fort William, the incredible landscape that surrounded us was so picturesque that I didn't feel scared at all. Just ten more miles to go for the day... Plus, by this point, I was feeling much more comfortable on my board than I had been back on that first day, blown out into the Atlantic at Land's End. Still, I was glad that we were heading inland and into smaller bodies of water where I felt less vulnerable and where I knew we were going to meet lots more people than we had in our weeks out on the sea. One aspect of adventure that I really love is that serendipity of bumping into other people and sharing stories, helping and being helped, waving and smiling. The sea isn't a great place for this social aspect to happen. I also missed exploring on land, even if I didn't go far – just taking an hour to go for a walk by myself. I'd missed those opportunities during this expedition and I was looking forward to seeing what the new canal environment would bring.

Aileen got up from a nap and joined John on deck as I paddled alongside, all of us lapping up the scenery. Forested mountains, glistening water, still air – *this* was beautiful paddling. The afternoon sun warmed our faces as we quietly let the miles pass beneath us.

Having covered twenty-five miles in eight hours that day, I began to look out for the University of the Highlands and Islands West Highland College on the water's edge at Fort William. I wasn't entirely sure if I would be able to pick it out from my board, but I was hoping to have a good look as I'd been asked to speak at their graduation ceremony after they'd seen me on the BBC talking about my Irish Sea crossing.

As it turned out, I couldn't see the college from the water and, tired from a long day, I had the finish point fixed square in my mind. Every ten minutes or so I'd ask John, 'what's the tide doing? Is it still with us?' as I felt my pace slowing.

'Oh, you're fine. We've got plenty of time,' he reassured me, smiling. 'Keep going!'

Then, ten minutes later: 'how many miles are left, John?'

And ten minutes after that: 'what time do you think we'll get there, John?'

He could tell I was tired – and looking either for a stopping point or that nudge to keep going just that little bit longer – so, he gently encouraged me. I focused on the fact that it was still gloriously sunny and was glad of the lovely tail wind kicking in for the last push.

As we turned the corner – heading north towards the entrance lock to the Caledonian Canal – the water became much shallower in the middle of the channel, forcing John to take Shogun out wide while I pushed those last few hundred metres in the most direct line possible to finally reach a place where it made sense to stop. We'd hoped to get there slightly earlier and into the canal that night, but, as we arrived at 8.05pm, the last opening of the sea lock for the day had happened a few minutes before we arrived and we had to make do with tying up on the waiting pontoon outside the lock for the night.

Corpach was clearly a hot spot for the locals to hang out, with fathers and sons and groups of friends fishing in the shallow waters as dusk fell, the banks nearby buzzing with people enjoying the last of the day's sunlight. We made dinner and had a beer sitting on the back deck of the boat before heading to the local pub for a drink.

It was John's last night. He'd gotten me back across the Irish Sea and as far into Scotland as he could – but now he had a cycling race to take part in and needed to leave at midday the following day to make it back in time. I think that week had left John with different feelings about the expedition compared to when he had left us in Rosslare after my first crossing of the Irish Sea. In Scotland, he had seemed much more at ease and like he was enjoying the slower pace and different considerations of being on a sailing yacht, yet chugging away under motor for hours following a paddleboarder. Plus, the testing situation near Corryvreckan and the endless banter Aileen had brought on board had lifted our spirits and bonded us as a team. That night, John insisted on buying us a round at the pub to celebrate all that we'd each achieved together.

'Hello there? Morning! Is anyone aboard?'

We were all startled awake, but John jumped up the quickest and was outside in a flash greeting the lock keeper who had just acted as our alarm clock. It was 8am and time for the sea lock to open for the day ahead – and we were right in the way.

'Sorry, sorry,' I said blearily, clearly still waking myself up as I popped my head out. 'We'd tried to get here before the lock closed last night, but had just missed it!'

'No bother. We've got the big boat coming out first and then we'll get you in next,' she said, gesturing to the huge leisure boat towering over us, waiting in the lock to be let out. 'We just need to move you out of the way so we can open the lock gate, as the water will be a bit turbulent and thrash you around too much where you are right now.'

Being thrashed around certainly didn't sound like much fun, so we were only too happy to oblige, particularly as the lock keeper would be letting us straight in afterwards. Before we knew it, we were through and it was paperwork time.

The options were either a seven-day, single licence or a fourteen-day, return licence – it was a toss-up... We'd planned to be all the way through the sixty-mile canal in just three days, and then a further three days on the return journey south after reaching John O'Groats. If we managed this successfully a seven-day pass would be enough. But, if for whatever reason we got held up, we'd need the two-week pass. Still, I took a bet on the seven-day option and got us checked in.

Licence sorted, we were also given keys to the toilet – and shower! – blocks along the canal: we were all looking forward to having a proper wash on this leg of the expedition, what with the sad demise of Shogun's solar shower back at Lundy Island.

Before being able to paddle along the several large lochs that make up most of the Caledonian Canal, we first had to navigate our way through several sets of locks – including Neptune's Staircase. As described by Scottish Canals, the body responsible for the canal, the staircase is an: 'amazing feat of engineering, raising the canal by 19m (62ft) over a quarter of a mile of continuous masonry, and it takes around ninety minutes for a boat to travel up or down the locks. Built by Thomas Telford between 1803 and 1822, it is the longest staircase lock in Scotland. An ideal location to enjoy 'gongoozling' the boats as they travel up and down the lock flight!'

And, yes, people did gongoozle us as we brought Shogun through. For safety reasons I couldn't paddle this section as the turbulent water through the locks and the close proximity to other boats meant that it was far too dangerous. So, walking alongside, I helped with moving the boat where needed. As people checked out our boat, sometimes they'd notice the signs on the side of

Shogun – probably one of the only times anyone had actually been close enough to read them since Liam and Amy made them back in Padstow.

In full PR mode while she hauled Shogun through the locks, Aileen gleefully explained to onlookers what we were up to and what I was attempting to do. One couple was so intrigued they even wanted their picture taken with me, just in case I ended up being famous one day perhaps!

Just a few days earlier, Aileen had never been on a boat before, but I was really keen for her to experience all she could through the expedition. With five days' boating experience now under her belt, John and I felt that it was time for her next challenge. It was time for her to try her hand at skippering. Plus, if there's nothing ventured there's nothing gained, so, before John left, Aileen was set to get her first skippering lesson within the confines of the lock walls. She didn't know it, but it was also a good test to see if there was any chance she might be able to skipper me further along through the canal after John left until Liam was due to return in four days' time.

I remember my first few driving lessons at the age of eighteen. Getting behind the wheel for the first time is always daunting – you have to take complete control of this large, metal object and try to get your head around the basics (and nuances) of handling an engine. During every single one of my driving lessons I would get so nervous and sweaty, feeling well and truly out of my comfort zone.

But having had a driver's licence for over ten years now, driving a boat didn't feel that different for me. OK, I definitely needed to learn a lot about how a boat moves in the water, wind and tide, but the actual mechanics of steering and handling an engine came much more naturally with that experience behind me.

Aileen, on the other hand, had never driven a car or any kind of motorised vehicle before. So, this was like those first ever, nerve-wracking driving lessons for her. Except this vehicle didn't have any brakes or solid land beneath it, and it needed to be carefully moved from one 25ft x 10ft lock to the next on a tight schedule – each time with a solid, stone wall rising up to the left, a towering door looming behind, and three other (far more expensive) boats packed within that same confined space. Plus, of course, there's all those people 'gongoozling' you... No pressure, then!

With John by her side, patiently talking her through what to do, she manoeuvred Shogun forward. Gently on the throttle to get a bit of forward momentum, keeping the boat a couple of feet away from the wall to start with, then nosing her in close as we reached our spot in the next lock.

She was totally bossing it. One lock, two locks, – but, as she progressed into the third lock, John and I could see that she was feeling the pressure. Aileen is never quiet and she hadn't said anything in a while. Intensely focusing on what she was doing, her eyes were darting between the front of the boat; the imposing wall to her left; and to calculating the distance to the other boats on her right. As she began to bring Shogun up to the wall, she slightly misjudged it and came a bit too close, giving the stone wall a little nudge.

I whooped and hollered to distract her from what had just happened. 'Woo hoo!' I shouted, jumping up and down at the side of the lock. 'You're doing bloody amazing! Look at you, you're a fully qualified skipper now!' But it wasn't enough. She was on the edge of tears and, once the gate had closed safely behind her, they began to run down her face. As Shogun reached level with land I checked out the small dent she'd added to the boat. Laughing, I said, 'mate, you didn't need to redesign the boat, I think she's streamlined enough!' She was half-crying and half-laughing, but I think she had had enough of skippering for the day.

In all, it took the three of us roughly an hour and three-quarters to get Shogun through the full set of locks. We spent the rest of the ascent up Neptune's Staircase chatting to the sailors on the other boat on our side of the lock. They were on the return stretch home to Denmark, having sailed around the world – two couples, probably in their fifties with a solid, sea tan that looked very hard earned – they were clearly old hands at manoeuvring their boat, but still very serious about the whole procedure. Their boat was around forty-five feet long and much newer than Shogun, with a sleek, polished design and two, gleaming steering wheels. To be fair to Aileen, driving a boat with a tiller is much more difficult than a steering wheel – and two wheels, well, that's just pure luxury!

At the top of the staircase, the lock keeper pointed us towards an empty mooring where we could tie up overnight. Before John had to shoot off to get back to Ireland and his cycling race, he was keen to have a go on the SUP as he'd never actually been on one before. Not wanting to fall in the water and trigger his pacemaker with cold water shock, he stayed kneeling and paddled around the canal. In moments he had a huge grin on his face and clearly saw the appeal.

'Yeah, it's pretty fun,' he conceded. 'But I still think you're crazy! There's no *way* you'd get me doing that on the sea.' he laughed.

Running out of gas

The next day, with Aileen now at least a little bit introduced to skipper life, I was keen to see if we could push on without John. It was Friday morning and Liam wasn't due back from his holiday for another three days. It would never have crossed my mind to push on without Liam, John, or another qualified skipper had we still been on the coast, but within the confines of the Caledonian Canal I figured it would be safe enough for Aileen to skipper – plus, I would be paddling close by, so I could hop back onto the boat and take over should anything go awry.

I reckoned that the next six-mile stretch from the top of Neptune's Staircase to the lock at the small hamlet of Gairlochy should take us about two to three hours – it seemed easily achievable and a good way to test out my idea of us going it alone.

Right after breakfast, we set out to give it a go. The headwind that day was brisker than I would have liked, which I knew meant that we'd need to be more forceful on the throttle in order to counter it and enable us to successfully manoeuvre Shogun away from the boats around us. I set her in gear, so that she was holding ground next to the pontoon, then untied the ropes. Pulling away from the pontoon, we were in the middle of the channel and moving forwards, so I stepped down the swim ladder and onto my waiting board. Then, all of a sudden, we were being forced sideways.

'Give her more power,' I shouted to Aileen.

'I am, but it's not working!' was her slightly panicked reply.

Seconds later, we were moving rather quickly towards one of the boats that had been moored on the pontoon in front of us. In a split-second decision, I jumped onto the swim ladder and grabbed the tiller. With the wind blowing us backwards, we needed to move it in the opposite direction to correct our course, as you would in a car. But Aileen hadn't yet had a single reversing lesson – for the boat or a car – and was unknowingly steering us in the wrong direction. I flipped the tiller to the opposite side and yelled, 'reverse, put her in reverse!' Aileen kicked her into reverse but it wasn't enough. *Four feet, three feet...*

As the stubborn wind continued pushing us towards the parked boat, its two male owners came out to stand just where we were about to hit and, rather than helping in any way, they simply stood there, arms folded, and stared. *Two feet...* 'More reverse… *full* reverse!' I yelled.

We swung backwards in the nick of time. We missed the boat and I steered us through a three-point turn, fighting the wind to get us back on course. Then it was full throttle to get clear of the boats and we were off. In hindsight, I should've stayed on Shogun until we were clear of the boats before handing over control. Sorry, Aileen!

I hopped back on my SUP and began to paddle. Aware that it was only the fact that I had still been tethered to the boat that had enabled me to hop back on board quickly enough to stop us crashing, I decided to keep it that way. It just meant that I had to be really careful that I paddled at the exact speed of the boat, keeping the line slack and making sure that Shogun wasn't aiding me at all. I decided that it was the best balance – this way, I was able to keep making miles under my own steam while John and Liam were away, but stick close enough to offer assistance should Aileen need it.

As we approached the bend in the canal just before Gairlochy, the lock keepers somehow knew that we were coming before we could even see the lock ourselves. They radioed over to us with instructions to hurry up as they were holding the swing bridge open for us, keeping traffic waiting on the road. I jumped back onto Shogun immediately, and made sure that we were OK getting through the bridge and then the lock.

Coming in nice and slowly, Aileen and I handled our very first lock together without a skipper on board. We managed to grab the heavy, blue ropes that they lowered down to us and kept the boat stable as the water flowed into the lock. On the other side were a series of pontoons and, beyond that, the canal opened out onto Loch Lochy. We decided to stop there while we were all in one piece. After going past the pontoons to check out the full range of berthing options we swung back round to park at the biggest open space we could find. It was the main stopping point for boats that would either have just come through the lock like us, or that had come from the loch and were waiting to go through the lock (all the lock/lochs! Are you keeping up?).

Triumphantly moored next to the shower block, we thought we had all that we needed to stay there overnight. That is, until we discovered that Shogun had run out of gas and that there was nowhere within a two-hour walk to get food. After trying and failing to find takeaways that would deliver this far out of town, we decided to make do with cold food for one night and went to bed.

Making plans for how I might be able to paddle more miles while we waited for Liam to return, I ran through a variety of options. *Perhaps Aileen could paddle with me on my other board along Loch Lochy and then we could hitchhike back to the boat. Or maybe I could just leave her with the boat, take my camping gear, get as far along as I could, then Liam and Aileen could catch me up with the boat on his return in a couple of days?* None of these options seemed right – plus I was keen to enjoy at least a little bit of downtime in this beautiful part of the country – so, I decided to stay put for the next day at least.

On our day off at Gairlochy, we were joined by Paula McGuire, who, just a month before, had become the first person to attempt to swim a lap around Britain with her adventure, Big Mad Swim. Setting off from Cornwall in April, she had self-funded a support boat, like I had, and we'd got chatting via Instagram. Back when we were both down in the south of England, I'd been hoping that she might know of a skipper who could help with SUP Britain, but she had been having just as much trouble trying to fill gaps in her own skipper schedule. With her husband as land crew, she'd had a skipper for the first week or so on her main support boat and a kayaker beside her in the water.

Having experienced anxiety for all of her life, a few years previously Paula had decided that enough was enough, medication wasn't the answer for her and she was going to bloody well get outside and face her anxiety head on. A stallion effort saw her swim an impressive chunk of the Cornish coastline – all while having a fear of the water – but it had soon become apparent to her that this was one fear she was happy to leave well alone. Not wanting to put her crew at risk when her panic attacks in the water became too bad, she called it a day and decided to spend quality time with her family instead.

Getting to the start line, as SUP Britain had proved to me, is the single hardest point in any journey. Whether you make it to your intended goal or not makes little difference – it truly is the journey that you go on in the pursuit of your dreams in the first place that makes life worth living.

Paula was awesome. She hopped aboard Shogun and, under the beaming sunshine, the three of us had a brilliant, long chat about adventure, sponsorship, getting speaking jobs and, finally, paddling. Paula's cheery and relaxed personality makes you feel like friends instantly. It was wonderful to converse so openly about our struggles and joys in taking on what seem to others like ridiculous challenges. Plus, both of us had fears which had propelled us to have a go and make a start where others might not have.

Cups of tea long finished, it was time to hit the water. Paula and I got onto the SUPs and paddled away from Shogun, past all the moored boats and towards Loch Lochy, the Highland mountains stretching out to meet us on either side. It was a calm, still, sunny day: the perfect weather for a novice paddleboarder and a great opportunity for me to share what I'd been doing with someone new. In true Paula fashion, she took herself for a swim back at the boat, clearly making sure to keep punching her old fear in the gut by getting into the water whenever the opportunity arose. After drying off, she kindly offered to take us into town in search of a new gas canister and some food, and we jumped at the chance.

The only bottle of gas at the only shop in town scanned through as £70 on the till, which – to both me and the cashier – seemed ridiculous. She spent some time checking with her colleagues about the price and looking for alternatives but we were out of luck. We just didn't need gas badly enough to pay double for it, so we opted to look for a local chippy instead. No luck! They were closed, so ice lollies it was, then Paula dropped us back at Shogun with a copy of her book, *Must Try Harder*, and we parted ways with tight hugs and promises to stay in touch.

It wasn't long before a boat with three retired couples pulled up next to us. Waving hello, one of the men wandered over to check out our boat. Stopping next to me, while Aileen sat on deck, he gestured to Shogun and asked, 'whose boat is this?'

I laughed and looked at him with an eyebrow raised, 'it's my boat.'

He looked searchingly at it and seemed confused, 'oh, so you have electric winches?'

'... No,' I told him in dismay.

'Oh! How do you pull on the ropes, then?' He seemed genuinely confused.

I wasn't entirely sure how to break it to him that women's hands work just the same as men's. *I'm as capable of pulling on a rope as you are, chappy.* Bemused, he went back to explain this deeply puzzling situation to his friends. You really couldn't make this stuff up...

Starting again

As Aileen and I sat on deck looking out over the water, she let slip that she'd never SUPed before.

'What? Well, now's your chance. It's the perfect conditions for it,' I insisted.

'Oh, no! I don't think I'll be able to stand,' she responded. But I wasn't having any of it and, knowing Aileen's weak spot, I began to push her buttons.

'You know back at Oban when those guys just jumped straight onto the boards without even kneeling down first? And the fact that Liam had never sailed before and has now skippered Shogun halfway up Britain?'

'Yeah...' she replied, knowing where I was going with this.

'Just imagine you're a man. You couldn't possibly fail!' I laughed.

'Damn it!' she said, resigned to the fact that she couldn't win this argument. 'But I don't have a wetsuit...' she tried anyway.

'Well, don't fall in then! Come on, Aileen... what would a man do?' I goaded, then went to get the board ready in the water for her.

From then on if she ever talked herself down or was hesitant to try something for fear of failure, I would simply ask, 'But what would a man do, Aileen?' which meant that she had no choice, she had to have a go.

'OK, you don't have to stand,' I reassured her, 'that's totally fine. Absolutely do it your way. But at the very least, you do have to try.'

She gingerly edged her way off the pontoon and crouched onto the board, feeling the water move beneath her, then, before she knew it, she was getting the hang of turning and pushing power through the paddle to cover laps past the boat and back again.

'See!' I shouted, filming her from the boat. 'You're doing it!'

As the sun dipped behind the mountains and the last light of day left a chill in the air, Aileen eventually came in off the board – totally elated.

'You're smashing the firsts,' I said, high-fiving her.

Over dinner we – once again – strategised our options to try and make some progress the next day. Despite a great start on the paddleboard that evening, Aileen didn't feel comfortable enough to set out to cover ten miles the next morning. So, we reached an agreement: we decided that Aileen would walk the length of Loch Lochy following the Great Glen Way, meeting halfway at a set point for lunch and, finally, at the far end once I'd paddled and she'd hiked the full stretch. Given that I could paddle around 2.5mph, I figured that this would effectively match an average walking pace of 3mph, so our timings should work out. From there, it would just be the small matter of getting back to Shogun...

The next morning, Aileen and I packed our bags for our respective adventures ahead and we each set off with a plan to meet at our designated lunch spot within a certain time window. As I paddled out into Loch Lochy with a dry bag on my board, Aileen was occasionally visible through the trees to my left as she traced the route along the water's edge. I felt the wind on my skin and it was an absolute dream to be moving again. The freedom!

The last time I'd paddled on my own had ended in tears, but this felt liberating – not scary. The Caledonian Canal really is gorgeous: dramatic mountains flank you on either side, some still snow-topped in June, giving way to lush, green trees and vegetation. I felt calmed by the human scale of the loch, as opposed to the sheer vastness of the sea, able to see land on all sides and having boats passing by.

Despite the weather being changeable at sea, in general throughout Britain it was a scorcher of a summer. London was stuck in a heat wave that didn't seem to end and even as far north as Scotland they were experiencing a proper long hot summer. Since travelling inland into Scotland the weather had maintained great conditions for paddling. Inland waters really are a much more hospitable place for paddling. But then again I'm glad to have not missed out on all that Ireland had to offer and the challenge of losing sight of shore.

You could argue this adventure was hard enough, what with me being a complete sea novice, and a terrified one at that. To my mind though, the sea is what presented the challenge to me. While I don't like canals or the idea of falling in them, the sea is where my fear was at its height and by choosing that route I felt like I'd tested myself more. I'd learnt about an environment that was totally alien to me. I'd acquired new skills, met new people and seen places I never would've done otherwise.

Having said all that, I'm not stupid and to stay on the coast and travel around Cape Wrath rather than opting for the cut through of the Caledonian Canal would have just been asking for trouble. And given the beauty that I was now passing through, I'm glad I took this combination of the Irish Sea and the Caledonian Canal.

It was a scorcher of a day, and I made it to our rendezvous point slightly quicker than expected. However, looking around, it was clear that it wouldn't be an easy place for Aileen to reach from the path through all the dense shrubs blocking her way. So, I calculated a second spot from Google Maps, sent her the new location, and paddled onwards.

As the depth of the water dropped away, it revealed a wide, shallow section with a beautiful, stony beach to my left. I came in to shore and sat myself down on a tree stump. Within fifteen minutes, Aileen had caught up with me and we got stuck into our food, comparing notes on our routes. We were making solid progress, even with the heat.

After a long hour – and a quick dip in the loch for Aileen – we pushed on. It was a boiling afternoon and being on the water was more than welcome: I dipped my hat into the loch and let the coolness drench my head. And, before long, Laggan was in sight. We made it to the locks at almost the same time, left my board near some of the boats, and went for a quick drink in the local, the Eagle Barge Inn. We asked around to see if anyone there was heading west towards Gairlochy that afternoon (back where we'd left Shogun), but the barman was quick to suggest that we wouldn't have much problem hitchhiking.

'Two pretty girls like you!' he exclaimed. 'You'll get picked up no problem!'

We smiled and left. I really don't think that men realise just how seriously creepy they sound when they say things like that and how much, in this context, it sounded like we were about to get attacked or killed.

Outside, we conferred. It was broad daylight and we're both pretty strong, so we figured we'd take our chances. Down at the roadside, Aileen enthusiastically waved her thumb at every passing vehicle. Nothing. Ten drivers came and went without so much as a glance in our direction. Then along came a lovely couple who smiled and invited us into their (air-conditioned!) car, then shuttled us back down to Gairlochy, even though it was a bit out of their way. Racing back along the miles we'd just covered under our own steam, we were glad of their kindness.

Our next challenge was getting Shogun up Loch Lochy to Laggan and my board, before dark.

Motoring out of Gairlochy, I think both Aileen and I were glad that I was on board this time. It's a *lot* to skipper a boat on your own, particularly when it's only your second ever day at it. As we set our course up the loch, the weather began to change. Hot, dry air gave way to wind whistling down the glen, forcing us to re-plot and seek out slightly more sheltered patches of water, hoping that the mountains would offer us some protection.

Not only was the strong side wind slowing us down, but it was throwing up quite a bit of chop. Reaching 20mph at its peak in the middle of the channel, Shogun was pitching to one side. I hate it when boats lean, so I tucked myself away on the stairs while Aileen stayed up on deck, trying to use the spray hood to shield herself. I started explaining how we'd had worse out on the Irish Sea, so while I was uncomfortable I wasn't concerned about these conditions – we could manage them no problem, I told her. She nodded, at which point a wave reared up and crashed over the side of the boat, completely soaking her. It really was magical timing and had us both in fits of laughter.

Arriving at the far end of Loch Lochy, we faced the challenge of parking Shogun in the still gusting winds, ripping down the glen to the lock. We clocked a good-sized waiting pontoon and aimed for that. Aileen had told me she felt scared when it came to jumping off the moving boat and onto the pontoon with the rope, so we agreed that I'd do that bit, while she would steer us in. With a better view from the front of the boat, I guided her on when to turn and how much power to give the throttle. Closer, closer, closer... Damn it! Neither of us had enough experience parking in the wind and we missed on the first go.

I directed us to circle round on ourselves and come in for another try, so Aileen brought us forwards. Suddenly, I noticed that I could see the bottom of the loch beneath Shogun. 'What's the depth reading?' I called, just as we hit with a dull clunk. I had to laugh. 'Reverse! Reverse!' I think this was becoming our go-to move...

Keeping to the deeper water for our second try, Aileen battled with the wind, but it was no good – we were being pushed away from where we were aiming for. Making an executive call,

I decided that we'd use our signature move and, rather than circling back yet again, we'd simply reverse onto the pontoon. Swapping roles, I took over the controls. And, as we came alongside, we both knew that we only had a matter of a few seconds before we'd be blown away once more, so it was now or never for Aileen to, quite literally, take that leap.

'Jump... jump! JUMP!' I shouted.

She overcame her fear and launched herself onto the pontoon. Landing breathlessly, she pulled us into position, both of us relieved to have made it at last.

Unfortunately I'd only managed to bring Shogun alongside right in the middle of the pontoon and so, aware that someone else might need to tie up, I tried to move the boat to one end or the other, but the side on wind was just too strong, pushing her away from the pontoon, rather than up or down it. So we had no option but to effectively park across two bays, whoops!

The next day, Liam was due back with us and we were more than ready to have his skippering expertise on board once more. After a bit of a detour, Aileen's dad, Alisdair, got him to Laggan. He was clearly refreshed, slightly tanned, and in renewed spirits. When we told Alisdair about our lack of gas supply, he kindly offered to take Aileen on a canister hunt in Fort Augustus. Unfortunately they had no luck, but came back with biscuits instead, which – to be fair – is almost as good. Alisdair stayed for a cup of tea and it was nice to get to know him a little: now in his sixties, he'd been a furniture-maker and artist before retiring a few years back, although he was finding himself just as busy as ever. After he hit the road once more, the three of us spent the evening swimming in the canal, eating food, and laughing. Liam and Aileen were getting along really well and I think he enjoyed having someone closer to his own age to hang out with. She was also brilliant at keeping him on his toes, which I loved.

The next day we were back into paddling mode and finally making miles again towards John O'Groats. Passing through the lochs was easy-going on calm waters, with Shogun and the dream team following behind me. Navigation was simple too: we just had to keep going forwards for the next forty-odd miles until we reached the sea.

However, as the summer heat continued to climb, it wasn't just people that were sweltering. Dotted along the Caledonian Canal are a series of swing bridges that move in and out of place to allow traffic to cross the water and boats to pass through, but – as it turns out – they have a very low tolerance for hot weather, expanding quickly and becoming stuck fast. While jammed bridges were no problem for me and my SUP, Shogun had to join the growing queue of vessels that couldn't get through at the top end of the lock ladder at Fort Augustus. It was midday and we could do nothing but wait for cooler temperatures the next morning.

Scrolling through social media that afternoon, I noticed an update from Cal with a familiar-looking sign in the background. She'd made it. She was at John O'Groats and what a sterling effort! She'd paddled solo through 30mph winds and pushed hard to get to the end. Truthfully, I was definitely gutted to have not made it first, no matter how slim the possibility had ever been, but I knew that it really made little difference to me. This was my adventure, and it came with very different challenges to hers – my fear being the main one. I was focused on looking forward to getting my own finish line, when the time came. But for now, I was happy just to walk along the banks of the loch and soak up the afternoon sun.

The following morning, as Liam and Aileen got ready to take Shogun through the first opening of the locks and down to the swing bridge at 9am, I made an early start and left before them. I was four miles down Loch Ness before they caught up with me, setting a great momentum for the day ahead. After the quiet frustration of waiting out the closed bridge, I was thrilled to be on the move again.

On what was a beautifully calm day, much more so than the previous, Loch Ness was a great place to paddle. The widest and longest of the lochs in the Caledonian Canal, Loch Ness is also the deepest. At about twice the depth of the Irish Sea, there was a full six hundred feet of water beneath my board, and who knows what was living down there? Monsters – hypothetical or not! – aside, the scenery was stunning. Mountainsides raked upwards from either edge of the loch, covered in thick forests with the odd house dotted amongst them, and the sky arched bright blue overhead. Making the most of the calm conditions, Aileen passed me a cup of tea and slice of ginger cake on my board, so I could recharge, after which she and Liam plunged into the water for a swim.

Conscious that the locks further up the canal were only operated until five o'clock in the evening, we wanted to get Shogun as far along our route as possible before then – after that, they'd be able to moor her up and wait for me to join them. So they pushed on without me; after all, here in Loch Ness, there were definitely no whirlpools to worry about.

Making my way down the canal on my own was very different to having my crew around. To some extent I liked the freedom of it, I felt calm and comfortable. Don't get me wrong: having a crew is great, but I also love the solo aspect of adventures. The time on my own, with my own thoughts, relying on only myself, and stopping when I want to with no impact on anyone else is liberating. Still, we'd grown used to spending all our waking hours together, so it felt odd not knowing how far they'd gotten and how their day was panning out.

Pleased with my momentum, I powered my way up the canal, glancing over for a little nosey at the boats moored up along the banks, without breaking my stride. One huge wooden boat was being renovated and then there was a slightly smaller, but still sizable, boat also under tarps with its newly built sections clearly visible. As I passed, the owner popped his head out and waved, shouting hello. I waved back and kept paddling.

But, unsatisfied, the man insisted that I stop to chat to him. It truly is amazing how so many men – especially older men – often have this real ability to put women on the spot, cornering us into feeling rude unless we do exactly what they want. *Actually, today, right now, I don't want to stop and chat to you, thank you,* I thought to myself. *I'm on a mission.* However, rather than picking up on my body language and unwillingness to indulge him, he launched into a monologue.

He began by explaining that, at the age of sixty-seven, he was 'very impressed' with me, gesturing vaguely towards my board. It might sound like a compliment, but it simply wasn't – he hadn't asked what I was doing and therefore had no idea about SUP Britain... he didn't know where I'd paddled from or where I was going to. So what was it that he was so impressed by? Was it merely the fact that I was paddleboarding, or was it because I was on my own? If he was going to be that easily impressed, then he clearly had incredibly low expectations of women. He finished off his riveting one-sided conversation by insisting that I look him up on YouTube and stop drifting away down the water while he was talking to me. Luckily, I had somewhere to be.

Further along the canal, I reached a couple of kayakers who invited me to a kayak/SUP marathon happening that Sunday. I told them that I'd be much further north by then, but it was lovely to enjoy a friendly, two-sided conversation with an adult man who was willing to use his basic social skills to read the situation and at no point insisted that I listened to his life story. I paddled onwards.

As I turned the corner, I saw Shogun tied up on a small pontoon on the left bank, just in front of a low, metal swing bridge. Clearly, the heat had become a problem again and the bridge was stuck closed, so this was as far as any of us would be going for the day. Rather far from the blue and green wilds of Loch Ness, we were very much in the outskirts of Inverness itself, with a fairly busy road running over the bridge. The trees that had guided me down the canal had disappeared, replaced with rows of grey houses.

As I got closer, I could see that there were other people on Shogun's deck with Liam and Aileen. In my slightly tired state I couldn't recognise them to begin with and my heart sank a little at having to be sociable to strangers. But then one face looked familiar – it was Aileen's dad, Alisdair, which meant that the others must be her mum, Clare, and brother, Murray. I was relieved to see friendly faces. Then, feeling a bit like I was intruding on a party on my own boat, I plumped myself down on the deck, slightly wet, very sweaty, and desperately in need of food and sleep. Aileen's family were very sweet and nipped off to buy us all fish and chips.

In the meantime, Liam proudly told me all about the kids who had come by to play in the river, and, when they had seen my spare SUP pumped up on the side of the boat, he'd offered to let them play on it. Rigging up a line to keep it tethered to Shogun so that they didn't float off down the canal, he threw it into the water for them to mess around on. I could see that Liam was back in his element. Being a water-based sports instructor for kids, this was what he'd known for the past few years and, just listening to him talking, I could see he really loved it. Having been a cycling instructor myself, teaching ten-year-olds to cycle on the road, I know that it's incredibly rewarding to watch children gain confidence through sport. Telling them stories of adventure, then giving them the skills to take on their own challenges, is a brilliant way to build confidence and nurture a curious nature.

Before long, the fish and chips arrived and so too did a spare gas canister. Aileen's dad had gone to extra lengths to track down a spare for us, after our struggle finding one at Gairlochy, Laggan, and Fort Augustus. What a gem. He really didn't have to do that – it was so kind of them all to be there supporting us, let alone feeding us and giving us fuel too. Ravenous, we all tucked into the delicious food, bobbing on the canal, as the day came to a close.

Back on the sea

The next morning, I was refuelled and ready to hit the water once more. With just two and a half miles left until the sea lock at Clachnaharry, the end of the Caledonian Canal, there was no point in me speeding off too much as I'd only have to wait for them to catch me up – and there was obviously no way I'd be going out into the Moray Firth on my own.

I knew that I was paddling through a major Scottish city, but the canal provided a quiet and secluded passage through to the north: the trees along the banks were dappled in the morning light, breaking up the grey beyond, and making this a lovely end to my inland stretch.

I paddled past what looked like some kind of yard where people fix up boats or strip down those that have come to the end of their life, before reaching the top of a series of locks leading down into Inverness marina. It was just a casual four locks this time, in comparison to the rather intimidating nine that Aileen and I had tackled with John back at the other end of the Caledonian Canal some twelve days earlier. I carried my board down past the locks, then paddled my way out to the Clachnaharry sea lock. *Less than an hour – not bad!* Now it was just the small matter of getting Shogun through.

I left my board down there and started the walk back to get to my team. Going through the canal had been far slower than I'd imagined it would be: I knew that I could have paddled the whole length in two to three days, had I been going for it. But even having pushed ahead with Aileen down Loch Lochy, the delays caused by waiting for Liam to return, plus two stuck bridges, meant that it had taken four times that. After all, as with any team, you can only go as fast as the slowest member, which in this case was Shogun herself.

It's always interesting speaking to other people who have been on both supported and unsupported expeditions. Of course, there are some adventures that you can only do supported. You've got no chance of beating Mark Beaumont's 80-day around the world cycle if you don't have a significant support team. But even despite this, by far, most people I've spoken to predominantly prefer to go unsupported. With no team you're free to go at your own pace, to stop when you want to and, most importantly, to push on when you want to. Plus teams are expensive, which means you need sponsors and therefore you add another layer of expectation, deliverables and potential stress.

On the other hand, sponsors mean more press coverage as you can leverage their PR machines, which means more on-the-ground support from the general public in most cases. Having people hear about your adventure and then offer to help with any issues you face is a huge practical and morale benefit – it's wonderful to have complete strangers bring you cake while out on the road. There are pros and cons, like anything in life, and it's been interesting to reflect on those for SUP Britain.

I found Shogun and my crew at the bottom of the lock steps waiting for the swing bridge to let them through. Running across just before it swung open, I jumped onto Shogun and helped take her through. Then it was time for cake and settling our bill. In the marina office I got chatting to the woman behind the counter and it turned out that I'd been emailing her back when I was organising the trip: she was delighted to see that I'd made it this far. I promised we'd be back in just a few days' time – after reaching John O'Groats – and said goodbye.

After getting through one last swing bridge and the sea lock, we were finally free to go and motored out towards the sea. As soon as we were clear of the lock, I threw my board off the back of the boat and jumped on. *The home straight!*

The section ahead consisted of three stretches: from Inverness up to Helmsdale, from there to Wick, and then the final fifteen miles to John O'Groats. I knew from my calculations that this initial section, closest to the city, was the trickiest, with a bridge, pinch points, and an exposed crossing.

The Kessock Bridge carries the A9, the main artery road leading from Inverness all the way up to the north coast of Scotland – I'd cycled northwards across it on my LEJOG bike ride – and it marks the meeting point of the Beauly Firth to the west and the Moray Firth to the east, leading out into the North Sea.

We were heading into a long stretch with a relatively significant difference between high tide and low tide, meaning that there would be a lot of water moving around and I was on my guard. Liam had changed a lot during the trip so far, mostly in a good way, but occasionally his newfound confidence got the better of him. In those first few months together, his nervousness and lack of ego had meant that he was considerate. He would explain his thought processes to me, sharing all the information we needed in order to make decisions about which direction to take if there was an obstacle up ahead. Not only had he been better at communicating in those early days, but he had also been more supportive, understanding, and forgiving of my lack of ability. While he might have become totally comfortable as a skipper, I was still scared of the sea. And just because he was more comfortable, that didn't make him in charge. I still needed to know his decision-making processes. In fact, knowing what was going on was what allowed me to make sure that we were taking the best course for me, for the boat, and for team safety. These were my calls to make.

Liam yelled at me from the boat to keep going straight and that they'd meet me at the other side of Kessock Bridge by the lighthouse. I couldn't help but be pissed off. He didn't explain his reasons and manoeuvred the boat away before I could reply.

I radioed over, 'Liam.'

'Yeah, what's up?'

'Liam, you can't just shout instructions at me and then leave. Why are you taking the boat over there?'

'Because it's too shallow on this side. We'll meet you at the lighthouse. What's the problem? I need to go get my camera... I think there's a seal over here!'

The problem is that I'm scared, Liam. I don't know what's up ahead and you've just left me. That's the problem, I thought to myself.

When I reached the lighthouse they still didn't seem to be changing course, so I took matters into my own hands, I decided it was time for a break, and landed my board on the pebbly beach that wrapped around Chanonry Point.

After ten minutes or so Liam called. 'Why have you beached?' he seemed genuinely puzzled.

'You guys didn't seem to be coming to meet me, so I'm taking a break... You need to explain what you're doing, Liam. You can't just leave and not tell me what's going on,' I told him. 'I need to know what's happening so that I can make sure I'm happy with the strategy.'

Frustration vented, I paddled over and they were annoyingly chirpy. But they offered me cake as an apology and we were soon distracted by dolphins. There was a crowd on the beach watching them play in the overfalls made by the tide rushing around this pinch point at the edge of the spit of land. The dolphins came close to the beach and I could see that they were much bigger than any of the ones we'd seen further south. But, more interested in playing than investigating visitors, they didn't come close and even seemed to stay away from me and Shogun.

Looking out past the dolphins, we spotted a canoe coming from Ardersier. It was Aileen's dad with a special cake delivery – what a star. He knew just how much of SUP Britain was cake-powered! Plus, it was also a great excuse for him to get out in his canoe and see the dolphins up close, something Alisdair had never done before. I was glad to have been a suitable excuse for him to finally get around to it.

The weather was dreamy until mid-afternoon when the wind picked up and became heady. I battled against it and started to cross over to the north side of the estuary – Liam had taken note of my earlier comments and, this time, was dutifully explaining his plan of action. I greatly appreciated it and felt much more comfortable.

I focussed and tried to push on, but the wind was just too much. Plus, the tide was turning against me. There was no way I could fight it out here, so I jumped onto Shogun to wait out the rough conditions. I had a nap, while Liam and Aileen kept watch as we stayed out at sea until the tide turned back in our favour.

After waking up a couple of hours later, I checked the digital chart on the boat to see where we were. Showing both our current location and a continuous record of the boat's route, it seemed we'd been motoring around in all directions while I was asleep. I was curious as to what happened, and it turned out they'd been trying to draw a dog with the boat tracker, which made me laugh, as I couldn't quite see the resemblance myself from the array of lines they'd created.

I paddled onwards through the unrelenting wind until just beyond the mouth of the Cromarty Firth, some eighteen miles north of the sea lock at Clachnaharry. However, it wasn't long before we decided that progress just wasn't feasible, and that it was best to duck round to Cromarty. This proved to be a good idea as the wind picked up even further and sent us pitching in the waves. Needless to say, it wasn't much fun on the board, or indeed on the boat, for that stretch.

Aileen got our dinner on as we motored into the Cromarty Firth, a haven with enormous boat cranes towering above us on the far side of the water. Pasta with vegetables was on the menu and, as I watched her fill up the pasta pan with water, I noticed that something was different.

'Er, mate, that's the wrong tap – you're using seawater!'

'Yeah, I know,' she laughed. 'I'm trying to save our freshwater supply. It's fine! I checked... as long as we boil it twice, it'll kill anything bad.' Peering into the pan, she confirmed, 'don't worry, I can't see anything swimming with the pasta!'

Intrigued, although not convinced our water supply was low enough to justify this, I watched as she carried on prepping dinner in the usual way.

Rolling on the sofa laughing at how dinner was turning out, I pointed out, 'I'm pretty sure you don't need to add salt to the pasta, Aileen.'

'Oh, no! I totally forgot I'd used sea water!' Aileen was now in fits of laughter too.

Once on the visitors' mooring and tied up for the night, Aileen served us dinner. On the face of it, it looked as yummy as ever, but the idea of eating seawater-flavoured pasta wasn't appetising. Liam, on the other hand, never turns down food and tucked straight in.

'It's still edible,' he said between mouthfuls.

Gingerly, Aileen and I tried it too, but we both grimaced. I'd never tasted anything so salty in my whole life. It was vile. In fact, it was just like when you've been rolled by a wave on the beach and you've accidentally drunk a bit of seawater and you can't help but retch. Bon appetit! Unbelievably, Liam ate a whole bowlful. Aileen and I opted for biscuits instead.

Back on the board at 5.40am the next morning, with pretty calm seas on my side, I made it up past Tarbat Ness lighthouse before the tide turned against me. We bobbed out the tide for five hours, then I carried on towards the next milestone, Helmsdale. Rather than following the coast, we made a beeline for the harbour across a ten-mile stretch of open water. More exposed and with a lot of chop, I ended up kneeling for most of it.

The north east coast of Scotland was making me feel nervous again on my board. For the most part, Ireland had given us dreamy paddling conditions and the Caledonian Canal had been gorgeous – both of which had helped my confidence to blossom, but this rough stretch put me on edge. It was probably the brush with Corryvreckan that had frayed my nerves and, while I knew that there were no more whirlpools to contend with, the North Sea isn't exactly known for its calm weather.

While I still had half the tide left to paddle, Liam decided to check in with Helmsdale to say that we were heading their way. It transpired that it was, in fact, a tidal harbour. The harbour master explained that if we wanted to be in overnight, we'd need to get ourselves there before low water at 10pm. It was 9.25pm. There was nothing else for it. I jumped on the boat and within five minutes we were under sail and motor, and really going for it. We arrived exactly on the deadline and had just enough depth to get in.

With no space left on the pontoons, we were directed to tie up alongside the seawall. As Liam was bringing Shogun in to park her, he got the timing wrong and from below deck I heard this almighty crunching sound. I ran to see what had happened, but Liam fobbed me off.

'Don't worry, we didn't hit anything. It's just the front port light caught on the metal ladder,' he said.

'So, you hit the wall and broke the light you mean?' I retorted.

'No. It's fine. We probably don't need that light and it was old anyway.'

'Er, we do need that light and it doesn't matter if it was old. It was working and now it's definitely not working. Please stop breaking my boat, Liam. We need it intact to get to the end!'

'Ha! I haven't broken that much on the boat,' he insisted.

'Day one of owning the boat, you broke the bucket and the deck brush,' I reminded him.

'Technically, they were probably already broken. And I fixed the bucket with some rope, so that doesn't count,' he contested.

'You broke the toilet roll holder with your bum... like you don't know how to use toilet paper or something,' I laughed.

'Oh, that was when I was changing into my wetsuit. Yeah, fair enough. I might get round to seeing if I can fix that,' he said sheepishly.

'And then there was the wooden cleat. How on earth you did that I have no idea. Those things are supposed to be strong!' He took my point.

Once we'd tied up, a good chat with the harbourmaster gave us some useful information for the next stretch of our route and we settled in for the night. Luckily, we didn't feel the boat list on the keel but it did bang against the wall once we had more water rising beneath us come morning. As the water lifted us up off the seabed, the lines holding us against the seawall slackened off, leaving Shogun's side to crunch against the stone with each pulse of the tide. Liam was beyond caring and didn't get up, so I nipped outside into the fresh morning air to tighten the lines at around 4am. Then at 5am. And 6am...

We were all tired and really feeling the sleep deprivation. Still, after heading back out to the last paddle point I made good ground towards Wick. On the tide turning, I jumped back on the boat, and Aileen and I slept, while Liam watched the men's World Cup England quarter final match and kept an eye on our position. As usual, we'd bobbed to wait out the tide.

The first we knew of its approach was the sound of a loud horn. And there was the clamour of shouting voices. Liam jumped on the throttle and motored away from them. They followed us. *What on earth?* Having been woken up suddenly by all the commotion, I was confused about who they were and what was going on. Still half asleep and below deck, looking up, I thought their aggressive shouting and the terrified look on Liam's face meant that we were being hijacked by pirates.

'Do they have guns?' I whispered to Liam, as I climbed up the stairs and cautiously poked my head out to see what was happening.

'What? No. They're fishermen,' he told me.

'What's going on? Why are they beeping at us and chasing us?' I was so bewildered

'I don't know. I thought they wanted to get to their pots, so I immediately moved us out of the way, but obviously not.' Clearly Liam was as puzzled as I was.

They were now closer and we could hear what they were shouting. It turned out that a member of the public had seen a yacht drifting in the tide and had thought that my SUP – which we'd left floating on the water and tied to the back of the boat as normal – was a rowing boat. They'd put two and two together and made fifteen, thinking that Shogun was somehow being pushed along by a rowing boat, which would, therefore, mean that she'd lost engine power and needed rescuing. After a phone call to the coast guard, a message was put out over the VHF radio to try and get hold of us or any other boats in the area that could help.

'But when you didn't respond,' the fishermen explained, 'the lifeboat was launched. It's on its way,' they concluded firmly, at which point we all turned around towards Wick. And there she was. That mighty, orange beacon of safety that you would pay a million pounds to see if you were in a real emergency and – as Liam kept pointing out – costs a lot of money to launch because of how much fuel it uses...

Crap.

As the lifeboat pulled up alongside, we all looked really sheepish. I explained what I was doing and apologised profusely. They all looked a little baffled, so I pointed to the sign on the side of Shogun, making it the third time in the whole trip the length of Britain that the signs had been useful.

They still didn't seem entirely sure what to make of us, so I assured them again that we were absolutely fine: we had power and were just waiting for the tide to turn. Then, realising that we'd had the radio on the channel from the last harbour, we made sure that it was on the correct channel, channel sixteen. The coastguard asked where we were heading to, when we expected to be there, and were happy enough to leave us to it. The fishing boat also left us after we thanked them for trying to help, even if they did seem a little perturbed that they'd come out of their way to assist and initially Liam had basically run away from them.

We felt incredibly guilty but there was nothing else for it but to push on, so, once the tide had turned (and England had won), I jumped back on my board. The weather, as well as my confidence, out on the north east coast was markedly different from that of the west coast. The overly choppy conditions were not fun, and I was eyeballing the storms as they rolled in from the vast expanse of the North Sea. It felt like the sea was raging and I didn't like it. Even so, we made it to four miles shy of Wick before calling it a day.

The next morning, we popped into the lifeboat station with two apology cakes – one chocolate and one lemon. We gingerly entered the quiet station and eventually found someone upstairs in the meeting room. As we explained the misunderstanding, he couldn't have been more relaxed about the whole thing, much to our palpable relief.

'Ah, don't worry about it. It's good training for us. We need to go out once a week anyway. Plus, that's what we're here for!' He seemed intrigued and wanted to know more about the adventure. 'You know, we don't get many paddleboarders out this way, so we're not used to seeing them up here. Where are you heading to next, then?'

He went on to share all of his abundant knowledge about John O'Groats harbour, including how incredibly shallow it is and pointing out which rocks to avoid. He also shared stories of the kinds of weather they get out this way, pointing to the pictures that adorned the walls – countless storms, rescue missions, and tragic stories that had claimed this unforgiving stretch of coastline.

Back in the harbour, I ran some calculations. Seventy-nine days in and it was just starting to feel real that John O'Groats was actually within my reach. I'd always known I'd get there – it had simply been a question of when and that when was now just two days away. Two days! That was all that stood between me and the finish line, when all I'd been working towards for the past eight months would be over. The drive to push past the start line, the struggle to find crew and financial backing, the tears and tendonitis: it had all been leading to this.

At least, in theory... In theory, it's the finish line that matters – getting a medal or a certificate at the end – but that's not what had pushed me this far. It had all simply been about a thirst for life and for adventure. I adored the challenge of it all, not knowing if it was possible but being bold enough to find out.

That's what had driven me the whole way, not the finish line itself.

Liam asked me if I'd thought about carrying on, making it into a round Britain adventure (not that he was offering to skipper it for me, I might add). It had crossed my mind, and, on the one hand I didn't want it to stop: I wanted to see how much further I could go. I wanted to find my limit. But, on the other, I was just incredibly happy with how far I'd come and what I'd achieved along the way – mostly, a sense of knowing that I can do whatever I put my mind to, one way or another. If I really want something, it's always possible.

It was the 8th of July and we had just enough of a weather window on our side to push on another seven miles, round past Wick to Noss Head, setting us up for the final, eight-mile push to John O'Groats. Overall, it seemed like it would be a fairly straightforward run to the end: we'd go directly up the last section of the east coast, before turning left once we ran out of coastline, bringing us to the home run into John O'Groats round the corner. However, we weren't alone in turning left there. At that point, the North Sea flows into the Atlantic, via the narrow gap between mainland Scotland and the Orkney Islands, creating a series of eddies, races, and overfalls, rather reminiscent of the conditions I'd met around Corryvreckan. Needless to say, I was feeling the nerves and knew that there was no way I'd let Shogun and my team leave my side.

Day 81: Tuesday 10 July 2018

We set off in beautifully calm weather, if rather misty such that we couldn't see land. I was so glad to be able to stand on the final day. My fear of the sea hadn't abated. Despite paddling almost 800 miles on my board I was still scared. But in the right conditions I felt able to control my fear slightly more than I had done at the start, which meant that I could stand when it was slightly choppier. Luckily on my final day I didn't need to combat chop, not yet at least.

It's always weird coming to the end of an adventure. It's what everyone naturally focuses on – the finish line – but the hours, days and weeks of struggle to get there seem a distant memory, like another life time ago or someone else's life.

At the start it's daunting how far I have to go, how much I have to get done to get to the end. Once underway though, it's just the next headland, the next harbour, the next 6 hours to think about. Sometimes the water will be glassy smooth and the sun will shine, others I'll be struggling to make any ground or crying my heart out, either way it's the here and now that matters. Each paddle stroke is what counts.

But that's the easy bit, really – making miles. Once I'm doing something, the momentum, the expectation, the rewarding feeling each time I overcome a hurdle along the way, it all keeps me moving. Overall it's much easier than I could have imagined. So long as I simply put one paddle stroke in, and then the next. Before I knew it there I was, just seven miles from the finish line, and that day I'd be about to do something that no one had done before.

Nearing the headland at the most northeasterly point of mainland Britain, we could see the water shifting. My heart started racing and I pulled closer to the boat for reassurance. As we approached, Liam started talking me through it, shouting instructions from the boat. I don't remember exactly what he said, something about how we'd go further out and round so it pushes us in the right direction. All I could think about was my experience near Corryvreckan. Liam hadn't been with us so I don't think he fully grasped what had happened and how utterly terrified I was. Being on a boat when the water is throwing you around is bad enough, but on a paddleboard – ooph! And this time, if I'd been pulled away from my team I wasn't tucked within the Scottish isles like I was on the west coast. Here there was nothing between me and Norway, some 300 miles away across the North Sea.

I dropped to my knees to steady myself in anticipation. As we started to be pulled through the choppy, swirling waters I was overwhelmed with fear. The helplessness I felt in those waters instantly took me right back to the west coast. I hated this. This was what I was most afraid of – losing control and my team not able to help me. I knew that they were right there this time, right by my side, but I was still anxious.

I shouted to Liam asking whether we should tie on a safety rope – a long line attached to my board and to the boat, like I'd done with Aileen on that first day in the canal. I'd keep paddling, keeping the rope slack so it wouldn't aid me in any way, but it meant if anything happened they could get me out quickly.

He looked at me puzzled, almost laughing, as he said 'no'. He was clearly completely unaware as to what I was feeling and why I was so panicky. Aileen, on the other hand, was leaning over the side, keeping a watchful eye on me to make sure I was OK. She could see the terror in my face. My attention darted across the sea's surface as I tried to work out where I would be thrown next, battling the shifting water to stay near the boat. A tear ran down my face. Aileen quietly mouthed, 'Do you want to come on board?' She was there on the west coast, she knew what I went through and how this felt so similar. She was paying enough attention to see how distressed I was and her offer made me feel safer. I relaxed a little as half of my fear was instantly replaced with determination.

There's only one way to get to the end, I thought, *and I do not want this bit to last any longer than it has to. Screw the overfalls – let's do this.*

As we approached the headland the fog cleared and the end was nigh. I paddled on, staying as close as possible to the boat. At least I felt far safer than last time with the support boat within touching distance. The closeness to the boat might have helped my fear, but it didn't help progress. Being so close meant I couldn't pick my own way through the swirling water and instead spent as much energy fighting to keep my board from being hit by the boat as I did trying to stay with it.

Once through the turbulent section, the wind eased off, and the brightly painted hotel next to John O'Groats harbour came into view. It was a relief to be past the overfalls, and with the water calm once again, I stood back up, moved away from the boat and paddled slowly, enjoying that final mile. Liam directed me towards the shore, holding back from the harbour itself. Once I was in position, and he was sure I wouldn't be pulled out into the North Sea, he took the support boat into harbour, making it in just before the ferry.

Of all the harbours we'd been in this was the trickiest. The boat's display showed a depth of just four feet as they moored on the outer wall of the harbour. Shogun's total depth is five and a half feet! (Luckily this is at the rear of the boat and the depth sensor is at the front, but this was still too close for comfort.) Despite his lack of experience, as ever Liam managed to skilfully position her without becoming beached. It took him and Aileen around 20 minutes to get in, tie up, and ensure Shogun was balanced such that when the tide dropped further and she inevitably did touch the sandy bottom, she'd lean safely towards the wall.

Once Shogun was sorted, Liam got out his drone and Aileen took his camera, readying themselves for my grand finale. It was odd bobbing about just outside the harbour waiting for them. Being at the end, able to see the John O'Groats sign, but not allowed to finish just yet. Having to wait there for half an hour felt a bit anti climatic. A few members of the public had spotted me, probably wondering what on earth someone was doing paddleboarding on the North Sea, but then when all I did was bob in one place most of them moved on and stopped watching me.

When Liam finally gave me the signal to paddle round into harbour, his drone attracted more attention. A young family had got chatting to him, plus a couple of other people, and as I rounded the corner of the outer wall, making my way past Shogun into the harbour they all cheered and whooped.

What a way to finish. I've never had anyone at the finish line for me before and this was a such a lovely, if rather surreal way to take my last paddle strokes – a drone following behind me, my crew supporting me all the way and strangers cheering me in. Aileen ran around with Liam's camera taking snaps as I touched down on the slipway at around 12.30pm and lifted my board out of the water, before walking up to the sign just metres away.

It's funny, the little things we worry about. The finish moment, when I touched down on the harbour ramp to get off my board had been in the back of my mind the whole way since Cornwall. I'd not had to be graceful getting on and off my board at sea, but the last thing I wanted to do was look like an idiot at the final point, in front of people other than my crew.

The ramp turned out to be quite slippery with seaweed but luckily I managed to hold my composure and not fall over or look clumsy with my board. In fact I was more comfortable with it than I had imagined – I'd actually started to feel at ease with my board, despite my fear of the sea. I walked up the ramp and headed straight towards the sign, awkwardly photo bombing someone's picture in order to make my grand finale by touching the sign and mark the end of a successful adventure.

With my final moments captured I put my board down a couple of metres away from the sign so the couple could continue taking their photos, this time without a weird paddleboarder ruining their shot. Aileen bounded up and gave me a big hug. As Liam came round from the harbour wall, he ran up the steps, put his drone down next to my board and lifted me into a big swinging hug – we made it! WE MADE IT!!!

To think that Liam and I had come so far together was really special. We'd both learnt so much about what we're capable of and faced our fears together. For all the issues along the way, it was great to share my expedition with him and Aileen, and all the crew that had joined me at various points from the planning stages through to the actual doing of it all.

The family who had cheered me in came over and their kids had a picture taken with me and my board. As we waited for a chance to take some pictures with the sign, tourists came over to enquire about what I was doing, some asked for pictures with me, most just thought I was crazy.

We packed our kit away and did the only thing you can do at the end of an expedition, go for a slice of cake and a cider.

I'd arrived. At the end of the beginning. I dared to start at Land's End and to keep starting each day despite fear, tears, financial and crew issues and a lack of belief from those that perhaps should've been supporting me most. More than any other adventure I've been on, this expedition taught me that the only assessment of what's possible that matters is my own. You may think I'm crazy, that this idea is impossible, certainly that *I* couldn't do it, that I'm just an amateur, that I don't have the qualifications or the experience.

But within all of that you've missed the vital ingredient needed to start. Admittedly it's something you can't see and that you'd never know if I or anyone else has it, simply by looking.

The confidence to start before I'm ready.

Throughout this trip I never let the possibility of failure enter my radar. It also never occurred to me until that message from David after I paddled across the Irish Sea, just how much it never occurred to other people that I *wouldn't* fail.

The thing that mattered most was to truly, wholeheartedly and unquestionably know that this was going to happen. I am going to fight to the end, I am going to find every way possible to go round, under, over or through any obstacles that stand in my way. I am going to keep asking questions, speaking to people, sharing messages and reaching out for what I need, and I won't stop until something so big is set in front of me that I'm forced to stop.

This is not arrogance, ego or blind faith. This is collaboration, communication, asking for help, being vulnerable enough and brave enough to admit that I don't know what I'm doing. This is testing and pivoting ideas, taking onboard advice and at least listening to those points of view I disagree with, even if not always acting on it.

I am not an island, and I couldn't have done this without so many people. Thank You.

After polishing off our cake and taking some final footage of me at the sign we loaded up Shogun and Liam gingerly reversed her out of the harbour, past the very shallow rocks and into deeper waters before the ferry came back. We motored back round Duncansby Head and down into Wick harbour 20 miles south of John O'Groats. After each grabbing a quick shower we headed out in search of a restaurant for a celebratory meal. Liam bought us a bottle of champagne to celebrate and we laughed at the tiny size of Aileen's panna cotta dessert, about the size of a two-pence piece.

It was so very special to have my crew with me at the end, to celebrate all that we'd achieved together, and individually, during SUP Britain. I had adjusted over the weeks to having crew with me, and all that comes with that. Relenting control, making sure everyone was happy where I could and ensuring cake supplies were optimised. Of course it hadn't always been plain sailing and being cooped up on a small boat for months on end was trying for all of us at times. But it was worth it for the camaraderie, for the incredible memories and because simply none of us could have gotten here without each other.

At the same time I was looking forward to some time alone. To find space and silence in lush green mountains, to wonder through forest tracks and hike up fell routes, to feel the solid land beneath me, and breath in fresh salt-free air. I think most of all though I was probably looking forward to relaxing in an indulgent bath and sinking into a huge comfy bed. It was the little home comforts that I craved.

It's rare in life that things turn out as I expect them to. And so it should be. If I'm doing something new that I've never done before, how could I possibly predict the outcome? From my experience I wouldn't want to either. Not knowing where I'll end up, or what it'll be like along the way is all part of the allure. The infinite possibility. The new connections and skills I never imagined I'd gain. And the incredible confidence that facing the unknown and coming out laughing gives me.

It was a pleasure to see my crew gain all these benefits too. They'd all lacked experience in some way in the things I asked them to do, yet they threw themselves into it. They stepped up and faced their own fears, they learnt about what they're capable of if they give themselves the opportunity and I hope they had a huge amount of fun along the way.

Alex had his day skipper qualification, but I don't think he'd delivered a yacht before.

Liam was a powerboat and dingy instructor, but had never sailed a yacht.

Sally had never been on a boat before, and now she's helped sail one 80 miles.

Ged had her day skipper qualification, but had never skippered on her own, yet did so at night.

Aileen had never been on a yacht or a paddleboard, she doesn't even have a driving licence, and we got her to skipper a 32-foot yacht through locks.

John, while the most experienced in the whole team as a yachtmaster with 50 years of experience on the sea, had never skippered a crazy adventure before which threw up completely new challenges.

Adventure is not a race. It's not about beating someone else's time, at least not for me. It's about discovery, of our world and of ourselves.

Epilogue

During the expedition, Liam and I had talked about him skippering Shogun back down south where I wanted to then sell her. But as we reached Inverness a couple of days after finishing, he decided to leave early to spend some time with Amy before he started his next job. Aileen and I stayed in Inverness for a couple of days, during which we had dinner with her family and explored locally until John joined us again and skippered us south.

It was funny being on the boat and going back the way I'd just paddled. Not because it was faster – it was only about two and a half miles an hour faster – but more so for the lethargy of it. You can't really do anything when you're on a boat, other than eat biscuits and drink tea. Which is fine, but it gets a bit boring after a while and after just a day spent cooped up on the boat I was dying to get off and go for a walk or do any kind of exercise to burn off some energy. I then realised how my crew must've felt for all those hours, days and weeks, particularly Liam when he was alone on the boat. I definitely had the least frustrating way to travel by being on my paddleboard.

As we sailed south we followed the same route past Corryvreckan. Seeing the swirling waters and feeling how it was throwing the boat around as we neared Crinan, I was so thankful to be on the boat and not on my board this time. Once at Crinan we said goodbye to Aileen where she'd first come aboard. A month had past and so much had happened. Tears, laughs and an endless number of firsts for both of us.

Having made it back down south with just John and I on the boat, we took her into Portishead marina near Bristol where I lived on Shogun for a month while I arranged to sell her. Chris hopped on his motorbike and came down to see me, checking out Shogun and hearing my whirlpool story first hand.

'I told you to watch out for it!' he said, laughing at me.

About halfway through the adventure I'd been contacted on Instagram by a guy called Alan Corcoran. An Irish adventurer, he'd previously run lots of marathons around Ireland and the previous year had attempted to swim the length of Ireland, from the Giant's Causeway in Co. Antrim to Tramore in Co. Waterford. However, a third of the way into the swim the rib that his support team had been using partly sunk in the harbour so they had to call the attempt off. Determined to go back and successfully complete the challenge, Alan was now on the look out for a more reliable support boat.

After I'd made it to John O'Groats, Alan got in touch to ask what I was planning to do with Shogun and when I said she was up for sale he immediately wanted to buy her. After a quick survey to check she wasn't going to sink we settled on £17,500 to include the tender and outboard I'd bought plus I threw in the extras like the new flare set and life jackets. Over the next year Alan prepped for his second attempt, and on 23rd July 2019 Alan successfully completed his swim the length of Ireland in 53 days.

It was great to see Shogun go on to support another crazy sea adventure, but I was definitely glad to be living on dry land again back in Bristol. After finishing the paddleboarding, even when tied up in the marina, I would occasionally wake up in the night in a panic that we were drifting and I needed to stop us from crashing into the rocks. There was something about the sway of the boat that told my body I was in danger.

While they weren't the focus of the expedition, it is nice to get recognition for the effort I put in. As reported by BBC Breakfast during the adventure I became the first woman to SUP across the Irish Sea. I also became the first person to SUP LEJOG on an inflatable board (I think anyone sensible doing it in future will opt for a hard board, as Cal had, as they're definitely more efficient) and, combined with my walk and cycle, I became the first woman to do a length of Britain triathlon.

In March 2019 I won the British Canoeing John MacGregor Outstanding Challenge Award for my contribution to the sport, which was such an honour. I took Erin along to the award ceremony with me as a thank you for all her support. It was wonderful to hear about the stellar line up of mainly women doing badass challenges who had also been up for the award.

Hats off to all of them; Anna Blackwell and Kate Culverwell kayaked 4,000 miles across Europe, Pip Stewart, Laura Bingham and Ness Knight became the first people to paddle the Essequibo River in South America from source to sea, Cal Major for her SUP LEJOG and Andy Sutton, a paraplegic kayaker who took on the Three Lakes Challenge.

Since finishing SUP Britain I've continued paddleboarding, this time in the mountains. Joining my friend Kris Roach we hike up to remote lakes in the Brecon Beacons with our boards, and I hope to explore more of Britain's remote lakes. I've also started wild swimming. But only in so much as I gingerly shimmy into a half a meter deep pool at the bottom of a waterfall or edge into the shallows of a lake desperately clutching a swim float and never going out of my depth. I'm yet to fully embrace the water and I'm definitely still scared of the sea.

My crew's stories

This adventure was not just about my journey. I was glad to offer up the opportunity for my crew to take on their own adventures, often starting before they were ready too. Here are their stories from SUP Britain.

Liam Morrell – Photographer-come-skipper

Living in the UAE as an outdoor instructor/photographer, I was looking for something different, something that would give me a new experience and help take my career in a different direction. A friend of mine had shown me Fiona's ad on Facebook calling for a photographer/PR person to document her expedition. I took a few days to work out if this is what I was waiting for. I decided I had nothing to lose so I threw myself into the unknown and sent over my details to Fiona. A few emails and Skype calls later I was in.

I met Fiona for the first time on our recce trip to Cornwall, our plan was to hunt for a boat and grab some photos and videos to help spread the word about the expedition. Over the course of this short trip I discovered some eyebrow raising facts about Fiona's... 'skill set'. Fiona had mentioned these points over Skype but I didn't quite realise the scale until this trip. She had all of the enthusiasm and her motivation was beyond comparison, however she had only paddled on the sea twice before she met me, had no knowledge of boats, tide, sea breeze and swell, to name a few. After the trip I thought *What have I got myself into* and at one point was close to pulling out, but thanks to some encouraging words from some good friends my bags were packed and we were on our way to Cornwall.

To be honest with you I thought I would be chilling on the boat taking photos and sending emails and the most stressful part of SUP Britain would be bringing the drone back into the boat... how wrong I was. Although that was very challenging it by no means came at the top of the stress list.

Day one and two went rather smoothly and I was feeling good about what was to come. But what came was not expected, we had got a boat (with a great sound system), we had cleaned her, loaded her up, put the sails on and were ready to go. Frustratingly for Fiona her skipper had not shown up and without him we were just sat in Falmouth. A day or so passed and the decision was made that I would skipper the boat for a couple of days until a replacement arrived. Now to give you an idea, I am not a skipper, I had only ever crewed a yacht for two days. I am,

309

however, a dinghy and powerboat instructor with good knowledge of winds, tides, swell etc. But it seems if you combine a powerboat and a dinghy you essentially get a yacht... apparently! We enlisted help from a guy called Alex who would skipper Shogun from Falmouth to St Ives whilst giving me a crash course on how the boat works and filling in all my knowledge gaps – without him I would not have had the confidence to take that boat alone.

With Alex now gone and all of Shogun's 32 feet solely in my hands, it's safe to say our first leg from St Ives was very nerve racking. I was bricking it, we had no more than 50 metres of visibility, I had to keep us on course, avoid crab pots and not crash as well as trying to get some photos – oh, and make sure I didn't lose Fiona. It was a lot for someone who had only ever driven a RIB and signed up to chill out and take photos.

The end of day one as a skipper brought possibly the scariest part of the expedition for me. Rather than the four-hour sail back to St Ives I opted to push to Portreath and anchor. I was happy with the anchor process and from what I had read, our anchor should be suitable for the sea bed. However as the fog lifted slightly at dusk I noticed we were surrounded by large cliffs and we seemed rather close to the beach, so we lifted the anchor and repositioned further out. The whole night I was terrified the anchor would slip. I had a drift alarm set on the boat's GPS, and an alarm set on my phone for every hour so I could check, but the other concerns were the noises the boat made, the sloshing in the bilge and whether or not the batteries would survive the night with the GPS and anchor light on. As dawn broke all was good, my nerves were shattered but we pushed on up the coast.

Every day I gained confidence in myself, the boat and Fiona: I slowly relaxed into it and started to enjoy boat life. We tried and tried and tried to get an actual skipper but we could not find anyone willing to join. So I just kept going, creeping up the coast until we found one. It just so happened we never did, apart from John who helped us cross the Irish sea and assisted Fiona when I went on a pre-booked holiday.

Fiona had good days, she had bad days – being scared of the sea and doing this is no easy challenge. She had essentially trusted her life to the hands of an inexperienced 22-year-old stranger, and I did my best to help encourage her to keep going when she was tired and to get on the board when she was scared. I soon learnt where the boundaries were and how far to push things.

I also had good and bad days; sometimes I'd be driving that boat for hours on end – the longest being 18 hours straight – mostly on my own as Fiona paddled so it was easy to get fed up. We got on well; just two exhausted people in a boat for three months was always going to be hard. We made sure we had our own space and actively sought to boost each other's morale. Food was key, it was an instant mood lifter and getting off the boat to do something different also became a big part of the trip. We'd SUPed together, played mini golf, swam, had visitors, walked and, of course, ate more food.

Whilst on the topic of food I must tell you my number one SUP Britain worst moment... sorry Aileen. It had been a long day, we'd finally got out of Inverness and were back on the ocean only a couple of days away from John O'Groats. We were all exhausted. Aileen had joined us a few weeks prior and was not only a very helpful crew member but was a massive morale booster for the two of us. She had kindly cooked dinner when we picked up a mooring in Cromarty. It was a wonderful, much needed pasta dish. I took a big old mouthful and to my horror it had been cooked with pure seawater. It was the saltiest thing I have ever eaten, horrific, but it was that or biscuits so I went for it and felt awful for the rest of the night.

My stand out moments from the expedition, bar many a beautiful sunset, would have to be waking up at Lundy island. After arriving in the dark we awoke at dawn to the most gorgeous day in one of the more beautiful places I have seen in Britain. I went for a quick dip – actually it was very quick as the water was still very cold – but all in all it was a magical moment. Another would have to be the hospitality we received in the Skerries, where we met up with some of my parents' friends who gave us such a warm welcome, treated us to our first proper Guinness and gave us cake. In such an isolated expedition this really touched home for me and was very much needed at the time.

I'm not going to lie, the last couple of weeks of the expedition were hard for me and at times I felt like I didn't want to be there any more. Exhausted and fed up of travelling at 2.5 knots, I struggled to find motivation. However, leaving so close to the end was not an option and with Fiona's undying motivation and Aileen's chirpy attitude we made it and what a feeling it was! To finally reach the destination you've been fighting to get to for weeks was such a profound moment that I will never forget.

There were so many amazing moments and challenges throughout the expedition it's impossible to talk about them all. All in all it was an incredible experience that grew me as a person, both professionally and personally. Being responsible for other people's lives whilst out at sea was a terrifying thought at the start but became simply the norm as time went on. It gave me a sense of purpose and the realisation that to overcome a challenge all you need to do is put your mind to it.

A few months after SUP Britain, one of Fiona's main sponsors, Red Paddle Co, was hiring a sales manager. I applied, spent a week camping and surfing in Cornwall and landed myself the job. I relocated to South Devon and my career has been taken in an exciting direction – I am currently loving my job and what I do. When I met Fiona I had a different sense of what adventure meant, now I realise it's all about challenging yourself mentally as well as physically. After helping Fiona complete hers, I am starting to plan my very own adventure, surfing, somewhere very cold and very remote.

SUP Britain was a truly memorable and humbling experience and I can only thank Fiona for choosing me to share it with her.

John Patrick – Skipper for the Irish Sea crossings

I noticed the ad on Facebook: 'Support skipper required for SUP length of Britain challenge'. Curiosity got the better of me and so a few emails and conversations ensued between Fiona and myself. It quickly became apparent Fiona had limited knowledge of boats, tides, currents and UK waters and so my brain started being picked. As a commercial yacht skipper it is engrained into me: plan, plan and then plan!

My first proper meeting with Fiona and Liam was in Milford Haven when I arrived to help with the Irish Sea crossing. I met a slim, quiet and relaxed lady, not quite what I had expected. So early, very early next morning we got to the edge of Wales.

The weather started to go downhill with a fresh breeze and it soon became apparent that Fiona was not comfortable. Despite considerable encouragement from Liam it was decided to abandon for the day. On the journey to our overnight anchorage I started to learn more: 'I did 3 days training before I started!', 'I don't feel comfortable in deep water!' she told me... *What have I got myself involved with* I thought.

The next day however, following another early start (hats off to Liam for his endurance) we launched Fiona back onto the Irish Sea – Rosslare far off as our target. It was a very different day with a flat sea, some mist and a very determined Fiona. Twelve hours later, as we approached the Irish coast, the water started to erupt with pods of dolphins. And then it happened, that trademark Fiona smile that spreads across her face and lights up everyone – I have done it, she said. You could even see that the dolphins were smiling as Liam captured them on various forms of media. The first woman to SUP across the Irish Sea!

My next involvement was when Liam left for a family holiday and I again joined Fiona and Ged in Bangor (Northern Ireland) to cover the passage up the west coast of Scotland. This would test me as I would be sailing waters I hadn't before. As we moved further north, my head spent more time in charts, weather forecasts, tide tables, almanac and pilot books, ensuring we optimised each paddling session. A crew change was to take place at Crinan, quite close to Corryvreckan, so even more planning went in as Fiona would paddle on whilst I changed crew and took on diesel ashore.

I pulled out of Crinan with my new crew, Aileen, eyes scanning the horizon for Fiona on her board. Nothing. Where was she? My eyes searched, my head filled with all my calculations trying to visualise where she should be. No reply on the radio. Then the frantic phone call – *at least she is still alive*, I thought. Aileen spotted her and Shogun's little engine was asked for everything it had to get to her. Five minutes later we were alongside – me as relieved as Fiona.

For the next three days whilst Fiona paddled I went over and over my calculations – *what did I miss? Did I work everything out correctly?* Nothing showed up. So even with the best planning in the world things still go wrong!

The next days were filled with sunshine, laughs, sea life and good progress to Fort William, my departure point on this occasion. I took no further part in the SUP challenge as Liam had returned, however I did deliver Shogun back to Portishead from Inverness with Fiona.

Shogun changed ownership to Alan Corcoran who then did a sponsored swim the length of Ireland 2019 and I was once again on board doing the deliveries first to Waterford and then Ballycastle. Shogun is now called Unsinkable II... another story!

I had a health scare back in 2012, when I was diagnosed with sudden death syndrome, which shook my confidence. This involvement with Fiona helped me realise that sometimes you just have to do it, get on with it and deal with things when they happen. Set yourself goals that reflect what you want to achieve and not what other people expect you to do. When people ask me why did Fiona do it, I reply because she wanted to, believed deep down she could, not many other people have done it and maybe for some reason she needed to.

This year, 2019, I set myself a little challenge to compete in an international 2.4mR sailing boat. This boat can be sailed by able bodied as well as less abled and male or female all on an even playing field. I attended the British, French and Irish Championships, where I became Irish National Champion. I have just returned from the world championship in Italy having towed the boat there and back through France.

Did I plan...? Maybe a little, but sometimes it's a case of, 'Just do it!'

Aileen McKay – Deck hand

'Please help. Come quickly...'

The signal on the skipper's phone was poor, but the words coming from the speaker could not have been more clear. Fiona was in trouble. John expertly coaxed Shogun out of Crinan harbour — knot by knot by knot — and instructed me to keep an eye out. I scanned the horizon carefully, hardly knowing what I was looking for.

Half an hour ago I'd been sitting by my heavy pack on the boatyard steps, rubbing stubborn sleep from my eyes after a night in my tent by the canal, where I'd pitched after hiking my way from Lochgilphead in the dark. I didn't know it at that point, but I wouldn't be back home for over a month. This wee boat was about to become my home.

She carried us out, out, out over the grey west coast waters near Crinan. I continued my scanning until... there she was: a tiny dot in the frothing waters!

John swiftly navigated us alongside, we got the ladder down and Fiona hauled herself aboard, shaking. *Thank fuck.* As she was drying off, clutching a mug of tea in her hands, we got around to introductions. I liked her immediately – Fiona is forthright and prone to grinning and it took us less than a day to forge a firm friendship.

As we pushed on northwards, there were some mornings when Fiona's mileage bid would hinge on a dawn start. With my own body clock wired rather more nocturnally, it was hellish. I'd quietly extricate myself from the warm embrace of my sleeping bag in my little nook by the engine to boil a kettle, spread peanut butter onto bread, and slowly cook up rich bowls of porridge. Yes, I felt like I was sleepwalking, but I also knew that it was worth it.

With the passing of each hour, Fiona powered through more miles, her paddle driving through the water surely and steadily. This was history being made. Day by day, Fiona would ink a few centimetres more of the black line making its way up her map of the British Isles — Crinan, Oban, Lismore, Loch Linnhie, Corran, Corpach, Neptune's Staircase, Gairlochy.

'But you're just two girls!'

I tried to keep the incredulity off my face as we gamely told the terribly concerned woman peering down into the locks that we would, in fact, be quite alright sailing Shogun to the far end of Loch Lochy ourselves. With our skipper, John, called away back to Ireland on other business and Fiona being single-mindedly determined, we knew that we would not be stuck in one location while the weather held and time marched on. No chance. So, in the baking heat, I hiked a speedy, sweaty twelve miles northwards on the Great Glen Way alongside Loch Lochy while Fiona propelled herself along its surface. We made it and the fates were clearly on our side – a kind-hearted lock keeper let us stash Fiona's board at Laggan and two sweet strangers drove us south back along the A82 to our starting point and to Shogun.

Neither one of us skippers, but both up for the challenge, we nosed her north, through twenty-knot winds and some serious tilt and swell, right the way back up Loch Lochy once more. Victory! At Laggan again, we demolished huge plates of hot, salty food in the pub and plunged into the cold canal for a swim, cleansing ourselves of the dust and heat.

My stomach threatened to eject the little I'd consumed that day. My skin was growing clammy. Having just learnt the ropes on the lock-laden Caledonian Canal, here I was flung from its slow, orderly security. This was the Moray Firth. Yes, it was the glorious view I'd grown up with outside my bedroom window for the first seventeen years of my life, but traversing it now was another experience entirely. Here, it met with the North Sea and the two fought like siblings.

My stomach burned and I'm sure it was sheer pride that stopped me from vomiting violently. It soon transpired that even Fiona's stoic kneeling tactics were no match for the swell and she, reluctantly but sensibly, called it a day. Later that night, tied onto a mooring buoy but not docked in harbour, and all of us finally ravenous, I carefully double boiled sea water for plain pasta, an earlier conversation about the need to be conscious of saving water from our limited freshwater supply weighing on my fatigued mind. The result was, of course, inedibly salty. I felt stupid. This simplest of tasks had escaped me. I struggled to see the funny side of not feeding my team properly and went to bed tearful.

Rosemarkie, Cromarty, Dornoch, Golspie... I began to accept the quiet thrill of realising that I was becoming more and more comfortable with the boisterous sway of the waves. Fiona would be on her board by blue dawn, steaming over the swell as the sky brightened. Somewhere out in the horizon, somethings and nothings broke and rolled. Every few minutes, a team of birds flew low, bellies touching the water and their bills leading them like the needle of a compass. Above them, orderly squadrons of sea birds silently pushed along, one by one, to take their place at the front of the line. Out here, nature's course was charted clearly – uninterrupted by the likes of us humans.

'Why's it called a bee line?'

'Oh, I dunno.'

'Me neither.'

'Yeah, doesn't make sense – a 'b' has a big old curved line in it whichever way you draw it...'

'Hmmm.'

'I've never thought about it before.'

'Me neither, but you think about all sorts of weird things when you're out at sea on a boat.'

In my small cabin, I rocked from half-dream to half-dream. The radio said my name. An old friend texted. I grew small. Then I woke. The vessel bounced one, two metres in every direction. I shut my eyes and the late afternoon sunlight filtered through my lashes. I fancied myself to be a tiny creature, folded softly into the neat white of someone's best cotton handkerchief and slotted into a roomy pocket. That morning's dawn start seemed at once to be somehow both three days and just a few minutes ago.

More idly than nauseously this time, I began to wonder if there are always stormy waves far out at sea the same way that there is always, always blue sky to be found above the clouds. The long days on the water morphed into one. Fiona's mission was the goal and our days became a great cycle of paddling, encouraging, eating, hydrating, tending to sunburn, and keeping her on the water as much as possible. Hour by hour, Fiona won her miles and the inked line on the map grew longer.

After a battle of wills with the weather, Fiona made it. Tenth of July 2018: John O'Groats was hers, the first woman in the whole world to complete a triathlon of the UK. First in the world! Bloody hell.

The sky was overcast and grey, but we were all the sunshine we needed. Everything up to that point – the long days, the choppy water, the cold nights – had all been worth it. Utterly, utterly worth it. And it was all possible because Fiona is a great believer in starting before you're ready; in saying screw it; in reckoning it's worth the leap of faith.

So, what's the moral of the tale? When a friend of friend you've never met before is out adventuring and needs a pair of helping hands on deck, you sign yourself up! It won't be what you expected – mainly because you will quickly learn to not put much in the way of expectations behind unknowns like this – but it will be absolutely amazing. You'll blast your comfort zone apart, you'll try new things, and you'll be so proud of yourself.

Thanks to Fiona, I was part of making a new history – one where women are, rightly, front and centre for their endurance, guts and ingenuity — and I've made a friend for life.

Author Note

Woo hoo – you made it past the start line and hopefully enjoyed reading about the ensuing adventure as much as I did writing about it. I would be ever so grateful if you could hop over to Amazon right now and leave my book a review. They really make the world of difference to how many people get to discover my work and I would love for you to help me out – even just a couple of words really do help me a lot.

If you'd like to find out about my wild swimming, mountain SUPing, or whatever adventure I dream up next, do sign-up to my newsletter for my latest and greatest ideas.

No spam, just cake, I promise.

www.FionaLQuinn.com/Newsletter

I'd love for you to get in touch and join me for a paddle.

Instagram: @FionaLQuinn

Twitter: @FionaLQuinn

Facebook: /FionaLQuinn

www.FionaLQuinn.com

Fiona@FionaLQuinn.com

Adventure Book Club

Founded by Fiona Quinn, Adventure Book Club is all about seeing the world differently. Adventures start with inspiration, but it's the people around you that will help you bring your ideas to life. We're creating a community to support you to read more, share more and do more.

Read about other people's adventures in the outdoors or adventurous approaches to life, and then come meet us in a field, on top of a mountain or at the beach to spend time outside and in the company of like-minded people.

If you'd like to read more about adventures near and far, join us
www.AdventureBook.Club

LEJOG Triathlon Routes

Cycle Britain

Walk Britain

SUP Britain

Maps provided by ZeroSixZero

Thank You's

A huge thank you to all of my crew: Liam, Alex, John, Sally, Ged and Aileen. I literally couldn't have done this without you. Your confidence to leap into the unknown, unending faith in me, and perseverance to push through the hard times mean more than you know.

To those who answered my stupid questions, guided me in the right direction and lent a helping hand, thank you – Sean, Mike P., Charlie, Rowan, Amanda, Kris, Tim, Alisdair, Clare, Murray, Eithne, Stephen, Mike and Daisy, Spike, David and Amy, and all of the harbour masters and lock keepers that we met along the way.

Liz Marvin and Aileen McKay, thank you for editing my book. Your honesty and encouragement helped me get through the last final hurdles of the writing process.

My sponsors, you helped me to believe in myself and keep pushing forwards – your kit ensured I got to the end in one piece. I can't wait to keep putting in through its paces on many more adventures: ZeroSixZero, Finisterre, SIGG, NRS, Aquapac, Red Paddle Co, SunGod, Odylique and dryrobe.

To my friends, especially Erin, who have supported me through the ups and downs – both those of you who believed in me and those who still think I'm mad, you challenge me to go bigger and I'm so grateful.

Mum, thank you for always supporting me and not freaking out too much at my wild ideas.

Kit List

For the geeks amongst you or those that fancy their own SUP-based challenge, here is a list of the key bits of kit that helped me through. Some were kindly donated by my sponsors, others I bought – it all comes genuinely recommended.

Boards:
Red Paddle Co 12'6 x 32 Voyager
Red Paddle Co 13'2 x 30 Voyager
Red Paddle Co Carbon paddle
Red Paddle Co 8' Coiled leash

On the board:
NRS Women's Sayan PFD (Personal Flotation Device)
SPOT Tracker linked to ZeroSixZero map on my website
Floating knife
Snack bars
SIGG insulated water bottle with carabiner
Aquapac waterproof iPhone case
Aquapac 'VHF Classic' waterproof radio case
Argos 2-way radios
SunGod Velans sunglasses
Baseball hat
NRS Women's Radiant 3/2mm wetsuit
Finisterre swimsuit

Finisterre board shorts

Finisterre swim top

Finisterre swim leggings

NRS Women's paddle watershoes

NRS High Tide splash jacket

Aquapac 25L heavyweight waterproof drybag with shoulder strap

Odylique organic sunscreen

Boat:

32ft 1984 Jeanneau Attalia

On the boat:

Dryrobe

Finisterre Nimbus insulated jacket

NRS Women's H2Core lightweight long sleeve top

NRS Women's H2Core lightweight hoodie

NRS Women's H2Core lightweight leggings

Lemon drizzle cake

Aquapac 70L & 90L heavyweight waterproof duffle bags

Aquapac 'PackDivider' ultra-lightweight drysacks, various sizes

Odylique Muscle Ease Oil, Repair Lotion and Moisturising Balm

About the Author

From taking on adventures large and small, Fiona tells stories of possibility, sharing how to build resilience and set your sights higher, to ultimately enable you to find new opportunities. Working with brands and organisations, she shares this adventure mindset through keynote speaking and writing. Having spoken at corporate events, award ceremonies, festivals, universities, schools, and on TV and radio, she enthusiastically challenges you to start before you're ready, face your fears, and change your view of what's possible.

Fiona believes that adventure gives us permission to try, to push our boundaries, to dream big, to look at challenges differently. But, most importantly, whether we succeed or fail, adventure renews in us a belief in ourselves. So, when the going gets tough, we dig in, we push through, we find another way and – sometimes – it gives us the strength to quit and start again.

Alongside working as a speaker and writer, Fiona runs AdventureBook.Club, sharing stories of adventure and helping others to get outside, and supports entrepreneurs to be more adventurous in their businesses via her three-month coaching programme, the Action Collective.

www.FionaLQuinn.com

Have you enjoyed this book?

Woo hoo – you made it past the start line and hopefully enjoyed reading about the ensuing adventure as much as I did writing about it.

I would be ever so grateful if you could hop over to Amazon right now and leave a review. They make the world of difference to how many people get to discover this book and I would love for you to help me out. Even just a couple of words really do make all the difference.

Thanks very much for your support.